Rochelle Jones is an award-winning reporter and writer whose articles have appeared in many national magazines, including *National Magazine, The National Observer,* and the *Congressional Quarterly.*

THE OTHER GENERATION: THE NEW POWER OF OLDER PEOPLE

ROCHELLE JONES

A SPECTRUM BOOK

PRENTICE-HALL, INC., Englewood Cliffs, New Jersey 07632

Library of Congress Cataloging in Publication Data

Jones, Rochelle.
    The other generation.

    (A Spectrum Book)
    Includes bibliographical references and index.
      1. Aged—United States.   2. United States—Population.
3. United States—Social conditions—1960–
4. Senior power—United States.   I. Title.
HQ1064.U5J68   301.43'5'0973   77-22306
ISBN 0-13-643064-3
ISBN 0-13-643056-2 pbk.

For My Mother

© 1977 by Prentice-Hall, Inc., Englewood Cliffs, New Jersey

A Spectrum Book

10 9 8 7 6 5 4 3 2 1

Printed in the United States of America

Prentice-Hall International, Inc., *London*
Prentice-Hall of Australia Pty. Limited, *Sydney*
Prentice-Hall of Canada, Ltd., *Toronto*
Prentice-Hall of India Private Limited, *New Delhi*
Prentice-Hall of Japan, Inc., *Tokyo*
Prentice-Hall of Southeast Asia Pte. Ltd., *Singapore*
Whitehall Books Limited, *Wellington, New Zealand*

CONTENTS

v

PREFACE

This is not a book about the problems of old people. Although the title, *The Other Generation;* refers to people who are over 65. It is a book about *us*, the vast majority of Americans who are not old. It is about the impact that the growing number of people who are over 65 are having on us and about what the increasing proportion of older adults in our society means to the rest of us.

There were more than 22 million people over 65 in the U-United States in 1976. Every tenth American was over 65. Much has been written about them. There is a growing body of academic literature written by gerontologists, who study aging and people over 65 and in the past several years a number of books aimed at the general reader have been published about older Americans. The problems of people over 65—their poverty, their struggles for enough food to eat, a decent place to live, and adequate medical care—have been well documented.

The plight of elderly Americans who suffer from the economic, social, and physical disadvantages of old age needed to be written about. Their condition is a national disgrace.

The people who feed off the old—the unscrupulous nursing home operators, the medical personnel who run Medicaid mills, the businessmen who exploit the needs of the old for hearing aids and other health devices—is a national scandal. Their existence needed to be exposed.

Yet, for the most part, these books and articles have tended to perpetuate the belief of the overwhelming majority of people under 65 that older adults are a race apart and that aging is something that happens to somebody else. Both beliefs are wrong. The growing number of older adults in the United States and the demographic shifts that are being caused by the increasing proportion of older adults in the United States concern every one of us.

In 1971, as a newspaper reporter for the *Palm Beach Post* in West Palm Beach, Florida, I was assigned to write a series of articles on the problems of the elderly. In the course of my research, I attended a seminar at Duke University for newspaper reporters, sponsored by the Southern Newspaper Publishing Association. Although the seminar concentrated on the problems of the elderly, a number of participants mentioned in their presentations the changing demographic structure of the United States, and hinted at its impact.

Fascinated by this idea, I spent several years talking to scores of gerontologists, hundreds of people over 65, and dozens of government experts on aging. I attended numerous conferences on the aging and read countless articles and books on the subject. I visited centers devoted to the study of aging, senior citizens centers, nursing homes, and retirement villages. This book grew out of those talks and visits.

I came away from my research with two conclusions. First, it became clear that increased longevity and the growing numbers of people over 65 were already changing the lives of the rest of us in ways that have not been generally recognized or appreciated. Second, I realized that fundamental changes are needed in our society if we as a nation are to come to grips with these demographic shifts.

This book deals with both conclusions. Its purpose is to make the rest of us aware of the impact of the changing demographic structure in our country and to help us to cope more effectively as a society with these changes by increasing our awareness of them. It describes the results that our present policy on aging has had for older Americans. It calls attention to the influence of the growing number of older adults on our public policy, our politics, our retirement system, our values, and our patterns of work, education, and leisure. It outlines the changes that need to be made in the future in response to these demographic shifts.

This book does not attempt to define once and for all the future of an aging society. It does suggest directions that we may take. The eventual shape of that society may be far different from what I have postulated, but it also will be far different from the society we know now. This book is intended to stimulate public awareness and discussion about the needs and problems created by a society that is growing older.

Finally, but by no means least, this book seeks to change the reader in a subtle but important sense. It seeks to heighten the reader's age consciousness. There *are* bias and discrimination against older adults. Ageism *does* exist. And older adults are often very different from what we imagine them to be. Unless we are sensitive to what society has done to older adults and what they are really like, we cannot possibly come to grips with what their growing numbers mean. This book is intended to alter the way most of us look at people over 65.

In writing this book, I have tried to appeal to both the general reader and the professional or student who is interested in aging. Therefore, I have tried to find a middle ground in referencing material. I have included references to material that would be of interest to the professional. At the same time, I have avoided adding footnotes that might simply impede the general reader. The overwhelming majority of the quotations that appear in the book are taken from my notes from personal interviews. Quotations from professionals in the field of aging and public officials are generally footnoted for clarification. Quotations from older adults are generally not footnoted. In any event, the conclusions are mine.

Before I started the initial research that eventually led to this book, my contacts with older adults were few and far between. Growing up in a mobile and age-segregated society, as most people under the age of 30 today have, I lacked sustained relationships with older adults. My grandparents were sketchy figures from the dimly remembered past. I never knew them or saw them as people who loved, hated, feared, hoped, dreamed. Through the years, several older adults offered enriching and rewarding friendships. But those friendships were neither frequent nor extensive enough to alter my generally negative notion of aging.

So I began work with the usual preconceived ideas. The idea

of growing old myself filled me with terror, and older adults themselves were people I feared and dreaded.

Getting to know older adults has been the most personally rewarding aspect of writing this book. I am grateful to hundreds of them for sharing their time, thoughts, and experiences with me. I am grateful to them for teaching me what it is like to grow old in the land of the young and what it means to be over 65. The physical defects, the poverty, the senility, the rigidity, the irritability—all the things we associate with age—are there. But warmth, energy, good humor, courage, and dignity are there, too. Their capacity to survive and even grow in a generally hostile environment is an example to the rest of us.

In short, I have come away from my research with a feeling of hope about my own aging and the future of our aging society. I am optimistic about the prospect of longer life. I believe the changes that will be forced upon us by the growing number of older people will benefit all of us.

Among the older adults who helped with this book, I wish especially to thank Billie Jones. She contributed to the research as a constant and unfailingly cheerful collector of possible reference material. Her constructive criticism is also appreciated.

I also wish to thank a number of other people. Gregory Favre, my editor at the *Palm Beach Post*, first got me interested in the problems of aging. Later on, he generously gave me time off from my professional responsibilities to undertake the initial research for this book. Norman Kirk enthusiastically supported the research and writing in the initial stages. Philip Perkins gave wholehearted support what it was sorely needed. The staff of the Duke University Center for Aging and Human Development were generous with their time. Florence Mahoney was enormously helpful in supplying research material on the biology of aging. Her contribution to the chapter on that subject was substantial. Last, but certainly not least, I wish to thank Peter Woll to whom I owe a primary professional and personal debt. Without his enthusiasm and encouragement at crucial times, this book would not have been finished. His advice, faith, and support are deeply appreciated.

A MATTER OF AGING

CHAPTER ONE

In the freewheeling, easygoing United States of the 1970s, very little makes Americans squeamish. On the contrary, we have a tendency to pride ourselves on our sophistication. We talk casually, sometimes with almost total strangers, about our divorces, abortions, and vasectomies. Hard-core pornographic movies, such as *The Devil in Miss Jones* and *Deep Throat*, have played at neighborhood theaters, while their stars have been featured on the covers of national magazines. The same magazines, available on the racks of any drugstore or supermarket, discuss the relative merits of the vaginal versus the clitoral orgasm. Best-selling books tell us everything we ever wanted to know about sex.

Seemingly, we have come a long way. But despite our frankness about these formerly taboo topics, we are not really as sophisticated as we might like to think. Our sophistication has limits—when we come to the subjects of old age and death, we tend to speak about them in the same embarrassed, uncomfortable tones that our Victorian ancestors reserved for sex. We talk about them in such a manner, that is, when we don't ignore them altogether. Typically, in the presence of these universal, inevitable events in the lives of almost everyone of us, we lapse into a sudden, uneasy silence. We are threatened by reminders that life is not forever and that youth is short.

Gerontologists, who study old age and the process of aging, perceive certain parallels between the attitudes of the 1970s toward aging and the attitudes of, say, the 1870s toward sex. In fact, Dr. James D. Birren,[1] director of the Ethel Percy Andrus Gerontology Center at the University of Southern California, suggests that old age and death have taken the place of sex at the top of our list of unmentionable topics of conversation. "Now that we know how to spell sex backwards," he said, "old age and death are the only two taboos left in our society."

Our unwillingness to look toward our future has extracted a price from us as a nation. We have largely condemned to invisibility one of our country's largest and most diverse minority groups, those men and women who are over 65. We have forced them into old-age ghettoes, denied them a meaningful role in society, and cast them back on their own, limited resources. This is unfortunate in itself. But the exclusion of so many men and women from society, as serious as it is, is only part of the cost of our reluctance to think about old age. Our fear has helped to obscure recognition of the fact that the population structure of the United States is changing. While we have been busy analyzing and examining the youth culture, the population of our United States has been growing older. The 1970 census turned up almost 20

---

[1]Personal interview.

million people who had passed their sixty-fifth birthday, and their numbers have continued to increase.

THE POPULATION SHIFT

In the 1970s we are in the midst of a population boom among older people that rivals and will surpass in its implications the baby boom of the post-World War II era. The presence of 22 million people over 65 in our society is the start of a totally new phenomenon caused by a steadily declining infant mortality rate and rapid technological advances that enable medicine to prolong life in ways that were previously impossible.

Until the start of the twentieth century, childhood diseases caused the death of many people before they reached adulthood, much less old age. But this is no longer so. Children today rarely die of diphtheria, whooping cough, or scarlet fever, to name just three of the diseases that often claimed the lives of children during the previous century. As a result, more people than ever are living to celebrate their sixtieth, seventieth and eightieth birthdays. Once they reach old age, technology is able to prolong the lives of many older people who would have died even 10 years ago. Advances in the treatment of cardiovascular disease and cancer, which are among the major causes of death after the age of 60, also enable many older people to live longer.[2] In 1974, for example, a man aged 65 could expect to live another 13.4 years; a

---

[2]In 1974 the death rate in the United States reached the lowest point since records were begun in 1900, according to the National Center for Health Statistics. The total number of deaths per 1,000 persons was 9.2. Although this figure includes deaths from all causes for all age groups, a major cause of the decline was the drop in deaths from heart disease, which decreased by 4.8 per cent between 1973 and 1974. See *New York Times,* February 4, 1976, p. 1.

woman of 65 could expect to live an additional 17.5 years.[3]

At the same time these things have been happening, the birth rate has been declining in the United States. We are approaching a zero population growth rate, meaning almost as many people are dying as are being born. This may be a direct result of our increased longevity. Some scientists have conjectured that there is a direct relationship between longevity and a society's birth rate. Dr. John Rock, known as the "father of the pill," said, " . . . it's been shown in many countries that as longevity increases, birth rates go down; that as the death rate goes down, birth rates go down. People have a sense of the necessity of replacing themselves if they feel they'll die fairly young. When they know they'll live longer, they don't feel the necessity of having so many children."[4]

When people expect to live to reach old age, it is hypothesized that their urge to reproduce themselves diminishes. They become preoccupied with other things, and they no longer feel compelled to have children at an early age. If they anticipate a long life and, therefore, an unlimited youth, they may pass the childbearing age before their desire to have children asserts itself. This may be happening —largely unconsciously—now.

Although the reason may be debatable, the result is not. The combination of increased longevity and declining birth rate is predictable. There are more older people, and they are comprising a steadily increasing percentage of our country's population.

Few people have realized that we are in the midst of a population shift that is unprecedented in terms of its significance and consequences. Even fewer people have been concerned with the implications of it. Academicians and gov-

---

[3]*Part I: Developments in Aging:* 1975 and January–May 1976 (Washington, D.C.: U.S. Government Printing Office, 1975), p. xvii.

[4]*Women's Wear Daily*, June 12, 1972, p. 12.

ernment bureaucrats occasionally discuss it among themselves, but their thoughts and articles rarely reach the rest of us.

Yet the impact of this population shift will be felt in the lives of all. It would be foolish to suppose that such a change could occur without causing, in turn, a variety of other changes. In subtle ways that often appear unconnected, the impact of this aging of the United States is already being felt. If we are to plan and adapt to this demographic shift, we must connect these seemingly random happenings.

The fact that in sheer numbers more people than ever are reaching old age might in itself justify a book that attempted to talk about them and their problems. The purpose of this book, however, is not to look at old age in America simply to pinpoint the rank injustices that accompany aging in our society, although they are many. The intent is not simply to document the problems of 22 million people that many would prefer to pretend do not exist. Although older people have many legitimate grievances, the purpose of this book is more far-reaching. Its concern is to go beyond the neglect that has been shown to older Americans. Its purpose is to try to give some insight into the impact that older people and certain of these population shifts will most likely have on the rest of us. Some of these changes are already taking place, and they will be examined fully in later chapters. Others are still ideas in the minds of gerontologists and government officials. Although they have not taken shape yet, they are definitely in the making. These changes will be looked at, too.

We shall see that there are, and we must prepare in the near future for, new ways of organizing our working lives and our leisure time in response to the challenge of longevity. As a consequence, our life-styles will be more flexible. We will have a greater range of choice. We will be able to choose, on a more or less individual basis, a far more personally suitable combination of education, work, and leisure instead of being forced to concentrate on education in youth, work in middle age, and leisure in old age in the form of retirement. As our leisure time grows, and we have to work fewer hours to earn it, our very values are being called into question. The Protestant work ethic, inherited from our Puritan ancestors, is being assaulted by the growth of free time. New professions, services, and institutions are being created, as older citizens make new demands on our communities.

We also shall be looking at the lives of older adults. Although other minority groups in our society have been written about, photographed, analyzed, and documented extensively, few researchers seem to want to recognize the existence of a subculture of the aging. We shall find that older people who have been shut off from the rest of society have been forming their own interesting, and sometimes surprising, ways of life. Whole communities inhabited exclusively by older adults have been springing up through the 1970's in places such as California, Arizona, and Florida, where many retirees flock to bask in the warm sunshine. In these communities, a down payment buys more than a house. It buys instant companionship as a shield against the terrors of old age and a sometimes dizzying round of activities to counteract the steadily contracting boundaries of a world that is increasingly populated by people and things that are unknown. In that leisure-oriented life-style, physical health and the ability to participate in the daily round of activities have replaced occupation and income as status symbols and measures of individual worth.

THE STATISTICS

To begin to understand the changes that have been taking place over the last 70 years, it helps to look at the population statistics. The aggregate figures are astounding.

Between 1900 and 1976, the number of people over 65 grew from 3 million to more than 22 million.[5] Although the population as a whole was growing at the same time, the number of people over 65 grew faster than the number of people under 65. By the time of the 1970 census, the 65-and-over group was almost seven times as large as it was in 1900, but the under-65 population was less than three times as large.[6] Between 1960 and 1970 alone, the number of older Americans increased 21 per cent, while the number of people under 65 increased by 18 per cent. In sheer numbers the older population represents a huge group, equaling the total population of all ages of our 22 smallest states. In terms of percentages, the growth of older adults in our population is equally impressive. In the last 70 years, the percentage of older adults rose from 4 to 10 per cent. One out of every 10 Americans was over 65 in 1976.[7]

The very old represent a steadily increasing proportion of those over 65. More and more people are living to reach their seventies and eighties, and they comprise the fastest growing of all the age categories. Between 1960 and 1970, the number of people who had passed their seventy-fifth birthday increased by 49 per cent over twice the increase of those between 65 and 74.[8] And one-hundreth birthdays are no longer so rare. More than 9,460 centenarians were receiving Social Security benefits in 1975.[9]

Women also make up a substantial proportion of the older adult population. In 1974 they constituted more than 60 per cent of the 20 million people over 65, an increase of

---

[5]*Part I: Developments in Aging:* 1975 and January–May 1976, p. xv.

[6]*Developments in Aging:* 1974 and January–April 1975, p. xvii.

[7]*Part I: Developments in Aging:* 1975 and January–May 1976, p. xv.

[8]*Developments in Aging:* 1974 and January–April 1975, p. xviii.

[9]Conversation with author, research division, Social Security Administration, June 21, 1976.

10 per cent since 1930. It is projected that the proportion of people over 65 will continue to increase at least through the year 2000. In 1890 there were 102 men aged 65 and older for every 100 women in the same age group. By 1974 the number of men had shrunk to 100 for every 143 women.[10] And by the year 2000, it is estimated that the number will shrink even further, to a ratio of 100 men to every 154 women.[11] As a consequence, the problems of the aging in the years ahead will be dominated increasingly by the problems of those in advanced old age and by the problems of single women.

None of these trends shows any signs of stopping or even slowing down. More likely, they will speed up. We will have more, not fewer, elderly people. Although predictions are chancey, by the year 2000, the total population of those over 65 is expected to be at least 30 million.[12] That is a *conservative* estimate. Other reliable studies put the figure much higher, and the estimates reach up to 50 million. The Bureau of the Census has estimated that, by the year 2030, the population of older adults will make up 16 per cent of the total population of the United States. If the present very low birth rates continue, that figure could be much higher. And no one is willing to predict the consequences of a major breakthrough in a cure for such killer diseases as cancer or cardiovascular disease. If cures were to be discovered, the number of older Americans would zoom off the now-existing population charts.

These statistics are useful signposts to the changing population picture. But they do not tell the whole story. The over-65 age group is not static. It is constantly changing as some old people die and younger people turn 65 and take

---

[10]*Developments in Aging:* 1974 and January–April 1975, p. xix.

[11]Ibid., p. xix.

[12]*Part I: Developments in Aging:* 1975 and January–May 1976, p. xix.

their places. Old age can be compared to a moving conveyor belt with some people getting on as others get off. Therefore, we can learn from statistics how many people will be in the over-65 age category in the year 2000, for example, but we can't tell how many will have passed through the old-age category between now and then. We can get some idea, however, from the fact that each day about 4,000 Americans celebrate their sixty-fifth birthday and about 3,000 aged 65 or over die, leaving a net increase of about 1,000 persons.[13]

We have been using "65-years-old" as a convenient and useful definition of old age, primarily because the pertinent statistics have been compiled with 65 as the dividing point between middle and old age. Consequently, we will refer to those over 65 with such terms as "older adult," "old," "aged," "elderly," and "senior citizen" throughout this book.

WHAT IS OLD AGE?

Although the sixty-fifth year and old age have become synonymous, there is nothing magical about turning 65-years-old. People do not age suddenly on the morning of their sixty-fifth birthday. We have given old age a social definition that ignores certain realities. Almost before we have left our youth, our mirrors show us the inexorable toll of the onslaught of years. Our hair turns gray and our once firm skin sags and wrinkles. Such biological happenings mock the fact that we shrink from our own aging. Physically we age continuously over the course of a lifetime. If we were to speak of growing old in physical terms, it would be more accurate to talk about aging instead of old age and refer to people as more or less aged rather than young and old.

But we have found it easier or more convenient, or perhaps less threatening, to accept society's tidy, if false, de-

---

[13] Ibid., p. xvi.

finition of old age. That definition stems from the Social Security Act of 1935, and it is a combination of custom and law, with a few interesting, individual exceptions. Many workers were already retiring at 65 when Congress decided to use it rather arbitrarily as the age of eligibility for Social Security benefits. Congress could have picked age 64 or 66 with equal ease. The passage of the Social Security Act crystalized custom into law, and many companies consequently adopted policies of mandatory retirement at the age of 65.

Congress tacked another requirement onto the original Social Security Act—it wasn't enough just to be 65. To be eligible to collect full benefits, a worker had to have retired from full-time participation in the work force. This has had a definite effect on our perceptions of old age. As long as people continue to work, they appear young to us. Physically and mentally, they may be no more vigorous than their retired contemporaries, but somehow they *seem* younger. The converse is also true. People who retire before the customary age of 65 or 62, or even younger—and the age of retirement is constantly going down—seem suddenly old. Society's view of who is young and who is old is reflected in the thinking of older people themselves. For instance, sociologists studying older people in Elmira, New York, a city of about 40,000, found those who were employed consistently refused to consider themselves old, while retirees of the same age more readily accepted the fact that they were no longer young. Only 18 per cent of employed people in their sixties said that they were old; 37 per cent of retirees of the same age did.

This arbitrary definition of old age has encouraged the thinking of those over 65 as some kind of alien group, somehow separate and distinct from the rest of society. We talk about the old as if the old were not once young and as if the young were not to become old. Marcel Proust, the French author, recognized the truth when he wrote, "Adolescents who live long enough are what society makes old men out of."

Fortunately, for some time now our whole concept of age has been in the process of being redefined. Our notions of youth, middle age, and old age are in a state of flux. Sooner or later all of us will feel the impact. Some felt it when the age of adulthood was changed. For years we assumed adolescence ended and adulthood began at 21, which was about as arbitrary as our assumption that old age begins at 65. When Congress lowered the voting age in federal elections from the age of 21 to 18, a whole new class of "adults" was suddenly created. Most states quickly followed by lowering the voting age in state elections to 18. At the same time, most states also granted a host of other adult rights, previously reserved to those over 21, to the 18-year-olds. By the passage of a few laws, millions of young people were suddenly considered adult enough to drink, gamble, and enter into legal contracts.

These changes, a reflection of the frenzy of our fast paced society, are having severe repercussions on the young. Many of the young feel old rapidly. In 1972 the *New York Times Magazine* ran an article by Joyce Maynard, a Yale University student, titled "An 18-Year-Old Looks Back on Her Life." The author said she was looking forward to a quiet and reflective time in her twenties after the turbulence of her teen-age years. She said she wanted to "retire" from the political upheavals and social movements of the 1960s that had been part of her life when she was still in junior and senior high school. Maynard wrote rather wistfully that she wanted to be a private person again.[14]

RETIREMENT

At the other end of our age spectrum, our tidy definitions of middle and old age are being upset by earlier retire-

---

[14]Joyce Maynard, "An 18-Year-Old Looks Back on Her Life," *New York Times Magazine,* April 23, 1972, p. 11.

ment. Recognizing this, retirement villages in many parts of the country are admitting people at the age of 55. One large development on the West Coast reports that 27 per cent of its residents are under 65. These people who retire in their early sixties or late fifties will have to accept a younger definition of old age or reject our social definition that old age begins at retirement. Such choices entail immeasurable psychological strains. Earlier retirement is forcing economists to talk about the problems of the "older worker" of 45 or even 40. This trend toward a "younger" old age has been underway for some time, however. A study of state employment agencies undertaken by the Department of Labor found that as far back as 1949 employers considered "older workers" to be those employees who had reached the age of 40 or 45.

This pushing back and down of the boundaries of old age has serious ramifications for 27 million working Americans between 45 and 64. They include 10.7 million between the ages of 55 and 64, who are on the brink of retirement and who are presumably already planning for their postwork years. Then there are 16.3 million in the older worker category who are caught in the squeeze between the shortening of work careers and increased longevity.[15]

This 45 to 54 age group illustrates most clearly our changing notions about who is young, middle-aged, and old. For that reason it is worth considering in some detail what is happening to them in the job market.

In the mid-1960s *Time* magazine featured this middle-aged group in a cover article on the "command generation." The article assumed that this age group controlled the country's economy, set its predominate values, and kept a firm grip on the positions of power. Although it is still true that large numbers of those who control the country fall

---

[15]*Employment and Earnings* (Washington, D.C.: U.S. Department of Labor, June, 1976), pp. 21–22.

within the 45 to 54 age category, it is equally true that large numbers of those in the same age bracket are being eased, more or less voluntarily, out of their once secure jobs.

Accurate figures on the number of early retirements in private industry are lacking, but there is general agreement that the number is considerable and increasing. At Ford Motor Company, for example, the number of early retirements nearly doubled between 1973 and 1974—621 employees retired before 65 in 1973, against 1,294 employees in 1974.

Forced retirement before the age of 65 is barred by federal law, but special financial arrangements or attractive pension supplements are often dangled before older employees as inducements for early retirement. Such lures are credited with boosting early retirements at the New England Telephone and Telegraph Company in Boston, and the Wells Fargo Bank in San Francisco. In an effort to cut its work force, the International Business Machine Corporation in 1975 offered a special deal to employees with 25 years service—50 per cent of their salary for up to four years plus their regular pension.

In other, more cruel cases, longtime employees are simply notified that they have "volunteered" for early retirement. A 56-year-old "volunteer" with 32 years service at his firm said, "I was in complete shock when they handed me the notice." Such pressure, according to a Department of Labor spokesman, is "quite widespread."[16]

The push into early retirement is not confined to private industry. Within the federal government, the average retirement age has steadily declined. Between 1964 and 1974, the average age of retirement from the Civil Service dropped from 62 to 58. In the early 1970s the Civil Service raised the annuity of those who retired at 55 by 6.1 per cent to encourage older civil servants to retire. As a result, one of

---

[16]"Early Out," *Newsweek*, April 7, 1975, pp. 67–68.

the largest groups ever to retire left the Civil Service in 1973—122,000, more than twice the normal average.[17]

THE UNEMPLOYED

For other older workers, the problems of unemployment begin in more humiliating ways without the cushion of extra money to ease the transition out of the work force. Some are laid off during a general slowdown in business. Others whose skills and expertise are considered out-of-date find that they are unwanted and unneeded. They are technological casualties. These men and women desire work, but prospective employers often shun them because of their age. Their numbers grew at an alarming rate during the first half of the 1970s. As a result of the recession, hundreds of thousands of older workers were laid off. In early 1975 there were 1.5 million persons over 45 on the unemployment lines. But this figure omits the substantial number of older workers who dropped out of the labor force after futile searches for employment and, therefore, were no longer classified as "unemployed." The "hidden" unemployed might have raised the actual unemployment figure to 2.9 million.[18]

Their ranks include workers from every conceivable job category—professionals, white collar employees, skilled blue collar workers and unskilled workers. Relative youth and a good education do not necessarily guarantee work. At a hearing before the U.S. Senate Special Committee on Aging, a 48-year-old lawyer, laid off during cutbacks by the National Aeronautical and Space Administration at Cape Kennedy, testified, "I've learned that the rule of thumb is not to hire lawyers over 40." In the course of answering every help-wanted ad and signing up with the employment agen-

---

[17]*Washington Star-News*, February, 21, 1974, p. 1.

[18]*Developments in Aging:* 1974 and January–April 1975, p. 64.

cies in his city, he sent out between 30 to 40 resumes and went to 13 job interviews over a two-year period. Despite good recommendations and high qualifications, he received no offers.

Once they become unemployed, many discover, as the lawyer did, that their age makes them unemployable. Although they are often the first to be fired, they are also the last to be hired. Employers are reluctant to invest time and money in training older workers who will retire in a few years, feeling, undoubtedly, that they will receive insufficient returns on their investments. In his opening statement at these hearings on unemployment among older workers, Senator Jennings Randolph of West Virginia commented, "Most people think in terms of 65 and older when they consider the problems associated with advancing age. But, in the case of unemployment, age may be a handicap 10, 20, or even 25 years before traditional retirement age." The bias against hiring men and women after the age of 45 is so pervasive, so deeply engrained, that employment agencies are apt to refuse such clients, knowing in advance that they will be difficult to place. A 58-year-old unemployed office clerk said that she had been turned away by the Florida State Employment Service. She said, "They told me not to come back. They said it would be a waste of time."[19]

Older workers who find themselves unemployed are generally out of work for many more weeks than younger workers. Even 15 or 27 weeks of unemployment is not un usual. Often, unable to relocate in a similar job at a comparable salary, unemployed older workers find themselves descending the career ladder. Eventually, they may unwillingly end up on welfare. In addition to the immediate financial loss caused by their unemployment, older workers must cope

---

[19]Author's notes, Hearings on Unemployment Among Older Workers, U. S. Senate Special Committee on Aging, Miami, Florida, August 11, 1971

with the loss of pride and sense of dignity. Although long-term unemployment during the middle years of life is obviously a problem in itself, it is not the whole problem. Unemployment or underemployment in the years before retirement reduces the income that a worker can expect to receive from Social Security or private pension plans after retirement. Economists fear that the business recessions and the resulting tight job market of the late 1960s and the first half of the 1970s will create a whole new generation of the elderly poor.

If these trends continue—and there is every reason to believe that they will not only continue but accelerate—one out of every six men in the 55- to 59-year-old category will be forced out of the work force by the end of the century into a premature and unwanted retirement before he reaches his sixty-fifth birthday. In 1960 the corresponding ratio was one out of every eight men. Before the start of the twenty-first century, the typical American might end up spending a third to almost a half of his life in retirement. Obviously, something is happening. In the course of a few generations the amount of time consumed by work over the life-span has been drastically reduced. For the first time, the national economy does not require people to put in 40 or 50 years of work to obtain a few years of leisure at the end of their lives. We can afford to have large numbers of people unemployed over long periods of time. Leisure, freely chosen or involuntarily imposed, is becoming available while people are mentally and physically able to enjoy it to the fullest.

A whole new life stage, a time that is neither middle age nor old age, but has some characteristics of both, is emerging. A few researchers have been studying, as they put it, the "postparental" phase of life. They are researching the years between 45 or 50, when the last child is grown and living independently and the parents are once again alone, and age 65, when old age has traditionally begun. But this new stage in the life cycle is not limited to people with children. Unmarried individuals and childless couples will be experiencing this newly evolved, yet largely unexplored stage of life. It would be more accurate to speak of a "post-work" life phase. Other sociologists, recognizing the blurring of distinctions between middle age and old age, have adopted the terminology "the young-old" for those between 55 and 65 and "the old-old" for those over 65. But these are hybrid terms that obscure more than they clarify. In short, we are confronted with a lengthy period of time that cannot be defined in terms of our present definitions of the life cycle. Reality has outstripped our ability to deal with it—or even to conceptualize it.

The preferred term in this book for those who are no longer middle-aged is "older adult," a phrase that seems to be less loaded emotionally and to carry with it fewer prejudicial connotations. It offers the further advantage of implying that aging and growing old occur constantly throughout life.

The terminology may not be overly important, but it *is* important that our arbitrary definitions are modified to take into account these changing realities. Obviously, people in their late forties and fifties will resent being labeled old simply because they are no longer employed. Although they may share many of the same social and economic problems of people in their sixties, they will not consider themselves, and will not want society to consider them, old.

Furthermore, the people who will be turning 60 during the next few decades will be vastly different from previous generations of older adults. Better educated, in far better mental and physical health, more capable of living independently and with more adequate financial resources, they will explode our notions of what it means to be old in America. To speak of them as "old," with its implications of physical and mental decay, will be a misnomer and one that they will rightly resent. Instead, we are about to see a new generation of those over 60, more vibrant and alive, with the capability of using their leisure to the fullest, who will want more from society than society has allotted to them in the past and who will make still unanticipated demands on society.

All of this—earlier retirement, shorter work careers,

and a blurring of our traditional definitions of age—points to another good reason for examining in depth the growing numbers of Americans over 65. They have been social pioneers, "immigrants in time," to use Margaret Mead's phrase, the first group to experience an early and long retirement. Their problems of maintaining a sufficient income during the postwork years, securing proper and adequate medical care, and finding useful and meaningful pursuits in their leisure time are the concerns of more and more of us. The old have been alerting us, if we would only listen, to problems of growing social relevance. They have been charting our future with basically inadequate resources and limited public assistance of any kind. Despite the growth and numbers of those over 65, America has yet to face seriously the question of the place of older adults in our society.

GOVERNMENT POLICY

Official public concern seems to fluctuate in two-year cycles. Little concern or attention is given to the problems of older Americans in nonelection years. But as election years approach and members of Congress prepare to face reelection, there are frequent speeches on the floor of the House and Senate about the need to honor our senior citizens, and bills to raise Social Security benefits gather support. Despite this rhetoric aimed at the over-65 voter, there is little agreement on such fundamentals as the place of older Americans in government-sponsored welfare and social programs or the level of benefits and the method for financing the Social Security system is still being debated decades after the legislation was initially passed. Government researchers, meanwhile, continue to fight over the amount of funds that should be devoted to basic research into the process of aging and into the causes of cancer and other diseases that attack young and old alike.

Moreover, little thought has gone into creating roles and meaningful pursuits for older people, who may be spending 30 or 40 years without the necessity of getting up and going to work in the morning. Older men and women are rarely asked what they would like or are capable of doing. Instead, the attitude of most sociologists and psychologists seems to be that life ends at about 40. They ignore older adults. Some gerontologists talk about the final third of life as a "consumatory" period suitable for quiet reflection and contemplation, but not much else. In *Childhood and Society*, psychologist Erik Erikson wrote " . . . healthy children will not fear life if their elders have integrity enough not to fear death".[20] That line of thought presupposes that older people are prepared to be content with teaching others how to die with grace and dignity.

Although the examples of our "nonpolicy" of aging are plentiful, the foregoing give some idea of the distance we are from a clearly articulated approach to the needs and wants of retired people. The former Commissioner of the Administration on Aging, John Martin, admitted. "The problems have come at us faster than the solutions."[21]

Few older people have been lucky enough to escape entirely the painful effects of this piecemeal philosophy of aging. For some, it means hoarding frayed dollar bills in order to eke out even a moderate standard of living in retirement. Others endure unnecessary pain because proper medical care is difficult or impossible to obtain. Even those who are fortunate enough to be healthy and to have sufficient financial resources are made to feel like second-class citizens. A retired dentist said he felt that he had been cut off from normal participation in the community when he retired. With a grimace that twisted the corners of his mouth,

---

[20]Erik H. Erikson, *Childhood and Society,* 2nd rev. ed. (New York: W.W. Norton, 1963), p. 320.

[21]Personal interview.

he said, "Look at these hands. I spent years learning how to use them. Now I'm supposed to make baskets with them."

Up to now, these 22 million men and women have been relatively silent about their problems. But this is changing. Older adults are growing restless. They are beginning to voice their grievances. They are talking with increasing frequency about political action. Like other minority groups with legitimate grievances, they are getting involved in politics. Many are joining senior citizens groups, hoping through joint action that they can force the country to sit up and take notice of them. Such groups are growing rapidly, and their frankly political membership pitch indicates that older people are responding to the call for political action. A surprisingly large number of people over 65 who were interviewed for this book felt that older adults were growing more militant. One said, "It hasn't been recognized yet, but the senior citizen is on the march." Many voiced similar thoughts in almost the same words.

This undercurrent of discontent, which promises to surface in national politics, cannot be ignored. A well-organized senior power movement under a determined leadership could have the same turbulent impact on the country's politics as the civil rights movement had in the late 1950s and early 1960s. In fact, some people in government think a senior power movement would have a bigger impact. In the same way that blacks forced politicians to take stands in favor of desegregation of schools, to support civil rights legislation, and to promise the appointment of blacks to government positions, older adults could force politicians to make similar concessions in their self-interest. The sheer number of older Americans who are eligible to vote indicates their potential political power. No politician can afford to ignore that many voters if he wants to get elected and stay in office. Such political power in the hands of older adults is not unprecedented, as we shall see in later chapters. At times in our history, older people have successfully exercised political power and manipulated politicians in pursuit of their own self-interests.

Years of talking at length to senior citizens, government officials, and gerontologists in and out of government has led me to the conclusion that we are in the midst of important social changes due to the promise and challenge of increased longevity. We need to reappraise our social and political institutions to enable them to respond imaginatively to the growing number of older people and retired people of all ages. We need to modify our life-styles and values as a consequence. Moreover, we need to do these things immediately. We have little time to waste. The urgency of this need is underscored by the research that is now going on in the biology of aging, research that holds out the possibility of even greater longevity by slowing down the process of aging.

WHY WE GROW OLD
AND WHAT CAN BE DONE
ABOUT IT

CHAPTER TWO

In the early 1980s a group of men and women should begin taking part in the most exciting and far-reaching experiment in the history of man. They will be the first people to participate in a series of tests that are expected to extend the human life-span and postpone the debilitating effects of old age. If the researchers are lucky and the tests are successful, some means of controlling the rate of aging may be known by 1985. By the early 1990s, a cheap, readily available and easy to take antiaging drug could be in our medicine cabinets. To begin with, we can expect a 10 or 20 per cent gain in our normal life-span. This would mean a minimum of 7 to 14 additional years of healthy, vigorous life. As the antiaging drug is perfected, this minimum might be increased.

Such was the scenario presented by Dr. Alex Comfort, an English biologist who is considered one of the world's leading experts on aging, at the annual meeting of the Gerontological Society in 1972. He stressed that his timetable was, if anything, conservative. "This," he said, "represents the lower limit of speed in development, given the present investment [in research funds], which is rather small."[1]

Other reliable studies predict a similar or even more dramatic extension of the life-span before the end of this century. The Rand Corporation, the highly regarded "think tank," predicts that we will be able to slow down the aging process by 10 or 20 per cent before 1990.[2] Smith, Kline and French, the pharmaceutical corporation, predicts the ability to control the aging process and a significant extension of life-span by 1993.[3] And Dr. Robert Prehoda, a specialist in technological forecasting, projects a 20 to 30 per cent increase in the life-span between 1980 and the year 2000.[4]

No scientist is willing to predict a generation of Methusalahs, but none is flatly ruling out the possibility either. Some say, on the basis of what is known now, there may be no upper limit on our life-span. In fact, biologist and former president of the American Association for the Advancement of Science, Dr. Bentley Glass said optimistically, "We are either the last of the mortals or the first of the immortals."[5]

---

[1] Author's notes, 25th annual meeting of the Gerontological Society, San Juan, Puerto Rico, December 17, 1972.

[2] T. J. Gordon and O. Helmer, "Report on a Long Range Forecasting Study," Rand Corporation, Santa Monica, California, 1964.

[3] A. Douglas Bender, Alvin E. Strack, George W. Ebright, and George von Haunalter, "A Delphic Study of the Future of Medicine," Smith Kline and French Laboratories, Philadelphia, 1969.

[4] Robert Prehoda, "Technological Forecasting, Longevity and Demography," paper prepared for Life Span Conference, Center for the Study of Democratic Institutions, Santa Barbara, California, April 13–17, 1970.

[5] Author's notes, 25th annual meeting of the Gerontological Society, December 18.

The very adjective that defines our nature, that is mortal, derives from the Greek for "those who must die." The immortals, of course, were those who were free of the exigencies of death and dying. Current research holds out the hope of postponing death. Man will be improving on the work of nature. For the first time, we will be able to push back the biological boundaries of life and conquer, even if just for a short while, our mortality. We shall be as gods. The consequences are immeasurable for man and for society.

There is a crucial difference between increases in our life-span, which is what we are talking about here, and an increase in longevity. We have been steadily increasing longevity for the past 150 years, and particularly during the last 70. Children born at the turn of the century could expect to live to be 47-years-old. Children born in 1973 can look forward to reaching their seventy-first birthday.[6] But for today's adults, life expectancy has not increased significantly. The young now live to reach old age, but the old die at about the same age they always did. At the turn of the century, a person of 65 could expect to live 13 more years. In 1974 the life expectancy of 65-year-olds was 15.5 years.[7] Although life expectancy at birth has gone from 47 to 70 years of age, an increase of 50 per cent, life expectancy at age 65 has increased by a mere two years, only 15 per cent. We are rapidly approaching a society where, barring unforeseen accident or disease, almost everyone lives to be 70, but nearly everyone is dead at 100.

Even cures for the leading causes of death among older adults would not appreciably change this situation. Dr. Carl Eisdorfer, former president of the Gerontological Society, estimates that cures for cancer, heart disease, and

---

[6]*Developments in Aging:* 1974 and January–April 1975 (Washington: U.S. Government Printing Office, 1975), p. xix.

[7]*Part I: Developments in Aging:* 1975 and January–May 1976 (Washington, D.C.: U.S. Government Printing Office, 1975), p. xvii.

cardiovascular-renal disease would add another 25 years at the most to the life expectancies of older adults.[8] This is because different parts of our bodies can age at widely varying rates. A person of 65 may have a heart that is functionally 40-years-old and a kidney that is functionally 70-years-old. People saved from dying of cancer, for example, may die soon afterward of, say, heart disease. Doctors now spend a large amount of their time treating people suffering from various degenerative diseases. But patching up one part of the body makes little difference when another part will soon fail. Our bodies become like old cars in need of constant repair. The upkeep is expensive, time-consuming, and ultimately futile. Such treatment can only be palliative at best.

THE AGING PROCESS

We all know what happens as we age. Our senses dull so that we cannot see or hear or smell as well as we did when we were young. Our muscles are not as strong or as coordinated. Bones lose their calcium and become brittle and quick to break in falls. Connective tissue, the substance that holds together the various parts of our bodies, hardens and contracts so that our once erect posture may become stooped and bent. The changing connective tissue makes the skin stiff and thin and prone to wrinkles. Fat accumulates around the midsection. Our hair turns gray and starts to fall out.

The deterioration that accompanies old age goes on deep inside our bodies also. Organs function more slowly. The heart pumps less efficiently. Blood doesn't move as fast as it should through the body, and the kidneys filter the blood more slowly. The lungs breathe in less and less oxygen. The bladder's capacity is similarly diminished. The brain shrinks as 100,000 of its cells die each day. The flow of hormones

---

[8]Author's notes, June 1971.

from the ovaries, testes, adrenals, and pituitary gland diminishes. Sludge accumulates in our cells, impairing their functioning. The yellow-black sludge called lipofuscin may make up 30 per cent of the volume of our cells in old age.

The onset of these changes is controlled by the rate of aging, which, in turn, controls how long we will live. This rate of aging can be calculated mathematically, as any life insurance agent knows, since it forms the basis of actuarial charts. It means the possibility of dying increases geometrically throughout life so that we are more likely to die of natural causes at the age of 70 than at 17. The increasing chance of death as we grow older reflects the progressive accumulation of disease, injury, and deterioration. In *Ageing: The Biology of Senescence,* Dr. Alex Comfort writes, "If we kept throughout life the same resistance to disease, stress, injury, which we had at the age of 10, about half of us here today might expect to survive in 700 years' time."[9]

This rate of aging varies with the species, so that nearly all mice are dead at 3 years of age, dogs at 15, horses by 30, and men by 100. These differences in maximum lifespan reflect the differences in the rate at which the "biological clock" that times the aging process is set—the faster it runs, the shorter the life-span.

The case of mouse and man offers a good illustration. Both are physiologically alike with similar brains, livers, hearts, kidneys, and gonads. Yet, their average life-spans are vastly different. The changes that take place during the second year of the mouse's life are biologically disastrous. A man doesn't experience comparable changes until his late sixties. For example, collagen, the material that composes our muscle tendons, ages much more rapidly in mice than in men. Similarly, what we called age pigments accumulate at a faster rate in mouse than in man. In the mouse brain, the age

---

[9]Alex Comfort, *Ageing: The Biology of Senescence* (New York: Holt, Rinehart and Winston, 1964), p. 1.

pigments take up as much as 25 per cent of the space within the cells by the time they are two years old. In the human brain, they build up much more slowly, at a rate of slightly over .6 per cent of the total volume per decade. All of this indicates that the "biological clock" ticks faster for the mouse than for the man. Scientists are still searching for clues to the cause.

SLOWING THE AGING RATE

If we are to extend the life-span, we must slow down the rate of aging, in effect, reset the "biological clock" that controls our aging process. Scientists believe that if the aging process could be slowed down even a little, it would alter our lives dramatically. Dr. Bernard Strehler, a biologist at the University of Southern California, estimates that a slight decrease in the rate of aging would make the 70-year-old men and women of tomorrow look and feel, physically and mentally, like today's men and women of 56. Ultimately, people would take 90 years to reach the present physical and mental deterioration of the age of 70.

By slowing down the aging process, we will be able to extend the life-span without prolonging the mental and physical decline that often accompanies old age. Most of us, if we were able to choose, would probably opt for a long, active life followed by a quick, painless death. Unfortunately, scientists consider such a life to be biologically improbable. But although mental and physical decline might not be eliminated altogether, it is also unlikely that they will be prolonged if for no other reason than that an antiaging drug that prolonged mental and physical infirmities would be unlikely to win widespread acceptance. It would be available, but it would be unused. Strehler estimates that slowing down the rate of aging will result in the same proportion of the old "in all stages of disrepair" that exist now. In fact, he predicts the proportion will be smaller during the initial use of an antiaging drug.[10] We will escape the monstrous fate of the Struldbugs, the tragic immortals of Jonathan Swift's *Gulliver's Travels*, who were doomed to eternal life without perpetual youth.

The quest for just this sort of antiaging drug has preoccupied scientists and not-so-scientific researchers from the beginning of time. King David tried sleeping with young virgins to absorb revitalizing "airs" from their bodies. At the very least, as one writer pointed out, it kept him from feeling lonely. Achilles ate the bone marrow of young bears to increase his strength and courage. Suruta, the Indian physician who practiced in 800 B.C., advised impotent patients to eat the testes of tigers. Later on, those who wished to stay young were advised at various times to eat mandrake roots, partridge brains, Chinese birds' nest soup, sweet potatoes, and a powder derived from the tubers of orchids known as salep.

By the nineteenth century, those who wanted to stay young, and for most this meant sexually potent, were again experimenting with animal testicles, this time through injections. Dr. Charles Edouard Brown-Sequard, the son of an Irish-American sea captain and a French mother, tried liquid injections from bulls' testicles. He claimed that the liquid made him into a new man and that at 72 he was able to resume sexual relations with his young wife. He attracted thousands of patients who were eager to try the supposedly magical injections, but his conservative colleagues in the medical profession rejected his novel ideas of sexual rejuvenation, and he died a broken man.

In the twentieth century, spurred no doubt by advances in surgical techniques, young doctors began experimenting with various "revitalizing" operations. Dr. Elie

---

[10]Bernard L. Strehler, "Myth and Fact: Consequences of the Understanding of Aging," paper prepared for Life Span Conference, Center for the Study of Democratic Institutions, Santa Barbara, California, April 13–17, 1970.

Metchikoff, who won a Nobel prize for his work on white blood cells, theorized that the body absorbed debilitating poisons from the large intestine. He suggested that removing the large intestine would, therefore, postpone old age. In the early 1900s, some people actually had their large intestines removed in an attempt to prolong youth. They found that although the large intestine apparently had little to do with the aging process, it did play a vital role in the body's functioning, and many died as a result of the operation. Another doctor, Serge Voronoff, a reputable but eccentric surgeon, tried grafting chimpanzee testicles onto his patients in another attempt at sexual rejuvenation. His "monkey gland" treatment became very popular in the 1920s. But Voronoff was also scorned by his medical colleagues, and his dream of rejuvenating men by inserting slivers of chimpanzee testicles into their own collapsed.

Despite these exotic attempts to discover an elixir of youth, a true "cure" for aging is more likely to grow out of much less glamorous, but far more rewarding, research in molecular biology. Although many things about the aging process remain a mystery, biologists, huddled over their microscopes and test tubes, are rapidly expanding our knowledge about how our cells and their components work. When we learn how cells control life, we may be well on our way to discovering how to retard the aging process. Let's see what our scientists have learned so far. To begin with, we age because our cells die. Some cells are simply incapable of reproducing themselves. Their number is determined at birth, and it remains constant throughout life. When such a cell dies as a result of injury or other, unknown causes, it cannot be replaced by surviving cells. Brain neurons are an example. The death of these cells actually causes the brain to shrink over the years so that it weighs 44 ounces at the age of 30, but only 40 ounces by the age of 90. Fortunately, most cells are capable of reproducing themselves, at least for a while, but they cannot reproduce indefinitely. They duplicate themselves for a time, then stop. Their life-spans are limited.

The discovery that our cells have finite life-spans star-
tled the scientific world when it was announced in 1961 by
Dr. Leonard Hayflick, chairman of the Department of Mi-
crobiology at the Stanford University School of Medicine.
Hayflick made the discovery quite by accident while doing
cancer research on human cells growing in tissue cultures.
Up to then, most scientists supposed that cells, supplied with
adequate nutrients, were capable of dividing forever. Our
cells were thought to be essentially immortal. But while experimenting with cells cultured from the lung tissue of a
human embryo, Hayflick found that the cells divided 50
times and then stopped. He tried interrupting the cellular
division by putting the cell colonies in a deep freeze after 30
divisions. When the cells were defrosted, Hayflick found,
they "remembered" how many times they had already doubled, and they took up where they had left off as long as 10
years before. They divided 20 more times, and then they
quit.

Hayflick does not think that we age simply because
our cells stop doubling. "That's nonsense," he said bluntly.[11]
He believes that we do not live long enough for our cells to
double the maximum of 50 times. But he does believe
that aging is a reflection of changes that occur in our cells
before they lose their ability to divide.

Evidence of this comes from the unfortunate victims
of a rare disease called progeria. Afflicted children, such as
Ricky Gallant of eastern Canada, seem to crowd their entire
biological life cycle into a few short years. When Ricky died in
March 1967 at the age of 11, he was chronologically young
but physically old. Wrinkled and bald-headed, suffering
from hardening of the arteries, Ricky looked like a wrinkled
old man.[12] Scientists know that cells taken from progeria

---

[11]"Aging," *Medical World News,* October 22, 1971, pp. 46–57.
[12]*Toronto Daily Star,* March 8, 1967.

victims double only a few times when they are cultured in the laboratory. The same defect in the hypothetical genetic clock that prevents their cells from dividing normally could also cause their premature aging.

If aging can be accelerated by mistake, as in the case of Ricky, we may be able to slow it down on purpose. Scientists are studying deoxyribonucleic acid or DNA, the genetic material in our cells, in an attempt to find out how the genes affect the aging process. DNA contains all of the information that is needed for our bodies to function correctly. It tells our cells to breathe, digest food, eliminate wastes, and reproduce. Somehow, scientists suspect, DNA loses some of this vital information as time passes.

Just how this information loss occurs is still being guessed at, but there are two main theories. The first holds that errors occur as the genetic materials are reproduced again and again. The DNA continues to transmit information, but with the passage of time it begins to make mistakes. Because of these errors, essential substances, called enzymes, cannot carry out chemical reactions that are essential for the survival of our cells, and eventually the cells die. This can be compared metaphorically to the scratches that build up on a long-playing record with repeated playing. At some point the scratches become so numerous that the record can't be played at all. If information is lost through cellular errors caused by "scratches" on the DNA, scientists say it will be relatively easy to slow down the aging process. In effect, some way can be found to lubricate the record so that it plays properly despite the scratches.

The second theory is that aging is genetically programmed into our cells. Within the DNA is a genetic program that causes us to deteriorate and die. The program starts at birth and plays for the next 90 or 100 years. When the program ends, cell functions ceases and life is over. If such is the case, the search for a "cure" for aging will be greatly complicated and take far longer. Scientists will have to devise a way to reset the genetic program so it plays at a slower speed. The effect will be like playing a 78 rpm record at 45 rpms. The program will then take longer to reach the end. To do this, scientists will have to locate the precise gene that controls aging, then alter it in some yet unknown way so that the aging process is substantially slowed. Such sophisticated genetic engineering is beyond our present capabilities.

Whether aging is caused by accumulated "scratches" or genetically programmed, its control depends on keeping the vital information contained within the DNA in good shape and continuously available for use by our cells.

Strehler, the leading proponent of the genetic theory of aging, suggests that we age because some control genes turn off the manufacturing of various parts of the body. All our cells, an estimated trillion or so, contain the same exact information that was present in the original fertilized egg. Because the DNA is the same and the cellular environment is the same, we should be able theoretically to replace malfunctioning parts of the body. If a kidney was not filtering blood properly, we could grow a new kidney, and a new heart could replace a clogged artery. Scientists believe that there is a relationship between the aging of our cells and the ability of the control genes to read the manufacturing instructions— hundreds of thousands of messages, all about the length of a written paragraph—on the DNA. At some point, the genes may lose their reading abilities. The "cure" for aging may be a remedial reading course for these genes. If the lost reading abilities can be restored, our cells may stay young. Dr. J. Ilan of Temple University in Philadelphia has done intriguing experiments along these lines. He tried injecting old cells with cellular extracts from young cells. Apparently revitalized, the old cells began reading genetic messages that had been previously lost to them.

In addition to genetic research into the aging process, scientists are exploring other ways of reaching the goal of a long, youthful life. Some research is based on entirely different theories of aging. Not all scientists believe that the secret of growing old is hidden in our genes. Other research is aimed at retarding some of the undesirable results of the aging process even before we understand what causes it. After all, we don't have to understand electricity to turn on a lamp. This research has concentrated on the effect of diet and temperature on aging, along with a fresh look at a previously discredited youth drug.

OTHER POSSIBLE CONTROLS

Let's look at the fascinating research on the aging process to see other ways in which aging might be controlled.

Autoimmunity. We may age because of a progressive failure in our body's immunological system. Antibodies and specialized white cells produced by the immune system are supposed to recognize and attack invading viruses and bacteria. But as we age, the system seems to go beserk, losing its ability to distinguish between our own body and its enemies. In short, we grow allergic to our bodies. The results are those changes that we associate with age.

There is fresh evidence that this may be the case. In the course of studying the relationship between senility and the loss of brain cells, Dr. Kalidas Nandy, associate professor of anatomy at Emory University School of Medicine in Atlanta, found that the immune system caused the death of nerve cells in aging mice. He also discovered that antibodies against the nerve cells were present in the blood of old mice but absent in the blood of young mice. When young mice were inoculated with the blood of old mice, thus exposing them to the antibodies, Nandy reported that they, too, showed signs of immunological damage.[13]

---

[13]Author's notes, 26th annual meeting of the Gerontological Society, Miami, Florida, November 7, 1973.

Nandy's experiments also suggest a way of correcting immune defects in aging. We might be able to deposit our disease-fighting white blood cells and antibodies in a deep freeze during youth and use them in old age to revitalize our failing immune systems. Thus bolstered, the immune system might function as it ought to, instead of turning against us.

Cross-linkages. Chemist Johan Bjorksten argues that aging is caused by molecules that get tied together as the years go by. "The effect," he writes in *New Scientist,* "is like what would happen in a large factory with thousands of workers, if someone slipped a pair of handcuffs on one hand of each of two workers, to tie them together. This, obviously, would reduce their ability to do their work, and if the process were allowed to spread through the factory, even at a slow rate, it would ultimately paralyze the entire operation unless means were found to remove the handcuffs faster than they were being applied."[14]

Bjorksten believes that we can control and "within limits" reverse aging by breaking down the cross-linkages. He suspects that this should not be difficult to accomplish. Soil bacteria, he points out, do this regularly. Otherwise the world would be littered with protein fossils. It might not be necessary for all of the cross-linkages to be broken. Instead of breaking the cross-linkages, the cross-linked molecules might be broken into fragments that could be easily excreted by the cells. This cleaning of the cells would revitalize our cells and, hopefully, our bodies.

Free Radicals. Another suspected cause of aging is a group of substances called free radicals. They are bits and pieces of molecules that are roaming free, looking for other molecules to latch onto, like convention delegates who have left their wives at home. They are commonly found in and

---

[14]Johan Bjorksten, "Could We Live Longer," *New Scientist,* 15, 552–54.

out of our bodies. The yellow smog tnat covers industrial cities like thick mohair blankets is partly composed of free radicals. They disintegrate leather and turn butter rancid. and, according to Dr. Denham Harman, professor of medicine at the University of Nebraska, they have an equally disastrous effect on our bodies.

Harman suggests that the free radicals are released when oxygen combines with polyunsaturated fats in our bodies. Once released, they thrash around in and out of our cells, disrupting the proper functions of cell membranes and worker enzymes. The result is tissue damage and, sometimes, death.

The proper diet, according to Harman, may minimize the disruptive effects caused by free radicals. By restricting the amount of polyunsaturated fats in our diets and adding antioxidants such as vitamin E that act as free radical traps, the number of free radical reactions might be reduced. The proper combination, Harman believes, could increase our healthy useful life-spans anywhere from 5 to 15 years.[15]

Blood toxins. The major aging agent may be toxins that accumulate in our blood over time. This theory, first proposed in 1923 and long forgotten, is currently being tested in a major research project by Dr. Norman Orentriech, a New York dermatologist. In recent years, more than 100 volunteer patients have been treated by plasmapheresis, a form of "blood washing," which entails withdrawing blood from the patient, removing its plasma content, and returning the blood minus the plasma to the patient. Some patients have the treatment weekly, others only once or twice a year.

Orentreich believes that blood plasma is a key factor in aging. "To make up for the lost plasma, the blood creates new plasma that behaves like the plasma of a very

---

[15]Denham Harman, "Chemical Protection Against Aging," *Agents and Actions*, 1, no. 1 (1969), 3–8.

young person," Orentreich said. "It speeds up the rate of cell growth and division throughout the body. Patients feel better and look better."[16]

The discovery of the cause, and subsequently the "cure," for aging will have a profound impact on our society. But the impact will be partially dependent on the cure. Our ability to buy and use an antiaging agent will vary. Some agents will be widely available; others, because of cost or inconvenience, will probably be reserved for the elite few. In such an event, the words "right to life" will acquire a new meaning, with moral implications for all of us.

In "Technological Forecasting, Longevity and Demography," a paper prepared for the Center for the Study of Democratic Institutions, Prehoda examined some of the possible consequences of aging research. He took three theories of aging, hypothesized that any one of them might be the primary cause, and examined the consequences to society if the "cure" for each one was in widespread use.[17] Here are his predictions:

1. If cross-linkages are responsible for aging, the discovery of an enzyme capable of severing them could mean a 35 per cent increase in the life-span. The enzymes will have a different effect on people of different ages because destroying the cross-linkages will allow some rejuvenation.

Some enzyme treatment will be fairly expensive. Enzymes will have to be injected with hypodermic syringes, and the syringes and learning how to give the shots will add to the treatment costs. Since enzymes are sensitive to extremes of temperature, they will need to be kept at a constant temperature, which will also increase the price. However, these costs might be partially offset by mass production. The consequent cost cutting might eventually bring the cost as low as $3

---

[16]Ted Burke, "The Controversial Rejuvenators," *Town and Country* (September 1972), p. 5.

[17]Prehoda, "Technological Forecasting."

or $5 a day, or $1,000 to $3,000 annually per person. Obviously, many will be unable to afford such youth treatments.

Perhaps as high as 25 per cent of the adult population in technologically advanced countries will be taking the injections in the first two decades after its discovery. As a result, the population of these countries will probably grow between one and two per cent by the start of the twenty-first century. More dramatic population gains can be expected in the second half of the twenty-first century as the original users of enzyme therapy reach advanced old age.

2. If free radicals cause aging, antioxidants should increase the human life-span by 35 per cent or more. Antioxidants, including vitamin E, can be manufactured cheaply in large quantities, bringing antiaging drugs within the reach of the entire population of developed countries and the relatively affluent in less-developed nations. Most likely, the antioxidants will be swallowed in pill form two or three times a day, at a cost of 20 or 30 cents, perhaps even less. Shortly after its introduction, half of the world's population might be taking daily doses of antioxidants.

For maximum effect, the antioxidants would probably have to be taken from adolescence on. A 60-year-old might gain five extra years, while an 80-year-old could expect only a modest one or two additional years of life. The population increase would be felt slowly and then only in the developed countries. A population bulge of 35 per cent would occur by the middle decades of the twenty-first century. Initially, however, the increase would be much smaller. The developed countries would grow about six per cent by the year 2000, but on a worldwide basis, the growth rate would average out to two or three per cent a year.

3. We can expect vastly different results if blood toxins turn out to be the cause of aging, and plasmapheresis, blood washings, the prescribed treatment. The blood washings would be roughly comparably to kidney dialysis, a highly technical treatment requiring the use of highly sophisticated

medical personnel. A reasonable treatment program might require two blood washings a week, or some 100 treatments a year. The cost for the use of the machine plus charges for hospital rooms and blood plasma would be about $10,000 to $20,000 per patient a year. The cost of treating the entire adult population of the United States would exceed the total gross national product that is predicted for 1980. Even if a way could be found to cut costs in half, they would still be astronomical. The cost of treating just 10 per cent of the adult population would run about $100 billion a year. Given the cost of the treatment and the relatively small number of people who could afford it, the population increase would be small, probably no more than one per cent in the most advanced countries by the year 2000.

Along with basic probing into the causes of aging, scientists are experimenting with ways of controlling it. As far back as 1934, Dr. Clive M. McCay of Cornell University showed that he could double the life-span of rats by restricting the number of calories in their diets. Later he experimented with alternatively feeding and starving mice. Dr. McCay found that he could double their life-span by feeding them their normal caloric intake for two days and starving them on the third. In an effort to update these now classic experiments, Dr. Morris H. Ross of the Institute for Cancer Research in Philadelphia discovered that the life expectancy of rats was related to the proportion of protein and carbohydrates in their diets as well as to the total number of calories consumed.

Whether these restrictions would work for us, too, has not been tested, but scientists are studying several long-lived people around the world in hopes of finding an answer. The residents of the valley of Vilcabamba in Ecuador, noted for their longevity, live healthy lives on diets that contain half the calories of the typical American diet. These people and the residents of Hunza in Kashmir also eat relatively little meat and diary products, with only about two per cent of their diet consisting of these saturated fats. The Abkhasians who live in the Soviet Union and are often studied by gerontologists because of their longevity also prefer fresh fruits and vegetables to meat and eggs.

Lowering our body temperature might be another environmental means of controlling aging—at least it appears to do so in cold-blooded animals. Dr. Roy L. Walford, professor of pathology at the University of California at Los Angeles, doubled the life-span of the fish Cynolebias by lowering the water temperature by five or six degrees. And at the National Institute of Health, Dr. Charles H. Barrows, Jr. found that he could double the life-span of rotifers, submicroscopic animals that resemble exotic flowers, if he reduced the water temperature from 35 to 25 degrees Centigrade. Obviously, we are not fish and rotifers. Yet some biologists speculate that we, too, would benefit if our body temperatures could be lowered a few degrees. "It would be very surprising," said Strehler, "if man were the only exception to the rule." Strehler estimates that a small decrease, perhaps even two or three degrees below our normal body temperature of 98.6 Fahrenheit, could add 20 to 30 years of useful life.[18]

Gerovital H3. Meanwhile, tests are underway in the United States on a product called Gerovital H3, developed in the 1950s by Dr. Ana Aslan of Bucharest, Romania. Gerovital H3 is composed largely of the standard pain killer procaine, best known under the trade name of Novocain, along with some other, secret ingredients. Aslan claims that it is the combination that gives Novocain its revitalizing power.

Aslan discovered the possibilities of procaine in 1949 while treating a young medical student with a stiff knee. She tried injecting a sizeable amount of procaine into an artery; almost at once the student was able to use his knee, and his pain vanished. Not long afterward, she started treat-

---

[18]Strehler, "Myth and Fact

ing elderly patients with procaine plus the secret ingredients, and in the following 10 years she treated more than 10,000 older people.

The results, according to Aslan, were astounding. She claims to have restored failing memory, relieved impotence, and improved hearing. Depressions vanished. People who were unable to walk because of crippling arthritis walked again, free of pain. Skin tone improved so that patients looked 10 years younger. Some patients who were bald were reported to have grown new hair, while the gray hair of other patients was said to have turned dark again. From the initial reports, published in 1956 in a German medical journal, Gerovital H3 seemed to do everything that the Fountain of Youth was *supposed* to do but didn't.

Hundreds of thousands of the known and unknown flocked to Aslan's Institute of Geriatrics. Nikita Khrushchev was reported to be one of her more enthusiastic patients. He is reported to have said that Gerovital H3 made him feel more "robust." John F. Kennedy, Charles De Gaulle, Sukarno, Ho Chi Minh, Marlene Dietrich, and Konrad Adenauer are also said to have benefited from Dr. Aslan's treatment. Throughout Europe, the drug is widely available and used.

Understandably, the medical profession looked askance at the seemingly extravagant claims for Gerovital H3. Nevertheless, in the early 1960s, five studies on the drug were carried out in the United States. Although the studies did not prove all of Aslan's claims, they did show that patients treated with the drug improved physically and mentally. Still, the American Medical Association remained adamantly opposed to the drug, and the Food and Drug Administration refused to license it for use in the United States.

In the early 1970's the Food and Drug Administration approved a new series of tests for Gerovital H3. Researchers are now investigating its effectiveness in treating depression among older people. The results of the first series of tests were reported in 1973 by Dr. Keith D. Ditman, a psychiatrist in Beverly Hills, California. He reported that 85 per cent of the patients noted "prompt and dramatic" improvement after being treated three times a week for four weeks.[19]

At the same time, other investigators were trying to discover a scientific basis for the rejuvenating effect of Gerovital H3. Seemingly, they have found it. Dr. Josef P. Hrachovec, a researcher at the University of Southern California, reported in 1973 that the drug appears to work by inhibiting the action of the enzyme, monoamine oxidase, in liver and brain tissue. This enzyme builds up in the body as a person ages, and in some yet undiscovered manner, it interfers with the hormone balance in the body. The result may be the phenomena of aging. Hrachovec said that Gerovital H3 may postpone aging by blocking the buildup of monoamine oxidase.

MENTAL AGING

Of course, we age mentally as well as physically. What happens to our bodies is only half of the aging process. More important to most of us is what happens to our minds with advancing age. We are afraid of our bodies outliving our minds, so that we spend our last years unaware of who we are and what we have been.

A few famous individuals have retained their remarkable mental powers into old age. Titian was still painting at the age of 99 when he died of the plague, and Michelangelo was working up to his death at 90. In our own

---

[19]Keith S. Ditman and Sidney Cohen, "Gerovital H3 in Treatment of Depressions: Preliminary Results," presented at the 26th annual meeting of the Gerontological Society, Miami, Florida, November 9, 1973.

time, Pablo Picasso painted canvasses of monumental beauty in his nineties, Leopold Stokowski was still conducting at 90, and Pablo Casals was giving cello concerts at 95. Yet such men are geniuses or near geniuses, and their ability to continue to create despite advancing age often appears to be as much of an aberration as their talent. Their ability to bring to their work the gusto of youth in old age seems to have little relevance to those of us who live and work in a more humdrum fashion.

Although such superhuman achievement in old age may be beyond the capacity of most of us, we should be able to retain the use of most of our mental abilities through new discoveries in hyperbaric medicine. At medical centers in New York and Florida, gerontologists are restoring the mental abilities of people who are considered hopelessly senile. They are returning to active life people who might otherwise languish in nursing homes or mental institutions.

These scientists believe that we deteriorate mentally because our brains do not receive an ample supply of oxygen. As a person grows older, the arteries that supply his tissues with life-giving oxygen tend to harden. The inner linings of the arteries thicken, the passageways fill up, and less and less oxygen-carrying blood reaches the brain. As a result, the inadequately nourished brain cells function less efficiently.

Corrective treatment is amazingly simple, considering the astounding results. Patients undergo repeated sessions, anywhere from 15 to 30, in a hyperbaric chamber that looks like a large iron lung. Each session lasts for an average of 90 minutes. While the patients are in the chamber, they breathe pure oxygen at an extremely high atmospheric pressure. The oxygen is thought to reactivate dormant brain cells that are alive but not functioning because of oxygen deprivation. The result has been a dramatic reversal of some of the mental deterioration that accompanies aging.

Doctors at the State University of New York at Buffalo and the Buffalo Veterans Hospital have been working since 1971 with patients who were considered hopelessly senile, many of whom had been hospitalized for years. Before the treatments, the patients who ranged in age from 53 to 76 showed little or no interest in the world around them. They were unable to perform routine tasks or to recall events that occurred that same day. After the hyperbaric sessions, they began caring for themselves again, slept better, and asked for newspapers or magazines to read. Their scores on memory tests improved by 35 to 300 per cent. Several were able to go home for the first time in years.[20]

And at the Miami (Florida) Heart Institute, normally cautious researchers used such words as "startling" and "almost miraculous" to describe the results of their hyperbaric treatments. "It's as if they've awakened from a long sleep," said research director Dr. Edwin Boyle. "They're more alert and more communicative in most cases. Their reaction times are going down and their physical coordination for the most part goes up." He envisions the day when, as a result of hyperbaric treatment, thousands of the institutionalized elderly will "go home and start mowing the grass and taking care of themselves."

Most of the 30 patients who were treated initially said that they noticed a definite improvement. One elderly woman passed her driver's test for the first time and got her driving license. An ardent golfer, James Russell, 67-years-old, said, "I certainly feel a considerable improvement. I've gone back to playing golf about every day and I just didn't feel like playing before I started (treatments)." Another man in his late seventies said that he was convinced his memory and mental functioning improved sharply. "Even though I've had only a couple of chamber treatments, I'm beginning to

---

[20]Eleanor A. Jacobs, Harry I. Alvis, and S. Movchly Small, "Hyperoxygenation, A Central Nervous System Activator?" *Journal of Geriatric Psychiatry,* 5, No. 2 (1972).

remember better—beginning to grasp the names of the people I meet," he said. "I used to forget them."

Boyle thinks the oxygen treatments may have limits. Those with advanced mental deterioration may be beyond help. "My impression is that people who are very old, in their eighties and over, who may be severely deteriorated, respond less and respond at a slower rate," he said. "The younger and less deteriorated, in their sixties and early seventies, respond more positively and more rapidly."

The middle-aged may eventually benefit the most from current research in hyperbaric medicine. Boyle said that treatment may begin in the forties and fifties and perhaps even younger in the future. Citing studies that show our mental abilities peak about the age of 25, he noted that a 45-year-old "is already 20 years down the slope." Middle-aged people, he believes, learn to compensate for the decline 'n various ways, "including a better secretary," so their loss of mental ability will not be noticed. With hyperbaric treatments, such compensation may turn out to be unnecessary.[21]

Given the possiblity of a "cure" or at the very least control of aging, society is morally obligated to speed up its present research into the causes of aging. We worship youth too much to tolerate aging and the aged. Dr. Glass says the conquest of aging is our next national imperative. "Man can do whatever he imagines," he said. "If he can imagine it, he can will it." Consequently, he envisions the government embarking on a crash program, similar to the one that put man on the moon, to find the secret of aging. "I can see a kind of breakthrough program like the space program," he said. The slogan "We will put man on the moon by 1970" becomes "We will be immortal by 1990—or before."[22]

---

[21]*St. Petersburg* (Florida) *Times*, March 5, 1972, p. 1.

[22]Author's notes, 25th annual meeting of the Gerontological Society, December 18, 1972.

A NEW GENERATION GAP

CHAPTER THREE

The middle-aged comprise the most powerful age group in society. They are the establishment generation. They hold the positions of power in our social institutions—in government, in business, in education, in the church, and in the family. They make our laws, determine the goods and products that find their way into our stores and eventually our homes, raise the children who are our future, and educate the youth of our country. By doing so, they shape the lives of all of us, and, in the process, they determine our social values—whether, for example, a person's worth is to be judged by material achievements or humanitarian contributions to the community.

45

THE GROWING PRESSURES

Despite their power, the middle-aged have never been less secure. They are trapped between the claims of the young and the old. The middle-aged have always assumed responsibility for their children and the young in society. The demands that children place on their parents and society for emotional and financial support are part of our accepted social order, long assumed and taken for granted. Now the middle-aged also are called on to assume responsibility, emotionally and financially, for their parents, both individually and collectively.

The growing number of older adults puts unprecedented pressure on the middle-aged. Their economic support is an increasing burden on the working population. Their political demands are challenging the present allocation of our nation's resources. Their leisure life-style threatens the underlying work ethic of society. Their sheer presence alters our notions of family responsibilities.

Younger adults and older adults are a lot alike. Both are alienated from the mainstream of society, largely nonproductive and dependent on others. Both are adrift in society and beset by confusing and sometimes conflicting social expectations. A college student summed it up: "We really have a lot in common. Neither of us has much money. It's not right for either of us to have sex. It's hard for both of us to get jobs. They've been rejected by their sons and daughters, and we feel rejected by society and our parents."

Caught in between, the middle-aged must assume the burden of both. The middle-aged must often begin what sociologists term "parenting the parents" as soon as their children are grown, and sometimes before. The emotional needs of older adults in our society can be insatiable. Failing mentally and physically, bereft of spouse and old friends, surrounded by an unknown and increasingly hostile world, older adults can require constant reassurance of their children's love and affection. For loving children, the pressure can be intolerable, forcing wrenching choices on them.

This happened in a family that I know, a decent loving family until the pressures of aging in our society tore it apart. It began one morning when the grandmother, a feisty, independent woman of 89, whom we'll call Mrs. Smith, slipped on her bathroom floor. She lay helplessly for several hours until a relative happened to drop by and find her. Afraid that she might fall again and not be found, her son and daughter-in-law persuaded Mrs. Smith to move in with them. The situation seemed ideal at first. The house was large enough to insure Mrs. Smith's privacy, and since she had an income of her own, she would be able to retain her financial independence. But trouble began almost immediately.

Her son did not realize that the move would undermine his mother's emotional security. She was used to her own home and her own ways. She was unable to believe that she was really wanted or welcomed in her daughter-in-law's home. "She turned into another person," her son said. "She was always so loving and giving, but not anymore." When her constant demands for reassurance were unmet, she accused her daughter-in-law of plotting against her. She knew how to turn the emotional screws. She would say, "I know you don't want me here. You want me to leave. Well, it won't be long now before I'm gone. Then you can have your house to yourself again."

At night she greeted her son with endless complaints about his wife. The wife had spoken harshly to her. The wife had done this and not done that. Some things were missing from her room, and Mrs. Smith was sure that her daughter-in-law had taken them out of spite. Maybe they would be happier if she left. "No matter how much we tried to do for her, it was never enough," the son said.

After several years, both the son and daughter-in-law were taking tranquilizers, and their marriage was nearly destroyed. After much anguish and mutual soul-searching late at night, they agreed to put Mrs. Smith in a nursing home. She ran away twice. Finally a judge ruled that she was mentally incompetent, and her son had her committed to a state mental hospital. Shaking his head, he said, "I still can't believe I did it. Putting my own mother away like that. But what else could I do? My marriage was just about over. It got to the point where I had to choose between my mother and my wife. I chose my wife." Now they are seeing a psychologist once a week, trying to salvage their marriage and resolve the guilt that they both feel toward Mrs. Smith.

Although few children are driven to such harsh choices, few also, confronted with the emotional needs of their parents, are able to escape feelings of guilt. The feeling that "something more should be done" is difficult to avoid. The middle-aged often feel that they are damned if they do and damned if they don't. Resources and help are scarce. Either the child assumes the entire responsibility or society does. There are few half-way measures.

When the middle-aged children have children of their own, the responsibilities, and often the guilt, are doubled. There is no way to calibrate precisely who owes what to whom. Responsibilities and obligations cannot be measured. The middle-aged flounder, doing the best they can, sometimes meeting the needs of their children and sometimes meeting the needs of their parents.

A 40-year-old woman, herself the mother of two young children, has been caring for her invalid mother for years. She is caught in a confusing swirl of emotions as she tries to balance her duties as mother and child. "All the time I'm taking care of my mother, I feel I should be with my children," she said. "When I manage to get away from her, I feel an enormous sense of relief. Of course, that makes me feel guilty. After all, she took care of me when I was growing up. So I devote more time to her and end up feeling guilty about neglecting the children. There's no end to it."

When three generations share a house, the middle-aged are literally and physically caught in the middle, refereeing clashes between parents and children. "My father-in-law was the dearest, sweetest man in the world," said one woman. "But there's no way to constantly reconcile the needs of an 80-year-old man and a seven-year-old girl. I was always in the middle of their arguments. I was always explaining to my daughter why she should be quiet so Grandpa could get some rest and explaining to my father-in-law that it's just in the nature of things for seven-year-olds to be noisy at times."

When middle-aged persons are pulled in two different directions by two different generations, something has to give. And it does. We have paid scant attention to the impact of these pressures on the middle-aged, but a psychiatrist who has is Dr. Robert Butler, director of the National Institute on Aging. He believes that the emotional needs of older adults can create severe emotional disturbances in their middle-aged children. Butler believes that this emotional irresponsibility is manifested in figurative or literal flight. Some resort to heavy drinking. Others seek solace in extramarital affairs. Still others desert their familes. The expense of supporting two sets of dependents traps others in stale jobs. They are unable to risk change despite constant boredom or tension.

CRIME AND THE OLDER ADULT

Older adults are able to prey emotionally on the middle-aged because so little is expected of older adults. There is no useful social role for them to fulfill. Society has fostered a juvenile dependency in them. The consequences for society, in the opinion of some of our pessimistic psychiatrists and gerontologists, can be dire.

In the 1960s there was another population bulge. The post-World War II baby boom was growing to maturity in a society of unprecedented affluence. Little was required of them except to get an education and have a good time before settling down to the responsibilities of adulthood. As a result, those who had the inclination also had the money and/or time to drop out, turn to drugs, riot at rock festivals from coast to coast, and adopt antisocial life-styles.

The parallels between then and now, between a leisure class of adolescents and a leisure class of older adults, are obvious. Writers have raised the possibility of a crime wave among older adults. They have envisioned the day when police would once again march down Sunset Boulevard, breaking up crowds of 70-year-old hippies who have been harrassing pedestrians, getting stoned, and throwing rocks at passing squad cars.[1] If the prospect of grandmother and grandfather turning to senile delinquency seems bizarre today, the prospect of the sons and daughters of middle-class America at the barricades seemed unlikely in 1959. In fact, criminologist Steven Lubbeck said, "The interesting question is: why aren't there senile delinquents? Adolescents are in limbo. No one knows what it means to be an adolescent. They are not tied into the social order so it is easy for them to raise hell and screw around. Old age is also a time of ambiguous social expectations. They, too, are outside social constraints. They also are adrift."[2]

There has been an actual increase in crime by people over 65. The Uniform Crime Reports, prepared by the Federal Bureau of Investigation, show criminal activity by older adults on the rise. The increase has been higher for older adults than for the population at large in a number of

[1]Richard A. Kalish, "Four Score and Ten," paper prepared for the Life Span Conference, Center for the Study of Democratic Institutions, Santa Barbara, California, April 13–17, 1970.

[2]Personal interview.

categories. Since many crimes are not reported, the actual increase is undoubtedly higher. If this trend continues, we will find a growing number of older adults who are committing an increasing number of criminal offenses.

Table 1 compares the increase among people over 65 with the increase among the total population over a five year period. Since these statistics were compiled in the 1960s, interestingly enough, the FBI has stopped collecting and compiling separate data on arrests among people over 65. The Uniform Crime Reports, it should be stressed, show *arrests* by law enforcement agencies among the total population and among people over 65 in each category. The figures are not conclusive, but they are provocative.

Table 1
Criminal Offenses Compared

Offense	*Increase In The Population At Large*	*Increase Among People Over 65*
Homicide	57	144
Burglary	36	38
Larceny	48	67
Carrying and possessing firearms	92	101
Driving under the influence of alcohol	−46	60
Total property crimes	41	62
Total crime index	42	54

If criminal activity can be linked to lack of social status and ambiguous social expectations, we can expect an upswing in crime among retirees. We can also anticipate further conflicts between youthful, vigorous older adults and a society that denies them a meaningful place and role.

THE CHANGING MARRIAGE SCENE

Because older adults are set apart from society, they are able to re-examine our social institutions. They are free to change and adapt them to their own needs. The social institutions most likely to change, since they are the least functional for older adults, are marriage and the family. Commenting on longer life-spans, biologist Dr. Alex Comfort said, "It will certainly increase the tendency for life-styles, and families, to be serial, so that each individual has the option of continuing in one pattern, or of entering a wholly different one, at the age when in the traditional family one was preparing for dependent senescence."

Over the last half century, the pace of family life has quickened. People marry earlier and have children at a younger age than their parents or grandparents did. Children leave home when their parents are 50 or 40 years old. Husband and wife are left to contemplate, with the prospect of longer life, 40 or 50 years of togetherness. Marriages that have survived up to that time because children provided a buffer against extensive interaction may be doomed when children leave home. After all, most marriages of 200 years ago rarely lasted more than 25 years. Soon we will anticipate 80-year marriages. Under those circumstances, "forever and ever" and "until death do us part" can become frightening. A redefinition of marriage vows is inevitable. Under no other circumstances would we try to hold a 20-year-old boy and girl to a contract, binding for 80 years, without an opportunity to revise the terms.

A new, more flexible concept of marriage is certain to emerge. Increasingly, traditional reasons for marriage are obsolete. Few people marry to have children to insure support in their old age, or to carry on the family name, or to provide a source of cheap labor in family-run businesses. Fewer and fewer women need to marry for financial security. The economic rational for marriage has been steadily eroded. Fewer people of either sex need to marry to obtain sexual satisfaction. Instead, people marry for more nebulous reasons. They expect marriage to increase their happiness, but people define "happiness" differently at different times in their lives. Because of this, we might need different kinds of marriages at different life stages.

Margaret Mead has proposed that society sanction two types of marriage contracts. She envisions one form of marriage that would be childless, easy to enter into and to get out of, and a second form that would be for bearing children, binding and difficult to dissolve. Although Mead anticipates that the nonbinding union would occur at an early age and the marriage for the purpose of bearing children would be entered into later, there is no real reason for such a sequence. People could enter into a binding marriage for bearing children fairly early in life and form several nonbinding unions after the children are grown. With the obligations of childbearing and rearing behind them, older adults should not be coerced by society to honor marriage contracts that cause unhappiness.

A total revamping of traditional marriage to meet the needs of older adults is suggested by Dr. Victor Kassel, a physician specializing in the treatment of the aged.[3] Kassel advocates a limited polygyny after 60, enabling any man over 60 to marry two, three, four, or even five women over 60. This radical suggestion would give widowed women, who outnumber older men and who face 15 or 20 years of widowhood, a chance to remarry. Obviously, no woman would have to enter into a polygynous marriage, but she would have the opportunity if she wished. She could enjoy an

---

[3]Victor Kassel, "Polygyny After 60," *Geriatrics* (April 1966), pp. 214–18.

active sex life again, since many older people, believing that sex is morally wrong outside of marriage, refrain from sexual activity.

Kassel feels that both the man and the women in a polygynous marriage would gain. They could share the expenses of a home, they would have help in times of sickness, and they would know that they are not alone. Polygynous marriages would be a dramatic departure from our traditional concept of marriage, but some kind of drastic changes are necessary in a society confronting the crisis of longevity. Limited polygyny could be for some a solution to many problems of an aging society in which single women heavily outnumber single men.

Other older adults, like their grandchildren, will reject marriage entirely, choosing instead personal rather than legal commitments. A sexual revolution among older adults is in the offing. Postmarital sex might be a good way to describe it. Like the change in premarital sexual mores, the postmarital sexual revolution would make sex acceptable and readily available to those who are single or whose spouses have died. In the 1960s, the Social Security Administration was shocked to learn that many pensioners were living together—"in sin"—because they could not afford the loss of their Social Security benefits, which would be the result of marrying. Those Social Security regulations have been changed so that elderly couples are no longer penalized if they marry. Nevertheless, some older adults continue to live together without a marriage license. This is true even in conservative, traditional, middle-America areas such as Des Moines, Iowa. A Des Moines social worker, commenting on postmarital arrangements, said, "That's their business. If there's sex, more power to them. I don't think they are going to have babies, so I think they can follow the same reasoning a lot of kids have proposed." He meant that marriage is necessary only if children are planned.

Not all older adults, of course, will choose divorce and serial marriages or polygynous marriages or postmarital liaisons. Some will always prefer traditional marriage or none at all. The important thing is that older adults will have choices for the first time, because increases in life expectancy require changes, an opening up of our socially accepted forms of male and female relationships. We need a variety of socially sanctioned relationships to meet the changing needs of people who are living vigorous lives into their eighties and nineties. These couplings and uncouplings of older adults will complicate family ties. Those ties are already growing complex without additional mix-ups caused by divorces and remarriages in the oldest generation. The four-generation family has become increasingly common. In fact, it has been replacing the three-generation family structure of grandparents, adult children, and grandchildren as the norm. Over 40 per cent of the people 65 and older are great-grandparents. Thus almost half of our country's older population is already part of a four-generation family. Yet, even as we become aware of this change, the four-generation family is being replaced by the five-generation family.

THE NEW FAMILY

Four- and five-generation families are the inevitable result of longevity. We are the first society in history to create such families, so we will have no help as we try to sort out the baffling network of relationships. Our concept of family responsibility will have to be revised. There are numerous questions that need to be asked, and most of the answers will have to be worked out through trial and error. For example, what kind of relationship is possible between a great-great grandmother of 90 and her 45-year-old grandson? What about her three-year-old great-great granddaughter? Is 87

years and five generations too much of a generational difference to be spanned emotionally? Can we realistically expect
the grandparent generation to shoulder financial, physical,
or emotional responsibility for the great-grandparent generation? And what about the middle-aged, who may find themselves at age 50 at the mercy of parents, grandparents, children, and grandchildren? To whom will they owe their biggest obligations?

Sociologist Elaine Brody has warned that we are faced
with the prospect of whole families composed of aging
individuals—grandparents in their eighties, parents in their
sixties, and grandchildren in their forties.[4] In the aging family, all of the members are struggling to come to grips with
their own aging. Each generation experiences in a unique
way the physical, psychological, social, and economic stresses
of aging. Although the problems overlap, individual members are too absorbed in coping with their own aging to offer
much support to others. These aging families are fragile, like
unstable houses of cards ready to fall apart at the first blow.
Brody's survey of applicants for admission to the Home and
Hospital for Jewish Aged in Philadelphia showed that a
major reason behind the requests was the death or severe
illness of an adult child or an adult child's spouse.

The middle-aged grandchildren bear the biggest
burden. As their parents and grandparents place more and
more demands on them, their own energy is waning and
their anxiety about their future dependency is growing. The
burdens intensify their own conflicts about growing old.

The other generations have to cope with special burdens, too. The parent generations—those in their sixties will
find their retirement suddenly threatened by their parents
who are still active in their eighties and nineties. Such a situation poses complex moral and emotional problems, exceed-

---

[4]Elaine Brody, "The Aging Family," *The Gerontologist* (December
1966), pp. 201–7.

ingly difficult to resolve. A newspaper advice columnist specializing in the problems of the elderly published a letter that dramatizes the situation. The writer said: "I'll concede that children are a blight on retirement, what with their indifference, but what in heaven's name can a man at age 62 do when his wife's mother moves in and expects to be catered to? My wife's mother is in her mideighties, is active and domineering. She has ample money of her own, but will pay us only a pittance for her keep. I could stand that, but she is robbing us of privacy and is wrecking any hopes I have for an early retirement." The columnist advised consulting a minister and, if the minister agreed, telling the mother-in-law to leave the house.

The survival of people into their eighth and ninth decades will mean that the family as we now think of it —nuclear and three-generational—will be rendered obsolete. A new, more inclusive, more compassionate family can emerge to take its place. The people who will benefit the most from this deemphasis on the nuclear family, just as they have been the ones most hurt by the emphasis on it, are older adults. They have been isolated from their children and grandchildren, forced to try to be independent, thrown back on their own, often meager resources. In an attempt to cope, many older adults are seeking retirement communities inhabited exclusively by people of their own age. In these communities, we shall see in a later chapter, older adults are forming their own subculture. They are finding companions of a similar age to share the joys and problems of the later years of life. But retirement communities, even the best of them, cannot hope to meet the needs of everyone who is over 65. We need a new definition of the family, just as we need a redefinition of marriage. We need a definition of the family that is based on the voluntary commitment of people, whether or not they are related, to share each other's happiness and to lend joint support during times of crisis to each of the individual members. Such a freely undertaken commitment is more important in determining if a group of people constitutes a family than ties that are formed by birth or marriage.

A circuit court judge in Orange County, Florida, has issued a ruling that substantiates a new definition of a family. The case involved a group of older adults in Winter Park, a suburb of Orlando in the central part of the state, which has been experimenting with a new definition of the family. The group, incorporated under the name of the Share-a-Home Association, consists of 12 elderly men and women. They share the expense and work of running a 27-room mansion nestled between a tree-shaded winding road and a small lake. Although the Share-a-Home Association considers itself a family, shortly after they moved in, neighbors sued on the grounds that the association violated the area's single-family zoning. In a courtroom packed with emotional supporters, relatives, and friends of the older adults, the judge ruled that the Association met the legal definition of a family. In a potentially far-reaching decision, the judge held that any group that pools its resources with the intention of sharing the joys and sorrows of family life is a family.

The Share-a-Home Association, which was formed in 1969, believes its experiment can bring a new way of life to thousands of older adults who are without family or friends and who are unable to live alone. In another community, these men and women might be placed in nursing homes or state mental institutions because they lack the physical ability or financial resources to maintain their own homes. For the most part, they are physically infirm and have low incomes.

Surprisingly, the Share-a-Home Association was not founded by older adults. It was organized by the James Gillies family, a deeply religious group that conceived of the idea while studying the communal life of the disciples. Gillies said, "If it worked for them 2,000 years ago, we figured it could work for us today." The Share-a-Home Association has no religious overtones, however. People of all faiths—or none—are welcomed. Although Gillies family members manage the house and receive a salary for their work, the Share-a-Home Association is set up independently of the Gillies family. It could fire them and hire new managers. Furthermore, the title to the house is held in the name of the Share-a-Home Association.

The older adults in the Share-a-Home Association —or family as they call it—contribute between $200 and $425 a month, depending on financial ability, to the Share-a-Home Association bank account to cover mortgage payments and maintenance on the house, food, trips, and the salary of the Gillies family. Most members have private bedrooms, although a few relatives share rooms. Privacy is strictly respected and members may be as social or unsocial as they please. Most meals are prepared by the Gillies family and eaten together, but the older adults often use the kitchen to whip up a batch of chocolate chip cookies or a late night snack. By sharing costs, the Association members are able to maintain a standard of living that would be impossible for them alone. However, the older adults are equally attracted by the idea of communal living and of being part of a family again. They enjoy being around the Gillies children and grandchildren, who wander freely through the rambling house.

Jesse Bush, an 85-year-old family member who shares a room decorated with greeting cards and treasured keepsakes with her 81-year-old sister, said, "I was in a nursing home for a while, and it was depressing. Nothing but old people. This is a real family. We share everything—our newspapers, our books, all our goodies. Sometimes we even fight like a family, but the arguments don't last long."

A stately, dignified woman who speaks in slow, measured tones, Miss Bush moved in several years ago from a nursing home. Although she did not need intensive nursing care, she was not capable of managing her own household.

She said, "I'm not physically able to keep house. Even if I were, I couldn't afford a decent furnished apartment. If I weren't here, I guess I'd have to take up residence on a park bench."

Although members are free to leave the Association at any time, they rarely do. With a few exceptions, those who have left have done so because of failing health. Although most of the older adults are infirm to varying degrees and need the reassurance of communal living, the Share-a-Home Association is not capable of caring for bedridden members. One of the family's few rules requires members who need intensive nursing care to leave.

Although "families" like the Share-a-Home Association cannot solve the myriad problems of aging in our society, they offer significant benefits for older adults and their children. First, the older adults live in a home, not an institution. The Share-a-Home Association is set up in such a way that the house is truly the home of the older adults who live there. By splitting living costs with others in similar circumstances, they can maintain a higher standard of living than they could afford alone. Second, the Share-a-Home Association relieves the middle-aged sons and daughters of some of the financial and emotional pressure of caring for their aging parents. The middle-aged who cannot bring their parents into their own homes for various reasons are not forced to put them in institutions. Instead, they know that their parents are living and sharing a home and family life with others.

Older adult families are being formed in other places. Gillies is starting two more Share-a-Home Associations, one on the West Coast of Florida and another in Cleveland, Ohio. The Richmond Fellowship of America, a nonprofit organization that specializes in making living arrangements for persons with special needs, organized an older adult commune in Washington, D. C., in 1976, with 10 more planned for the area.

The Richmond family is similar, although smaller. It requires members to be at least 60 and mobile and to agree beforehand on a plan of care if they should need institutionalization. The Richmond Fellowship acts as landlord and the members pay a nominal rent of $80 a month. The members are independent and on their own. There is no staff. Members take care of the house themselves and work out their own living arrangements and rules. David Harre, the director, said, "Our message is one of enhancing independence. We want to provide the security that is gained by being together and to enable people to expand their lifestyles."

The Richmond Fellowship, which was formed to provide aftercare for the mentally ill in England in the late 1950s, hopes to become the catalyst for a nationwide movement of older adult communes. Harre said the response to the family, following an article in the *Washington Post,* was overwhelming. He explained that the goal of the group is to organize at least 12 families in other parts of the country by 1978 through working with other nonprofit groups.

A DISTORTED VIEW

The much-maligned institution, the American family, needs to be reshaped for other reasons. Those of us under 65 are growing conscious of what it means to older adults to be isolated from the mainstream of society. We are learning that this corrodes their self-esteem, self-respect, and sense of dignity. We realize their overwhelming loneliness. We know older adults, like all people, need to be needed. Our psychiatrists warn us that the high incidence of suicide and mental illness among the elderly is often a direct consequence of estrangement. Yet we pay little attention to what it means to the rest of us to be isolated from older adults. We, too, pay a price, difficult to measure, but very real.

Increasingly, we live in age-segregated communities. College students live in college dormitories, then move into communities of young people, who, like everyone else around them, are starting their careers. In "swinging singles" complexes, apartments with "no children" clauses, and youth ghettos in big cities, young adults are isolated with others of their own kind. After marriage and children, young couples move to the suburbs for the next few decades to raise their families. The three-bedroom ranch homes and split levels are compactly designed for Mother, Father, Dick and Jane, but unlike houses of a previous generation, there is no room for Grandmother or Grandfather, much less a stray aunt or two. As a result, millions of people spend most of their lives without day-to-day contact with older adults. In fact, we may not know any older adults at all in any meaningful sense, including our own relatives, who may be living thousands of miles away in retirement communities in Florida, Arizona, or California. Our visits may not be long enough or frequent enough for us to grasp the rich texture of their lives.

As a result, our view of old age is warped. Lacking personal knowledge of older adults, we pigeonhole them, accept the stereotypes that distort and demean them. We read a lot about older adults in nursing homes and institutions. Since our world is bereft of older adults, we assume wrongly that most of them are institutionalized. We read about the plight of older adults and infer that the years between retirement and death are inevitably whiled away like the cards in an afternoon game—aimlessly, randomly, without plan or design.

We come to fear and dread the latter third of our lives. Butler said, "The contemporary imagery of old age—the picture of unproductive, dependent, lonely, wizened, rigid, old people—is hardly calculated to attract youth into their own future. There is little to look forward to. Among the diseases produced by the benevolent and curative process called retirement is one that goes beyond its effects on the retired themselves."

This distorted view of old age foreshortens our youth. Because we lack models of active, assertive older adults to imitate, we end up conforming to the warped picture of old age as a period of inevitable and irreversible decline. One woman in her early sixties, fingering the keys of her daughter's typewriter, said, "I always wanted to know how to type. There are so many things I wanted to learn, but I guess I never will now. I'm too old. It's too late for me." Of course, it wasn't too late. Statistically, she could look forward to another 20 years of life, plenty of time to learn and use all sorts of skills. However, thinking and believing that it *was* too late made time run out. Such people come to the office of Dr. Adriaan Verwoerdt, a psychiatrist at Duke University Medical Center, with amazing regularity. "I see it all the time," he said. "People in their early sixties, even fifties, start to slow down, back off from life, years before they need to. They start to think they're old so they start to act as they think old people should act. Pretty soon they even look old. It's a waste. They conform to the picture they have of old age, and it's a crippler."[5]

CHILDREN AND OLDER ADULTS

Most disturbing of all, children are growing up without savoring the unique rewards of friendships with older adults. Such friendships between the old and young can be infinitely rich, filled with rewards that are difficult to define because they are felt rather than articulated. In a letter to a syndicated advice column, a mother wrote, "My small children are underprivileged because they can't know their grandparents better. My children and I love their grandmother very much. But she lives thousands of miles away, and I cannot afford the air fare more than once every three or four years. Some children, I know, look to their older parents only from the point of view of 'How much are they

[5]Personal interview.

going to leave?' Grandparents have much more to offer than money—things like love, family feeling, sharing nuggets of wisdom. Then there are grandma's tales of the old days and grandpa's stories of his exploits in the great war. My children are losers because they don't get these, and when I see children or grandparents who don't care, I want to cry."

When I was a child, my grandparents lived in another part of the state, but an elderly lady—she seemed ancient to me then, although she was probably in her sixties—lived in the neighborhood. When I was seven and eight, we passed lazy afternoons in an orgy of salted peanuts, soft drinks, and lemon drops that were pleasantly tart to suck. She taught me Chinese checkers, canasta, and Parcheesi. We played with a fierce competitiveness. Both of us played to win; neither of us gave an inch. She did not condescend to my youth; I did not concede to her age. She usually won, but when I did, I felt a surge of gloating triumph that could not be matched by beating my seven-year-old contemporaries. In those long hours at the card table, something intangible passed between us. I suppose I kept her from being lonely. She gave me a feeling for a past that I would never know. She communicated a sense of another time and place, of books that had been read long ago in other houses and finally preserved behind the thick glass doors of her credenza, of rooms and corridors where she had lived, down which I would never go. I remember her distinctly, although I have not seen or heard from her in over two decades. And I recall her more vividly than I do my young friends at the time.

I suppose I was lucky. Most of the people in our neighborhood were families with young children, along with a few middle-aged couples whose children were grown. It was the kind of middle-class suburb that contains few older adults today. The children who live in them are the losers. They grow up thinking of older adults as a kind of endangered species that has gamely survived into the present time.

The absence of grandparents and other older adults can turn suburban ranch homes into simmering pressure cookers, in constant danger of bubbling over. Parents and children live so close together, physically and emotionally, that the anxieties, pressures, and tensions of daily life are turned inward. There is no relief from the closeness. Without buffers, parents can easily inflict their own neuroses on their young. Dr. James Howell of the Palm Beach County Health Department said, "I can't prove it, but I think from what I've seen that children in such nuclear families grow up more neurotic than children from other families."

Children from pressure-cooker homes grow up defining their community and their place in it in narrow terms. They lack a sense of reaching out and extending themselves to others, according to a study by sociologists T. R. Sarbin and W. J. Van Spancheren, Jr. Such children grow up to form their own pressure-cooker families of Mother, Father, Dick, and Jane.

Juvenile delinquency. Children need the sense of continuity and tradition that comes from older adults. Traditionally, the elderly teach the young the morals, values, and ethics of a society. Despite a growing number of older adults in our society, we have lost our elders. We lack a group of older people who use their wisdom and experience for the collective good of the community. When the lines of communication break down between the oldest and youngest generations, society as a whole is weakened. The loss of figures worthy of respect, even awe, has disastrous consequences for the young, according to Dr. Maurice E. Linden.

Linden believes that juvenile delinquency is directly linked to our attitudes toward the elderly. He points out that cultures such as the Chinese, Indian, and Hebrew, which hold high esteem for older adults, also boast a low rate of juvenile delinquency. He says "common sense logic" implies that an increase in "arrogance and willfulness in the young" would accompany a decline in respect for the old. Without respected authority figures and guidelines formulated by them, the young become their own arbiters of right and wrong. Linden believes the young need to grow up in an atmosphere that includes authority "enriched with warmth, humanism, and charity, yet firm in its leadership, independently motivated, and oriented around group principles." Lacking close relationships with older adults, the young grow up with an exaggerated sense of their own importance and authority, leading to warped characters and fragmented personalities. The results show up ultimately as police statistics recording the number of juvenile arrests.[6]

Affiliated families. Children and older adults can be brought together again through affiliated families, three-generation networks of individuals, not all of whom are related.[7] Affiliated families would be composed of any combination of husband/father, wife/mother, and their children, plus one or more older adults. The older adults, although not related, would be part of the family. They might even be called by a kin name.

Affiliated families can take numerous forms. The possibilities are as infinite and as varied as the individuals who compose the affiliated family. The older adults might or might not share a home with the parents and children. They might or might not recieve money for their help with the house and children, depending on their financial and emotional needs. Along with other details of setting up and maintaining the affiliated family, these things would have to be worked out by the individual members themselves. Each family would fashion its own arrangements. All families, however, would share a voluntary commitment to responsi-

---

[6]Dr. Maurice E. Linden, "Relationship Between Social Attitudes Toward Aging and the Delinquencies of Youth," *The American Journal of Psychiatry* (1957), pp. 444–47.

[7]Sylvia Calven and Ethel Vatter, "The Affiliated Family: A Device for Integrating Old and Young," *The Gerontologist* (Winter 1972).

bility for one another. Like the members of the Share-a-Home Association, the members of the affiliated family at the very least would commit themselves to sharing their joys and lending emotional support in times of trouble.

Children of an affiliated family would learn that aging is not an aberration, but a normal, inevitable part of life. Older adults would know again the warmth and concern of family living. Parents would benefit, too, especially working mothers who are frequently forced to accept makeshift arrangements or none at all for their children during working hours. With an older adult in the home, younger women could develop their job skills at a time of life when they are needed the most. Single working mothers would be able to share the responsibilities of child rearing. They would have help in raising their children and making decisions about their children's future. They would not confront this formidable task alone.

In St. Petersburg, Florida, a young mother talked about an arrangement with an older woman that meets the definition of an affiliated family. She is not familiar with that term and does not call it by that name. It is one, nevertheless. When Mrs. Brown and her husband were divorced several years ago, she went back to work. Her daughter Stephany started school the same year. "I was really worried about her," Mrs. Brown said. "It seemed like a lot of changes in her life in one year, losing her father, starting to school, me going to work. I felt like I should be with her more, not less, but financially that just wasn't possible." By chance, she mentioned her problem one afternoon at the supermarket to Mrs. Gould, a widowed woman who lived several blocks down the street. Mrs. Gould volunteered to come by after school to look after Stephany. Mrs. Brown offered to pay her a small amount, and the arrangement was settled. Mrs. Brown said, "It's been a godsend."

Over the last few years, what started as a convenience

has turned into a family. The Browns and Mrs. Gould are together more than the few hours a week that Mrs. Gould takes care of Stephany after school. Mrs. Gould joins the Browns and their relatives on holidays. They exchange birthday and Christmas presents. Mrs. Gould said, "I don't do it for the money. I never needed it. I do it out of love. It's like raising a family again."

Stephany calls her "my other grandmother." And Mrs. Brown knows that Stephany is being looked after by someone who loves her. "She just wonderful," Mrs. Brown said, referring to Mrs. Gould. "I don't know how we'd get along without her. She's just like a member of the family."

EXAMINING OUR VALUES

The presence of large numbers of retired, older adults is forcing a re-examination of two of the most cherished and deeply embedded values in our society—the value of life itself and the meaning of work, which gives a structure and focus to life.

Although scientists are pursuing ways of extending the life-span in their laboratories, our medical advances up to now have succeeded mainly in prolonging dying. Refined medical techniques and technology are enabling people to survive physically long after they have suffered irreversible mental, emotional, and spiritual deterioration. They remain alive only because drugs and machines keep their failing organs functioning. They linger, often painfully, on the brink of death for months. As a result, our hospitals are filled with elderly patients who are slowly dying of long-term degenerative diseases such as heart ailments and terminal illnesses.

THE RIGHT TO DIE

Public debate is growing over death with dignity, the right to refuse extraordinary medical treatment even when refusal means death. Proponents of death with dignity and living wills believe emphatically that the terminally ill and those who have suffered brain death should be allowed to die with a minimum of pain and cost. This issue exploded on the front pages of newspapers across the country in 1976 with the case of Karen Ann Quinlan, a young New Jersey girl who had suffered what doctors termed irreversible brain damage. But the Karen Ann Quinlans are few, and older adults are in the center of this debate.

Large numbers of older adults have put us on a collision course with some of our deepest-held values. The Judeo-Christian ethic holds that life itself is an absolute that is not to be tampered with. Life in itself is seen as good and to be preserved at all costs as long as possible. With modern medicine, "at all costs" and "as long as possible" becomes virtually open-ended. Doctors, trained to provide the best possible care to all their patients, find that their best is escalating all the time. Highly advanced and expensive equipment is technically keeping alive people who will never return to active life.

Our religious values, however, conflict with our economic ethics. Our society is geared toward helping people who can contribute and produce economically. Those who are unable to work are left to fend largely for themselves. When our resources are distributed, their share is small. The sacredness of life is a expensive value to try to maintain. Sociologist George Maddox, director of the Duke University Center for the Study of Aging and Human Development, said, "The Promethean myth runs deep in the Western world, but we're running into practicalities. We can't maintain this value."

If we admit this, if we concede that some lives are more sacred than others, that some lives should be maintained and others should not, we are then adrift in a murky world where there are no rules.

Although doctors and clergy are not on the verge of reaching a consensus on the right to die, courts and state legislatures are moving ahead. By the twenty-first century, the right to die may be as firmly established in our statutes and common laws as the right to life.

Florida became the first state, in 1973, to enact death with dignity legislation, giving residents the legal right to refuse extraordinary medical treatment and protecting doctors from civil or criminal liability for carrying out the wishes of a terminally ill patient. The law also permits the next-of-kin of a terminally ill patient to request doctors to discontinue "medical treatment designed solely to sustain the life processes." In the case of a terminally ill patient who has not signed what is called a "living will" and who has no next-of-kin, extraordinary medical treatment can be stopped by the agreement of three doctors. California adopted similar legislation in 1976. The California law allows a doctor to shut off life-support equipment for a patient whose death is imminent if the patient has signed a living will.

The Florida legislature considered death with dignity legislation for four years before it was passed with virtually no debate. Other states probably will want to consider carefully and thoroughly such emotionally loaded legislation before passage. As the number of older adults increases, however, death with dignity legislation will be enacted by all of our state legislatures. It is no accident that Florida, the state with the highest percentage of older adults, was the first. The legislation received the support of senior citizen groups. Many older adults, dreading lingering deaths, wrote their state legislators to pass the bill. The bill was also supported by many middle-aged people, who had seen the lives of their hopelessly ill parents needlessly prolonged.

Although courts have refused to prosecute doctors accused of hastening the death of hopelessly ill patients in several incidences, the right to die was dramatically affirmed by a circuit court judge in Dade County, Florida, in 1971. In that case the judge ruled that a 72-year-old Cuban refugee, hospitalized with hemolytic anemia, had, "a right to die in dignity." For two months, doctors treated Mrs. Carmen Martinez through continual blood transfusions that involved surgically opening her skin and forcing blood into her veins. Weak and in constant pain, she pleaded with her daughters, "Please don't let them torture me anymore." Her doctor, however, feared that yielding to her wishes might lead to his being charged with aiding suicide, while denying her requests might lead to being charged with violating Mrs. Martinez's civil rights. The doctor took the case to court, and the judge decided "This woman has a right not to be hurt." The painful transfusions were immediately stopped, and on the day after the court decision, Carmen Martinez died peacefully.

LEISURE—CURSE OR BLESSING?

Along with our attitudes toward life and death, our attitudes toward work and leisure are changing. Longer lifespans and earlier retirement are giving rise to a new leisure class of older adults. There will be, by one estimate, 50 million people over the age of 55 in retirement by the year 2000. More people will have more leisure over a longer period of time than ever before. Yet this leisure can be a curse instead of a blessing, because of our ambivalent attitude toward work and leisure. As a society, we have never been comfortable with leisure. We promote retirement as a reward for a life of hard work. We tell the about-to-be retired that retirement is an opportunity to do all of the things they have always wanted to do. We encourage the retired "to take life easy." At the same time, we abhor the thought of our own retirement. We dread the day when we will be expected to "sit on the front porch" as the world bustles around us. Some people are so wrapped up in their work that psychiatrists have labeled them "work addicts" or "workoholics." Moreover, American society invests heavily in work, but not play. Bus lines, for instance, run frequently to the business sections of our cities, while they run less often to the parks and recreation areas. We educate people to earn a living. The idea of training people to enjoy leisure seems ludicrous.

It is easy to see why retirees look askance at their unaccustomed leisure. At Leisure World, a retirement community in Laguna Hills, California, the name itself hindered sales at first. Prospective buyers, who associated leisure with idleness, shied away. But leisure and idleness are not the same. Idle time is wasted time. Leisure can be active, creative, purposeful. The word "leisure" is derived from the Greek for school, and for the Greeks leisure was not empty time. Their leisure was used for the benefit of one's community and one's self. Leisure is the very opposite of a variety of activities pursued for the sole purpose of filling up the hours of the day. Leisure is sloth when not used constructively.

Leisure needs to be made respectable. For many workers, leisure time is their only creative time. Much work today is not meaningful. To insist that it is emotionally as well as financially rewarding ignores the reality of the twentieth-century working world of assembly lines, conglomerates, and agribusiness. Much blue- and white-collar work is repetitive and boring, stifling the mind, numbing the body with fatigue, and creating an overpowering urge to run away or escape through alcohol and other tranquilizers. Leisure can make a person feel human again. Take an assembly line worker who welds together parts of an automobile frame, the same two parts hour after hour as the hours spin into days, weeks, months, and years. Perhaps in his leisure time he customizes cars, spending hours at the kitchen table working out the design, searching for the right parts, rebuilding the chassis and motor, and ending up finally with a car that fulfills his personal vision of what a car should look like and be. Which is creative—the welding or the customizing, the work or the leisure? Take a secretary who works in a 50-woman secretarial pool, arriving punctually at nine and departing at five, being careful that she never takes an extra five minutes for lunch or her two regularly scheduled coffee breaks. Maybe she goes home, picks up her knitting, turning different wools and stitches into one-of-a-kind sweaters for her family and friends. Which is fulfilling—the typing or the knitting, the work or the play? We need to banish once and for all the idea that activities that pay are valuable, while activities that do not pay are unimportant.

We need a theology of leisure that will give it the sanction that the Protestant ethic gave to work. The Protestant ethic held that the pursuit of wealth was a duty, and work was not merely an economic, but a spiritual, end. It has been almost a century since Max Weber's *The Protestant Ethic and the Spirit of Capitalism* was published, but his spirit continues to haunt our leisure, which is seen as a means of recuperating from work instead of a rewarding and productive end in itself.

European theologian, Jurgen Moltmann, has suggested a way to free leisure of guilt. In *Theology of Play,* he proposes a new way of looking at leisure and play, which can give them the validity we now accord work alone. He calls for a radical Christian interpretation of leisure. He argues that leisure should be a model for revolutionary change. He claims that leisure and play are, at present, ways to tranquilize the work force to build good morale so they will be better workers. Leisure is diversionary instead of revolutionary. Leisure should be an opportunity for people to design a more humane future. Through leisure, men and women can achieve a "humanizing emancipation" from their present condition. Consequently, Moltmann calls for an expansion of leisure time to test alternatives for our future. He calls for Christians, as the first liberated people, to lead the way to the future by creating congregations of the liberated rather than churches of the idle. Moltmann gives the moral sanction to leisure that his Calvinist predecessors gave to work.

Older adults of today are exploring the leisure frontier. They are the liberated, social pioneers, feeling their way and ours into the future, giving us guidance for the predicted time in the twenty-first century when we will shift from a work (scarcity) society to a leisure (abundance) society, when work will be deemphasized. The elderly are the first group in our society, outside of some of those with inherited wealth, to sever the link between work and income. For generations, we have been taught that if we want to eat, we have to work. This is no longer true for older adults. Amendments to the Social Security Act have enabled older people to enjoy increases in their standard of living without being required to increase their productivity. They are not required to "earn" their Social Security raises by increased output. Although older adults are at present the group in our society with an abundance of subsidized leisure, all of us will soon have more time and money. Through longer vacations, more paid holidays, and shorter working weeks, we already have considerably more free time than our grandfathers.

Although we distrust leisure, we are, nevertheless, greedy consumers of it. The statistics on the amount of money we spend on leisure and the ways we spend it are dizzying. An estimated $105 billion was spent on leisure in 1972. We spend each year about $1.3 billion on skiing, $50 million on tennis equipment, and $2 billion on golf. We own some 4 million camping vehicles, 1.9 million snowmobiles, 2 million minibikes, and 1.5 million surfboards. Yet our glut of equipment can bore us. We all have rushed out at some time to buy some new leisure "toy," only to relegate it to the back of the closet after a few uses, much like a child who tires of a new Christmas toy even before the wrapping paper is cleared away. Older adults can warn us of the pitfalls that lie ahead in a leisure-oriented society. They can teach us how to live with our new-found leisure. They have the time to work out satisfying life-styles. We will be the future beneficiaries. Many older adults have the opportunity and challenge of using their experience, imagination, and wisdom to create the future for the rest of us.

MIDDLE-AGED VALUES IN A BIND

The work-based values of the middle-aged are undermined by the growing numbers of older adults with increasing leisure time. In fact, many of the values of the middle-aged are becoming the values of a minority.

In a broad study of three-generation families conducted by the Ethel Percy Andrus Gerontology Center at the University of Southern California, interesting differences between the generations cropped up. Generally, the young and old ranked humanitarian values significantly higher than the middle-aged. Both the young and the old rated such values as a world at peace, service to mankind, and equality for all mankind highly, while the middle-aged considered them of lesser importance. The middle-aged put achievement at the top of their list of values. Older adults valued loyalty most. The young picked friendship as the most highly prized value.

When the Methodist church polled its members in the early 1970s, it also found that the attitudes of teen-agers and people over 55 were remarkably similar. The young people and the older listed aiding minorities and ethnic groups as the number-one problem facing the church. They listed working for world peace as number two on their list of priorities. The young and old said that the church should involve itself more in the social affairs of the world around it. The Reverend Dr. Virgil Sexton of Dayton, Ohio, a research specialist on the staff of the church's program council, said, "Surprisingly we found in the sample that the expressions of youths and persons over 55 were practically the same on most questions." The most conservative views in the survey were those of the middle-aged, the 45- to 54-year-olds.

These are some of the social changes that can be expected as the number of older adults in our society grows. They are not the only changes, however. A demographic shift such as the aging of our population will have consequences that cannot yet be seen.

The middle-aged will find their society shaken by the emerging subculture of aging. Some resentment and hostility are inevitable among older adults, whose needs and wants have been neglected for so long. But the result of responding to these needs and desires will be a more open and flexible society for all. New forms of marriage and the family will increase the range of choices for older adults. This will in turn expand the choices for the middle-aged and the young. We will have a new freedom to enjoy leisure fully, unmarred by nagging guilt and anxieties. And the emerging right to die will provide a new personal autonomy, enabling us to choose, in the face of the ultimate, between life and death in accord with our most deeply held moral and religious beliefs.

"AGEISM"—
ANOTHER FORM OF BIGOTRY

CHAPTER FOUR

Two stories offer an interesting insight into the troubled relations between older adults and the rest of society, an estrangement that is not new, although it is assuming new importance. The stories were told or written hundreds of years and thousands of miles apart, but they treat older adults in a similar manner. From the days of oral literature around the campfire to the most avant-garde playwriting of recent years, the place of older adults in society has changed little.

A common European myth tells the story of a family who would not let the grandfather eat at the table with the rest of them. Instead, they placed his food in a little wooden trough some distance from the others, and there, out of their sight and hearing, the old man ate his meals. One day the middle-aged father came across his young son hammering some nails into a couple of boards. "What are you doing?" the father asked. Glancing up from his work, the son replied, "It's for you when you get old." Shocked by that glimpse of his own future, the father hastily invited the old man to rejoin the family at the table.

In a modern play by Edward Albee, a middle-aged couple give the grandmother an army blanket to keep her warm on cold nights, her very own dish, and a nice place to sleep under the stove. Eventually, the couple planned to give her a pretty toy shovel and then put her in the sandbox permanently. Older adults who have been shuffled back and forth among the homes of their children before being sent to a nursing home for the rest of their lives can easily recognize their own situation in the plight of Albee's grandmother.

These stories reflect certain unpleasant truths about the situation of older adults in society. The first is their isolation. They are shoved aside and prevented from participation in the ongoing life of their family or community. (This will be examined in the next chapter when we look at the emerging subculture of aging.) The second is the degradation of older adults. Our opinion of what people deserve is a reflection of what we feel they are worth, and we, in general, do not think highly of older adults. We feel they deserve less—a wooden trough for eating, a spot beside the stove for sleeping—simply because they are old. There is an extreme and unremitting bias against older adults, a bias so prevalent that it has been given a name—ageism—by Dr. Robert Butler, director of the National Institute of Aging.

WHAT IS AGEISM?

Why this bias exists and what causes it is a matter of conjecture at best. Ageism may grow out of a simple desire to end "aesthetic pollution." Older adults do not conform to society's youthful standard of beauty. Wrinkled skin, liver spots, and varicose veins are offensive in a nation that embodies its ideal of human perfection in the firm breasts and smooth thighs of young Miss Americas. We may want to get rid of older adults, put them out of our sight so that we are not affronted by their appearance.

Ageism may stem from impatience that older adults insist on hanging around after they are no longer needed. Society relies on the young to reproduce itself, something the old are generally unable or unwilling to do, so they are not needed for that. Economically they are rarely needed either. If they are retired or disabled, they are considered a drain on public funds. If they are still working, they are criticized for taking jobs that "rightfully" belong to the young. And the young may hunger after the money or power or position of older adults.

More likely, ageism emerges from our almost universal and overwhelming dread of death. As a result of modern medicine, most people who die are over 60. As Dr. George Maddox said, "Old people are people who are intimately involved with death. Age represents death. We are not comfortable personally or professionally in the presence of death."[1] Our discomfort before death translates easily into a dislike for those who, by their sheer presence, remind us that, we, too, will die someday.

To exorcise the fear of death, we make those who are about to die redundant and irrelevant while they are still alive. By rendering the about-to-die trivial in life, we lessen the fear that death holds for us. If the about-to-die do not matter, we reason, death may be meaningless also, and we need not be afraid of it. At the very least, we are able to reduce our anxieties about death to a manageable size.

---

[1] Personal interview.

OUR DOUBLE DEATH STANDARD

Our anxieties show clearly in our double standard of death. When a child dies, we grieve openly and fully. We mourn the loss of unfulfilled potential and the waste of undeveloped talents and abilities. Of course, this is true, but we are capable of mourning because the death of a child holds no particular terror for us. We are able to face it openly because, having survived childhood and being older, we are not reminded directly of our own mortality. We do not identify our future dying with the death of a child.

But society shows no such sorrow when an older person dies. We are not struck by a sense of sadness when we read the obituary of a person in his or her seventies or eighties. Instead, the death is considered "right" or "natural." And at the funeral of an older person, there is no general outpouring of grief except by members of the immediate family, and sometimes not even by them. In the minds of many who are present, the person has long since ceased to matter. Such funerals are to comfort the living, not mourn the dead. The family is offered the consolation that the end was quick and painless or that the deceased was spared further suffering. But the anger that accompanies the death of a child is lacking. There is no sense of outrage at an unkind God or cruel fate.

This was made real to me when my own father died. Quite unexpectedly, I found myself the center of attention at *his* funeral. Well-meaning friends consoled me for my loss, and although I appreciated their sympathy, it seemed a trifle misplaced. I had lost my father, but he had lost his life. After a while I wanted to scream, "You've got it all wrong. He's the one that is dead. Don't be sorry for me. I'm still alive. Be sorry for him." But realizing they meant well and were unlikely to understand, I said nothing. Of course, I felt a sense of sorrow and loss, and perhaps some self-pity as well. But beyond that I felt anger. I though of all he might have done and seen or even been if he had not died at the age of 67. It seemed, however, as if I were the only one at the funeral who harbored such thoughts.

Our double standard of death seems so natural to us that we have difficulty picturing things differently. But our attitudes are hardly universal. Sociologist Robert Blauner has written that some societies have diametrically different conceptions of death. Instead of mourning the death of the young, they mourn the passing of the old. Some societies do not even recognize the death of children. Those who die before a certain age are not accorded funerals. Not all of these are primitive societies, whose notions of death can be dismissed as "barbaric" or "foreign." During the long period of high infant mortality in France, pictures were rarely kept of children who died in infancy. The children were considered of so little value that they were not worth remembering. It was the remembrances and keepsakes of the old that were cherished.[2]

Such societies also had an entirely different view of life after death. They believed firmly in some sort of hereafter. With this unshakable faith, they were able to confront the death of older adults. They could face such deaths without fear. They were sure that the deceased, and eventually themselves, would transcend this life. As a society, our belief in immortality is, to say the least, shaky. Ageism, then, serves a protective function. Because ageism is part of our defense against death, helping to shield from our conscious minds those things we would rather not think about, we are able to feel little or no guilt about our treatment of older adults—in life or in death.

Although the underlying causes of ageism are debat-

---

[2]Robert Blauner, "Death and Social Structure," in *Middle Age and Aging,* 2nd impression, ed. Bernice L. Neugarten (Chicago: University of Chicago Press, 1970), pp. 531–40.

able, its existence is not. Surveying the problem from his vantage point as staff director of the Senate Special Committee on Aging, Bill Oriol said, "There is ageism in this country, and it is real and growing. The truth is most people consider the elderly expendable."[3] His concern is shared by sociologists and psychologists who are beginning to regard ageism with the seriousness they once reserved for racism. Researchers have begun to quantify the extent of ageism in society. Such statistical documentation, which will be looked at later in this chapter, can broaden our understanding of the depth of the bias against older adults in society, but it is not necessary for proof. Regrettably, there are too many readily available examples.

GOVERNMENT SPENDING

Ageism is rampant in government, and it pervades business. It is widespread in medicine and the sciences. The media reflects the ageism of the society it reports on and seeks to entertain. Even our speech and language is biased against older adults. The federal government gives low priority to older people. Neither the Executive Branch nor the Congress is equipped to deal seriously with the problems of the 22 million Americans over the age of 65.

In the Executive Branch, the Adminstration on Aging is a bureau of low rank and little prestige within the sprawling Department of Health, Education, and Welfare. The position of the Administration makes its head, the Commissioner on Aging, a poor advocate for the nation's older adults. Unable to report directly to the head of HEW, the commissioner must send requests for funds through the hierarchy of deputy chiefs and undersecretaries before they finally reach the department secretary. At each level, the budget comes under the scrutiny of people who have many

---

[3]Personal interview.

other, and usually more pressing, concerns than funds for aging.

The National Institute on Aging was established by Congress in 1974 to coordinate and promote research into the biological, medical, psychological, social, educational, and economic aspects of aging. But just as the Administration on Aging is the stepchild of the sprawling Department of Health, Education, and Welfare, the National Institute on Aging is the stepchild of the mammoth National Institutes of Health. It has been hampered by lack of leadership and lack of funds, causing the institute to flounder without direction. For the first two years, the institute lacked a director, and the National Advisory Council on Aging, which was required by law to draft a research program for the institute, delayed its initial meeting for an entire year.

In fact, the National Institute on Aging was in large part a simple reorganization move. Five of the six staff members were already working at other institutions. Office furniture, typewriters, and other supplies were borrowed from or shared with other institutes. Research already funded by the National Institute of Child Health and Human Development was simply transferred to the new institute.

The creation of the National Institute on Aging meant new lines on an organizational chart, but not much more money for research in aging. The institute is the smallest of all those within the National Institutes of Health. Its budget in fiscal 1976 was $15.74 million, less than one dollar for each older American. By contrast, the National Institute of Health's budget was $678 million and the budget of the National Heart and Lung Institute was $304 million.

The situation in Congress is worse. Former Congressman Robert H. Steele, who championed older adults for years, said, "Congress has inadequate structure for recognizing, identifying, and acting on the needs of the elderly."[4]

---

[4]Author's notes on speech delivered to the 26th annual meeting of the Gerontological Society, Miami Beach, Florida, November, 1973.

Both the House and the Senate have special committees on aging. But unlike other Congressional committees, aging committees lack the authority to report legislation. They can hold hearings and recommend legislation, but they are unable to approve bills. The committees give visibility to the problems of older adults, but not much help. Programs that are aimed at older people must receive the approval of other congressional committees, pitting older adults against other special interest groups for money.

The result of this haphazard, fragmented approach toward the problems of older adults is to cheat those over 65 out of their fair share of the nation's resources. In general, programs for older adults are poorly funded to begin with, and in times of tight budgets, even this minimal funding is slashed. During the administrations of both Richard Nixon and Gerald Ford, older adults were the target of misdirected attempts to reduce federal spending. President Ford, for example, recommended a $52 million reduction in Older Americans Act programs in fiscal year 1976 out of a total budget of $245 million, well over 20 per cent. The penny-wise, pound-foolish budget cutting shows up in a number of areas. Budget cuts, for instance, called for termination of the Older American Community Service Employment Act. This program enables older adults to work their way out of poverty by helping others in their communities. It makes little sense to force older adults to collect welfare checks instead of salary checks.

Older adults fare poorly when they must compete with other age groups for government services and help. They have fared especially poorly under revenue sharing, the program of "no strings" fiscal assistance to local and state governments. Revenue sharing replaced categorical grants earmarked for certain specified purposes with money that could be used in general as the governments chose. William R. Hutton, executive director of the National Council of Senior Citizens, said, "There are currently a number of studies underway which will provide further documentation of the efficacy of general revenue sharing. The data that is available now is often conflicting and inconclusive. One fact, however, is not in serious dispute: Older Americans are not receiving their fair share of programs and services supported by general revenue sharing funds."[5]

When state and local governments are free to choose what they will do with federal funds, they rarely choose to help older adults. An analysis of spending by 219 governments revealed that only 28 spent any part of their money for programs and activities specifically and exclusively on older adults. Older adults received two-tenths of one per cent of the funds.[6] The exact amount of money that is being spent on programs and activities for older adults is unknown because, in reporting expenditures, the governments lump older adults and the poor into the same category. However, only two per cent of the total, about four cents out of every dollar, was spent for social services for either the poor or the elderly.[7]

When the federal government controls the purse strings, however, older adults are also slighted. They are consistently underrepresented in antipoverty programs, job training courses, and similar social service programs. To get an idea of the bias against older adults and the impact of ageism, consider the following examples:

1. Older adults, who have the most time for education, participate the least in adult education courses. The Office of Education reported in 1976 that 22,500 older adults out of a total of 750,000 participants were enrolled in adult education courses.

2. Older adults, who have the most difficulty in find-

[5]Testimony before the House of Representatives Select Committee on Aging, November 18, 1975.

[6]*Part I: Developments in Aging:* 1975 and January–May 1976, (Washington, D.C.: U.S. Government Printing Office, 1975), p. 174.

[7]"General Revenue Sharing: Reported Uses 1973–1974," in *Revenue Sharing, A Selection of Recent Research* (Washington, D.C.: U.S. Government Printing Office, 1975), pp. 411–64.

ing jobs, benefit the least from job retraining and public employment programs. People over 65 made up only 10 per cent of persons enrolled in the job training programs under the Comprehensive Employment and Training Act.

The government's preoccupation with cost-benefit analysis provides a ready rationale for ageism. Cost-benefit analysis measures the cost of the government in terms of dollars against the expected benefit to society as a result. It can argue that it is not intentionally ignoring older adults, but just trying to assure the maximum possible return on the taxpayer's dollar. The Secretary of Health, Education, and Welfare in the Nixon administration, Robert Finch, once stated this argument rather baldly. Programs for the elderly, he said, result in very little "payoff."

If the worth of programs is judged by cost-benefit accounting, this may be true. It may make sense on this basis to invest money in programs for the young instead of the old. They and society will certainly benefit for a longer period of time. But cost-benefit accounting is a narrow-minded, totally mechanistic way of funding federal programs. This dollar mentality overlooks other considerations that might dictate different priorities in the federal budget. Past contributions to society, need, and the ability to obtain help from other sources are examples of legitimate standards which, if they were applied, could modify the existing distribution of natural resources by the government. But this is impossible as long as ageism is a factor in government decision-making.

Our society, however, is geared toward the production and acquisition of material goods. The young are humored and indulged because they are producers- and consumers-to-be. The old are shunted off and penalized because they are no longer permitted to produce, and, therefore, lack the money to consume. Older adults are caught, as they so often are, going the wrong way in a revolving door. If they could produce, society would consider them entitled to help, but society keeps them from producing and then uses their lack of productivity as an excuse to deny them help.

They are doubly penalized for a situation they did not create and cannot change.

BUSINESS ATTITUDES

Ageism embodied in public policy spreads from government to business. In an earlier chapter, we spoke of the pressure on older workers in their late fifties and early sixties to accept a premature retirement. But ageism does not stop there. It influences business attitudes toward workers in their forties and early fifties. Employers still advertise for "young workers" or "recent college graduates." And corporate reports boast about the youthfulness of their executives.

In personnel offices, older job applicants are often rejected because they are "overqualified," a thinly disguised way of saying that the boss wants a young employee. Interviewers may refuse to place an older applicant with 10 or so years of experience because the job description calls for two to four year's experience. If older adults manage to pass these initial hurdles to employment, they may be rejected on the basis of a pre-employment physical, even though the job requires little physical exertion.

In such cases the bias may be more subtle, but the underlying corporate attitude is the same. In a working paper on age discrimination, the Senate Special Committee on Aging reported, "Age discrimination is the only form of discrimination that enjoys widespread social approval within corporate life." Being young, in fact, represents "an underlying corporate value."[8]

This ageism in business gets tacit approval from the federal government. The Age Discrimination in Employment Act of 1967 prohibits businesses from discrimination in the hiring of older workers between the ages of 40 and 65. But enforcement is notoriously lacking. Up to 1977, only 265

---

[8]*Part 2: Appendixes, Developments in Aging:* 1975 and January-May 1976, p. 175.

cases had been filed for violations of the act. Moreover, the Wage and Hour Division of the Department of Labor, which is responsible for investigating violations, did not have a single employee assigned full time to age discrimination cases. The act itself is an example of ageism on the part of the federal government. It protects workers up to the age of 65, but it ignores workers over 65, who suffer the most from discrimination. Sociologist Erdman Palmore of the Center for Aging and Human Development at Duke University points out, "It's like saying you can't discriminate against Negroes except for the very black."

The federal government, which should be leading the way, isn't. Senator Lloyd Bentsen of Texas succeeded in extending coverage of the age discrimination act to government workers at the federal, state, and local levels. But government employees in most states are still forced to retire at the age of 65. And in the federal Civil Service, most workers are forced to retire by the age of 70. Moreover, workers over the age of 70 are not eligible for regular appointments to the Civil Service. They are limited to temporary appointments subject to renewal. Federal employees, in fact, are subjected to heavy pressures to retire early. Older adults who want to work cannot look to the federal government for help. Some three million people over 65 are in the work force at large, 3.3 per cent of the total, but only 29,067 of them are employed by the federal government. Older adults comprise a mere 1.2 per cent of federal employees.

By not enforcing the act, the federal government forces older adults to lie if they want to work. It is as demeaning as it is unfair. One woman who looks 10 years younger than her age and acts 20 years younger solved the problem by dropping 10 years when she applied for a job as a salesclerk. She got the job, but for a long time she worried about the lie. But confronted by a divorce late in life and a teenage son to support and send through college, she saw no alternative. "If I hadn't lied," she said, "they never would have hired me. I know that." For 15 years until her voluntary retirement at 71, she worried, knowing that her job depended on maintaining her lie. If her boss had discovered her age, she said, he would have fired her, although she easily outsold clerks 20 or 30 years younger. Many capable clerks, she claimed were forced to retire because of their age. "If I hadn't lied about my age, they would have put me out to pasture with the others," she said. "The company would have died if they knew how old I really am."[9]

MANDATORY RETIREMENT

Mandatory retirement is by far the most serious and pervasive form of ageism. Society is gradually lowering the barriers to equal employment opportunities for minorities and for women. Vigorous and strict enforcement of the Age Discrimination Act would go a long way toward creating equal employment opportunities for people under 65. But mandatory retirement policies and laws condemn older adults to second-class citizenship in a society that continues to believe work is good and idleness is bad. They are a particularly virulent form of discrimination, which has been declared constitutional by the United States Supreme Court.

Robert Murgia of Andover, Massachusetts, had reached the rank of colonel in that state's police force when he was involuntarily retired at age 50, the compulsory age for retiring state police in Massachusetts. Murgia believed that he was mentally and physically able to perform his job, so when he was forced to retire, he went to court. His attorney, Robert City, said, "There are elaborate medical screening processes the state police use on personnel every two years until age 40. After that the exam is annual. Murgia passed all tests and met all standards, which meant he was fit." Murgia,

---

[9]Quoted by Delores Barclay, *Ft. Lauderdale News,* in "Retirement, A Bitter Pill for Some," June 9, 1976.

in fact, had passed a comprehensive physical four months before he was retired, and his ability was never disputed.

Murgia contested that the Massachusetts compulsory retirement law was unconstitutional on the grounds that it violated the equal protection clause of the Fourteenth Amendment. The case eventually reached the Supreme Court on appeal from the U.S. District Court that had ruled in favor of Murgia. The Supreme Court reversed that decision.

By its decision, the Supreme Court found that the right to work is not a fundamental right to be claimed by all citizens. The effect of the ruling is to deny some citizens the opportunity to hold a job, to earn a living, and to have a place in the community on the arbitrary basis of age alone. In its per curiam opinion, the Supreme Court noted "the substantial economic and psychological effects premature and compulsory retirement can have on an individual" before concluding, regrettably, that compulsory retirement laws do not violate the Fourteenth Amendment.

The Supreme Court opinion justified laws and policies that demean 22 million older adults and countless other workers who are subject to mandatory retirement. In his eloquent dissent, Justice Thurgood Marshall summarized the case against mandatory retirement:

> While depriving any government employee of his job is a significant deprivation, it is particularly burdensome when the person deprived is an older citizen. Once terminated, the elderly cannot readily find alternative employment. The lack of work is not only economically damaging, but emotionally and physically draining. Deprived of his status in the community and of the opportunity for meaningful activity, fearful of becoming dependent on others for his support and lonely in his new-found isolation, the involuntarily retired person is susceptible to physical and emotional ailments as a direct consequence of his enforced idleness. Ample clinical evidence supports the conclusion

that mandatory retirement poses a direct threat to the health and life expectancy of the retired person and these consequences of termination are not disputed by [the Massachusetts Board of Retirement]. Thus, an older person deprived of his job by the government loses not only his right to earn a living, but, too often, his health as well, in sad contradiction of Browning's promise, "The best is yet to be/The last of life, for which the first was made."[10]

PROFESSIONS AND AGEISM

It is most distressing perhaps to find ageism among doctors and scientists, the two professional groups that should be expected to give the least consideration to the age of the people they help. But, according to their own colleagues, doctors and scientists suffer from the same ageism that afflicts everybody else in society. There is, for example, only one practicing geriatrician in the entire United States, that is, one specialist in the medical problems of old age for 22 million older adults. Although it may appear ludicrous, it is scarcely surprising considering the lack of emphasis most medical schools place on the processes of aging. Few medical schools require courses in geriatrics. Less than a third of the medical schools in the country, 32 out of a total of 114, offer elective courses in gerontology within their regular curriculum.[11] Out of 20,000 medical school professors, only 15 are regularly engaged in teaching or full-time research in the field of aging.[12] In fact, some studies show that medical

---

[10]Massachusetts Board of Retirement et al., Appellants, v. Robert D. Murgia, U.S. Supreme Court, June 25, 1976.

[11]Conversation with author from the American Association of Medical Colleges.

[12]Joseph T. Freeman, "Medical Education in Geriatrics," in *Research and Training in Gerontology* (Washington, D.C.: U.S. Government Printing Office, 1971).

students become increasingly negative toward older adults as they progress through school. Butler said, "I've heard medical students use the terms 'crock', 'toad,' 'turkey,' and the one I heard most recently was 'dirtball'."

Slightly more psychiatrists have specialties or sub-specialties in the field of aging, but their numbers are scarcely adequate to treat the number of older people who are having difficulty coping with the problems of aging. Adriaan Verwoerdt, director of a graduate program in geriatric psychiatry at the Duke University of Medicine, says that it is extremely difficult to recruit psychiatrists to work with older adults. "The trouble with getting more doctors in my field," he said frankly, "is that most people don't like the old." The program, the only one of its kind in the country, is now 10 years old. It usually graduates two or three psychiatrists a year, but few have gone on to full-time specialties in aging. "Most psychiatrists just can't take full-time work with the old," said Dr. Verwoerdt. "The old are too depressing to work with."[13]

Similarly, few scientists engaged in basic research in the fields of biology or chemistry concentrate on the causes and possible "cures" for aging. Such research is hampered by the bias against the old on the part of the researchers themselves. Hayflick, the microbiologist who has been honored by the Gerontological Society for his outstanding contributions to research in aging, has chastised other scientists for neglecting the phenomena of aging. For too long, he said, research in aging has been considered the "stepchild" of the scientific community, not entirely respectable or worthy of the attention of serious scientists. Except for a "miniscule" number of biologists, he charged, the study of the causes of aging is believed to be "an impractical pseudoscience dealt

---

[13]Personal interview.

with by eccentrics and charlatans." The reason for this, he suggested, is the feeling that the extension of the human life-span is not desirable.[14]

THE MEDIA

Since ageism is so prevalent in society at large, it is hardly surprising to find ageism in the mass media, which expresses and, in turn, helps to mold popular opinion. Television has rarely showed older adults in anything but the role of grandparents, and even then they have been stereotyped. There have been exceptions, of course. The grandparents on "The Waltons" have always been popular, for example. But, in general older adults are portrayed on television either as doddering old fools who cause problems for their relatives or as wise old ancients who are always ready with a pithy saying or a piece of warm gingerbread. Old adults are almost never allowed to appear as individuals who love, hate, laugh, get mad at the injustices shown to them, and like the rest of us, attempt to cope with a myriad of problems to the best of their abilities. And when television tries to go beyond these stereotypes, the shows, such as Danny Thomas' "The Practice," are not big hits.

The lack of older adults on television has not been an accident, according to Harlan Ellison, a television writer. Ellison said that during his work on a science fiction series, "The Sixth Sense," for example, there was a policy forbidding characters over the age of 40. In one instance, he said, stories were planned about a colony of senior citizens, but the producer demanded that the locale be switched to a Rand Cor-

---

[14]Author's notes on speech delivered to the 26th annual meeting of the Gerontological Society.

poration "think tank" so that the characters could be about
35-year-olds. "This tends to promulgate the idea that growing old is bad," Ellison said, "that, God forbid, you should get
over the age of 30, you're dead!"[15]

Newspapers do little better. With few exceptions, they
write about older people as if they were an alien race. In
general, they ignore older people who are still active in their
communities. Instead, they feature retirees who, supposedly
by some stroke of luck, have lived to celebrate their eighty-
fifth birthdays, well-preserved physical culture addicts who
look 15 years younger than their age, and "old-timers" re-
miniscing about the "good old days." Or else, newspapers
focus on the problems of old age, contributing to the general
belief that old age is unmanageable and something to be
dreaded. After analyzing 265 articles on the subject of aging
that appeared in a large midwestern newspaper, Roderick
MacDonald, a graduate student in gerontology at the University of Nebraska, concluded that newspapers encouraged
their readers to hold negative images of older people and
aging itself. At a time when older adults comprise a growing
proportion of the total population, he found that newspapers carried, on the average, only 1.1 articles a day on aging
and older adults. Nearly 50 per cent of those articles were
human interest stories, which failed to educate readers about
the realities of aging in America today. MacDonald does not
think that newspapers create ageism. Instead, he believes
that they reinforce society's negative stereotypes of older
adults. "Until the news media find a few good words to say
about aging, we will continue to think negatively about old
age," he said. "We will keep on thinking about aging as something that can't be helped or dealt with."[16]

---

[15]Quoted in Associated Press dispatch by Jerry Buck, published in
the *Ft. Lauderdale News*, Ft. Lauderdale, Florida, under the title "Author's
Talk on Censorship," 1972.

[16]Roderick MacDonald, "Content Analysis of Perceptions of
Aging As Represented by the News Media," presented at the 26th annual
meeting of the Gerontological Society.

Unfortunately, ageism is too deeply embedded in our society to be eradicated simply by eliminating the biases of newspaper reporters and editors. If ageism could be eradicated that easily, we would have little to worry about. We would simply have to convince newspaper people to think more positively about those over 65, and the problem would be solved. But it goes too deep for that.

STEREOTYPING

Ageism is part of our popular mythology and speech. The saying "You can't teach old dogs new tricks" is only one of many clichés reflecting the bias against older adults, which, although false, society accepts as true and conditions the young to believe.

The stereotyping of older adults begins early and continues throughout life. Grade school children have already been indoctrinated with negative attitudes toward older adults and about growing old. When children between the age of 3 and 11 were asked what they knew about men and women over the age of 65, they often replied: "They have heart attacks at 90 and die," "They go to church a lot," "They have to have canes," "They talk funny," "If they are crippled or something like that, they can be sent to houses that will help them." Their views of older adults created a dread of their own aging. They foresaw a time when "My face will feel crinkled, my eyes will feel flurry." They believed they would feel "sad because I'll be dying soon, and I won't have the fun and joy I had when I was little."

At the same time, it is almost impossible to talk about people over 65 without resorting to the use of words that are denigrating and derogatory. For a long time, when I started to write this book, I puzzled over this very problem. In the parts of the Soviet Union where a person of 85 is considered young and people regularly live to the age of 110, they refer to people over a certain age as "long lived." It is a lovely word without any negative connotation. I searched for such a word to use in this book, but none was there. I was left with the unsatisfactory terminology offered by the English language. At the start, I rejected such euphemisms as "senior citizen," which seemed to cover up more than reveal. I wanted to write honestly and truly, and both seemed impossible if I compromised at the outset by my choice of words. Other words seemed imprecise or objectionable for other reasons. "Elderly" implied physical frailty, and many of the people I was writing about were not infirm. "Retiree" wasn't quite as objectionable but it was a sociological term, referring to people who had accepted their unemployment as a permanent condition, and that could mean a wide range of ages. I was writing primarily about people over 65.

For a while I favored the word "old," which seemed relatively neutral, a word based on an inescapable chronological fact. But, to a person of 18, someone of 30 may appear old, whereas to a person of 70, rebelling against society's ageism and refusing to acknowledge his loss of youth, someone may have to mark the ninetieth birthday before he is old. And, I realized, in our society, we lust after the "latest," "newest," "most modern," "all new," "just in," and "just out." Anything that is not new is undesirable and unwanted. In society's opinion, I realized the very word "old" was an insult, and although I disagreed—disagreed profoundly in fact—I would have to deal with it. And so I settled on "older adults," which has the advantage of avoiding the tricky word "old," while defining the group I was writing about in chronological terms.

The problem I had is the problem society has. The words we use to try to define the world, that we must use as we struggle to confront reality, force us to think about older adults negatively. Until we find new words for those over 65 or are able to change the connotations of the words we now use, we will have difficulty eliminating ageism in our society. It is not an accident that the civil rights movement placed such emphasis on what white Americans call those Americans who are not white. It is not a simple cause-and-effect relationship, obviously. Blacks are not now more equal because they are called blacks instead of coloreds or Negroes. But such linguistic changes have forced us to look at nonwhites in a new way. And a similar change would force us to see those over 65 in a fresh perspective. We can pass laws to prevent outright discrimination against people over 65, but as long as they are called "old," and to be old is to be unwanted, ageism will exist.

THE GROWTH OF DISCRIMINATION

As the number of older people in society has increased, ageism has grown also. In the opinion of sociologists Erdman Palmore and Kenneth Manton of the Center for the Study of Aging and Human Development at Duke University, ageism is a serious and growing problem in the United States, rapidly surpassing racism in prevalence. "Few people," they say, "recognize that there is any significant ageism in our society. There has been almost no recognition that the relative status of the aged is declining."[17]

In an attempt to assess the extent of these kinds of discrimination, Palmore and Manton measured the disparity between young and old, blacks and whites, and men and women in the areas of income, jobs, and education between 1950 and 1970. They found that blacks made small but significant gains toward equality with whites. Women barely managed to maintain generally inferior status. They dropped slightly behind men in level of education and employment, and stayed about the same in income. But older adults fell steadily behind the young and middle-aged on these

---

[17]Erdman Palmore and Kenneth Manton, "Ageism Compared to Racism and Sexism," unpublished paper provided by authors.

three scales. Trapped by a fixed income during an inflationary era, their per-capita income dropped further below the per capita income of 14- to 64-year-olds. The growth of free public high schools and universities has raised the educational level of the population at large so that more of the under-65 age group have acquired advanced degrees. Mandatory retirement means that there are fewer employed people over 65 than under 65.

Even though ageism is of increasing importance in a society where more and more people are living to reach old age, it is not new. The mistreatment of older adults has been the common and accepted custom throughout history, as Simone de Beauvoir, the French writer, documents in her encyclopedic study of old age, *The Coming of Age.*

CHANGING CUSTOMS

In tribal days when a society could not afford to support its entire population, some chose to sacrifice older adults. The ways were many and varied, but the result was the same—the older adults were killed so that the young might live. In times of scarcity, the Eskimos put feeble older adults on ice floats to freeze to death while they were fishing, gathering food to feed the surviving young. Nomads left older adults behind when they grew too sick to follow the tribe in the migrations to find new herds and pastures. Older adults were left with enough food to last a few days, and after that, it was presumed, death by starvation came quickly. Some tribes surrounded the killing of older adults with elaborate ritual. The Koryak, who lived in northern Siberia and followed the herds of reindeer across the frozen steppes, killed older adults with a spear and knife in front of the whole community after long and complex ceremonies.

The greatest security and highest status were enjoyed by older adults in relatively stable and agrarian societies.

Such societies, having accumulated a surplus of food and possessing ample shelter, could afford to support both young and old. The young were willing to share these things with the older because older adults possessed skills and know-ledge which were needed by the young. Then, too, longer life expectancy gave older adults enough time to amass large amounts of capital in the form of property. They could use their property to control their families since all of the relatives hoped for the largest share after their death. In public as well as private, older adults were respected.

These conditions existed in the United States during the first half of the nineteenth century. On the family farms of rural America, even the very old were needed. They could always do something—keep an eye on the children, gather eggs or separate the good from the bad vegetables before canning, all simple but valuable tasks. Often the farms themselves were owned by older adults. Their married children lived with them, instead of the reverse, and older adults were secure in their homes.

But only a few decades later, the initial rumblings of the Industrial Revolution drastically and permanently changed the status of older adults. With the rapid growth of industry, the importance of land as a source of income declined. Work shifted from the home to the factory. And in the industrial towns, there were few opportunities for older adults to participate in the work of the community. Only the young could endure the long hours and squalid working conditions of the factories. The number of employed older adults declined. Since they contributed less, it was easy to think of them as worth less.

By taking work out of the home, the Industrial Revolution began to break down the extended, multigeneration family. On the farm an able-bodied person always could be used. Consequently, there was room for people of all generations; an elderly aunt or cousin or two could be taken in. When the young and their families moved to the cities, older adults were usually left behind on the farm. In 1870, the average household in the United States consisted of 5.7 people.[18] By 1976, the number had dropped to 3.4 people.[19] Even if older adults moved with their children, there was relatively little for them to do compared to the farm. Factories supplied the family with goods that were once handmade, food was bought at the store, and the children went to school or work. Older adults became economically useless to the family and a burden to support.

Modern technology further devalued older adults. In earlier societies, time was conceived as linear and static. Change occurred so slowly over the years that those who lived the longest inevitably knew the most about life. But with the Industrial Revolution, our concept of time was altered. Time became synonymous with change, and change with progress toward a bigger, better, brighter tomorrow. Today matters little and the past not at all. As a society, we became future oriented. It was tomorrow that counted. Consequently, older adults, instead of being the repository of the collective wisdom of society, turned into the bearers of a dying culture. Everything they represent—tradition, custom, ritual—is devalued in the technological age. As immigrants in time, they have to struggle to keep up, much less lead the way.

CHANGING SELF-CONCEPTS

All of this has affected the self-concept of older adults. There have been scars. Older adults fear old age and hate themselves for growing old. What Joseph H. Bunz, a sociologist at the State University College of Buffalo in New

---

[18]Paul Glick, *American Families* (New York: John Wiley and Sons, 1957).

[19]Conversation with author from the U.S. Census Bureau.

York, terms gerontophobia, "the unreasonable fear and/or irrational hatred of the elderly by . . . themselves," is the symptom in older adults of the ageism that afflicts society at large. They, too, worship the young and denigrate the old. In a survey of 124 people ranging in age from 9 to 85, psychologist Dr. Boaz Kahana found that old age was considered the least desirable time of life by every age group, including the old themselves. "It is clear that the elderly share society's worship of youth," he said. "It is difficult to resist the temptation to see the different ages as grappling with various developmental tasks. . . . The aged concerned with maintaining a positive self-image in the face of a thankless and devalued position."

To maintain a sense of self-respect and a healthy self-image, older adults are forced to deny the fact that they are old, and old age is considered such a burden in our society that to deny it becomes a measure of social adjustment. In several small towns in the midwest, for example, 151 men and women over 65 years of age were asked to answer "yes" or "no" to such questions as "I never felt better in my life" by two social scientists, C. Terence Pihlblad and Robert L. McNamara. Afterward, the same people were asked if they considered themselves middle-aged or elderly. Over 60 per cent of those who considered themselves middle-aged also scored high on the social adjustment scale, while only 33 per cent of those calling themselves elderly ranked high on the scale. In effect, society's view of old age makes it extremely difficult for older adults to acknowledge their age in a positive, mentally healthy, and self-accepting way.

Instead, as a means of self-protection, older adults adopt a different perspective on aging. Aging is always something that happens to someone else. Old age is always 5 or 10 or 15 years later on. Society may consider people in their sixties, and certainly those in their seventies, old, but they don't. In my interviews with hundreds of older adults, I cannot recall one physically healthy person under the age of 75 who was willing to accept the idea that he was old.

George, for example, is a healthy, active man in his early seventies, who retired a number of years ago from a major oil company. After his wife died, he sublet their apartment in New York City and moved to Fort Lauderdale, Florida, to be near his children. Interested in a number of different things and hobbies, he always found plenty to do. He puttered around the homes of his children, doing odd jobs or played golf with his brother-in-law or read all the books he had never had time for. But, although he seemed happy, his children worried about him. They were afraid that even though he didn't say so, he missed his many friends back in New York. And so they urged him to go to a certain part of the beach where men of his age gathered in the morning to meet and talk. He was instantly and deeply offended. "Me? Go there?" he said. "They're nothing but a bunch of old men. I don't want to hang around with them."

Although most older adults, like George, recoil from people of their own age, others seek their companionship. Realizing they are considered undesirable and unwanted, they have been segregating themselves from the rest of society. They are forming enclaves of older adults where they live, play, and die with others of their own kind. Another and somewhat contradictory effect of ageism is the emerging subculture of aging. Let's see what it looks like.

THE SUBCULTURE OF AGING

CHAPTER FIVE

About an hour's drive south of Los Angeles, California, on the Santa Ana Freeway, nestled between purple hills visible in the west and the Pacific Ocean, unseen but not far away either in the east, is Rossmoor Leisure World, a retirement community of 14,000 people, with an average age of 72. The advertising brochures say that Leisure World, as it is more generally called, is a "whole new way to live," and this time the advertisements are right. Leisure World is the biggest and one of the best of the retirement communities that are springing up around the country.

Retirement communities started in the early 1960s on the West Coast, where warm weather and a relaxed way of life attract many older adults. They spread to Florida and

Arizona, and more recently to New Jersey and other Northeastern states.

Older adults are flocking to these communities by the tens of thousands, sometimes leaving behind children, family, homes they have lived in for decades, and lifelong friends. One gerontologist estimates that one per cent of the total population of older adults may someday live in retirement communities. If their popularity on the West Coast is indicative, this may be a conservative estimate. At popular villages in southern California, prospective buyers line up at dawn when newly constructed condominiums are scheduled to go on sale. During one buying frenzy, the Rossmoor Corporation sold $12.5 million of new retirement homes in a five-hour lottery, including all 59 homes in a special division where prices ranged from $99,900 to $127,900. As a result, some developers are already envisioning retirement communities with projected populations of 100,000, 400,000, or even 600,000 older adults.

Many retirement communities are new towns, designed specifically for older adults, such as the ones developed by Ross Cortese, president of the Rossmoor Corporation. Others have been created by influxes of retirees themselves to existing communities. Older adults have been migrating in unprecedented numbers to such areas as the hills of central Texas; the Ozarks in Arkansas and Missouri; coastal towns in the Carolinas, Virginia, and New Jersey; the Adirondacks and Poconos, the mountains of northern California and Oregon; Puget Sound in the Northwest; and the Upper Great Lakes.[1] In fact, although California ranked first and Florida fourth among the 10 states with the most numbers of older adults in 1975, seven of the states were in the East or Midwest—New York, Pennsylvania, Illinois,

---

[1] *New York Times,* February 1, 1976, p. 1.

Ohio, Michigan, New Jersey, and Massachusetts. The other state was Texas.[2]

Large areas of the country are now feeling the impact of the growing number of older adults. What is happening in many places is reflected in Clare County, Michigan, which ranks thirtieth among all the counties in the United States in the immigration of older adults. Since 1970, the number of people over 65 has increased in the county by 43 per cent. Older adults comprised 25 per cent of the county's population of 21,000 in 1976.

The result in this small northern Michigan community has been an economic boom—and demands for new services. Stores that once closed down after the summer tourist season stay open all year. In Harrison, the county seat, the police force has expanded from one to five full-time officers and is now on duty 24 hours a day. "They forced us to go to 24-hour police protection," said Police Chief Howard A. Haskin. "It's not fear of crime; it's fear of medical emergencies." The town bought its first ambulance after older adults began moving in.

Older adults have made their numbers and influence felt in other ways as well. The county has created a Commission on Aging, there is an active Federation of Senior Citizens, and a federally supported lunch program has been set up.[3]

LEISURE WORLD

Retirement communities obviously appeal to older adults. A look at the present and past life-styles of the resi-

---

[2]*Part I: Developments in Aging: 1975 and January–May 1976*, (Washington, D.C.: U.S. Government Printing Office, 1976), p. xxiii.

[3]*New York Times*, February 1.

dents helps to explain their popularity. Leisure World is a good place to begin.

Because of its location, Leisure World has been studied extensively by sociologists from the Ethel Percy Andrus Gerontology Center at the nearby University of Southern California. Their surveys add to our knowledge of Leisure World residents. Their findings basically agree with the conclusions I have drawn from my conversations with older adults in other retirement communities and appear to be generally true.

A visitor to Leisure World is immediately impressed by the atmosphere of total security and self-sufficiency. The entrance is guarded 24 hours a day by a private uniformed security guard and flanked by a 10-foot-tall world globe set in a lush garden of tropical plants and bubbling waterfalls. At night, giant floodlights cast beams of light across the entrance. Beyond the gate is a towering glass and concrete building that houses the offices of the nonprofit Leisure World Foundation, which manages the village for the Rossmoor Corporation and a shopping center. The shopping center consists of department stores, a bank, gas stations, a motel, five restaurants, and a barber and beauty shop. Beyond the shopping center, the village proper begins.

Leisure World sprawls across 600 gently rolling, meticulously groomed acres that are constantly seeded, weeded, and mowed by 170 full-time gardeners. The Spanish-style condominiums, mostly two-story interspersed with a few one-story buildings, are called "manors," and they are set back from the winding streets. Flower beds border the streets and perfume the air. The atmosphere is relaxed and gracious. There is a feeling of tranquillity, a sense of endless time to pursue and savor the good life, however it may be defined.

Shortly after 8:00 A.M., golf carts begin rolling through the streets to the 27-hole golf course, and some women mount their bicycles to pedal to the shopping center to pick up the mail and chat with friends over coffee and English muffins.

At 8:30 A.M., the oom-pah-pah sounds of organs drift from Clubhouse No. 1, the center for crafts and hobbies, signaling the start of another busy day of activities. At 9:00 A.M., the would-be organists are replaced by amateur painters, and so a typical day goes, continuing on through a Red Cross sewing workshop, the Aquadettes, pool and billiard tournaments, the ukelele group, classes in ceramics and world literature, and winding up 11 hours later with ballroom dancing at 7:30 P.M. On other days the schedule is crowded with classes in Spanish, scrabble, knitting, sculpture, bridge, mosaics, macrame, table tennis, Russian, acting, and French. Altogether, tnere are 101 different clubs, craft workshops, and assorted planned activities for Leisure World residents.

The tennis courts fill up early, and by noon those who can't get a court head for the riding stables or the two Olympic-sized swimming pools. The less athletically inclined can spend the afternoon bowling on the lawns or playing shuffleboard.

At night, residents can often choose among dances, concerts by guest performers, and plays by local Production Guild 500 in the community's 840-seat theater. Musical revues produced by the Production Guild periodically spoof life in Leisure World. A favorite skit is "Numbers Game," which shows a party guest spending the evening outdoors searching for the party, a not infrequent occurrence in a community of cul-de-sacs and dead-end streets.

Ed Olsen, director of Leisure World Foundation, says that Leisure World conscientiously avoids a "now we sing, now we dance, now we play golf" attitude. "We have tried to make things available so people can be as involved and as active as they desire," he said. "But if they prefer, they can stay at home and do nothing."

Even the stay-at-homes, however, are not forgotten.

They can tune in Channel 6, Leisure World's own cable television station. "The largest closed circuit TV station in the world" broadcasts a variety of shows. Some are educational, answering frequently asked questions about health and Social Security, while others are purely entertainment. These include "What Was My Line?" featuring panels and mystery guests from the community, since Leisure World has its share of millionaires and celebrities.

Leisure at Leisure World, Olsen insists, is "creative, not just play." The adult education department of the local school district offers regularly scheduled classes in many subjects at Clubhouse No. 1. And Olsen says, 'It's surprising the number of people who have become involved. Many who never would have done so are continuing their education here."

When future residents buy a condominium at Leisure World, they probably are making the last major purchase of their lives, and both they and the developers are well aware of it. The advertising brochures stress that Leisure World offers "total concept living." Once residents move in, they never have to leave the community, unless they want to, until they die. It is this that makes Leisure World "a whole new way to live."

Leisure World residents can live, shop, play, and worship in the seven churches and one synagogue within the community. But they can do so, more or less, in a number of retirement communities around the country.

SECURITY IS THE WORD

What makes Leisure World different, what Leisure World offers that others don't, is continuum care. Leisure World residents avoid the painful uprooting from familiar things and people that residents of other retirement communities experience if they become sick or infirm.

When Leisure World residents are no longer able to maintain their homes, they are able to sell the "manor" and move into Rossmoor Towers. The two high-rise condominiums feature private apartments with daily maid service and communal dining for those who are unable to shop or cook for themselves. If they get sick, they can check into the Leisure World Medical Center, which provides fully staffed, around-the-clock medical services. The multimillion-dollar center employs more than 80 doctors, including a full-time psychiatrist, nurses, and related personnel. (A full-scale hospital is also under construction.) And if they need extended care after leaving the medical center, they can transfer to the nursing home across the street.

Although this continuum of care is undoubtedly a lure for older adults, the real attraction of Leisure World is security. The true symbol of the community is not the illuminated world globe at the entrance, but the six-foot-high wall that surrounds it. Leisure World is a walled city in more ways than one.

Leisure World capitalizes on the concern of most older adults for physical and emotional security. The brochures emphasize "peace of mind at Leisure World." One advertising leaflet shows an older couple out for an evening stroll, pausing under a street light for a chat with a uniformed security guard. "Take a walk around the block in the middle of the night?" it asks rhetorically. "Why not!" It goes on to say, "For Leisure World residents, nothing can be compared to the overwhelming feeling of well-being; the comfort that comes from safety, security, and peace of mind."

Many agree, and they choose Leisure World for precisely that reason. A retired insurance executive from Seattle, Washington, C. Edwin Courtney, said, "The security feature is extremely important. To be able to turn the key and go on a trip without any apprehension about our home and belongings is a great thing."

The desire for physical security by older adults who

have worked all their lives to accumulate a few material possessions and who want to be assured of keeping them in old age is understandable. But their craving for psychic security is almost a fetish.

Social problems such as pollution, crime, narcotics, and unemployment are words in a newspaper for the most part in Leisure World. The residents read about them, even talk about them, but their closest contact to the reality these words represent is usually through the evening news. On the nightly news, such problems seem as interesting but as remote as a crop blight in Afghanistan. This is the way the residents prefer it. When *The News*, the weekly community newspaper, ran a story about two women being robbed in their condominium, residents complained. The editor said, "Some of them want us to print only the good news." The residents want to keep their illusion of total tranquillity, even if it is false.

FINANCING

None of this comes cheaply. Leisure World is definitely not for the older couple or single individual struggling to get by on Social Security. The cheapest one-bedroom, one-bath condominium starts at $50,000 and goes up from there. Monthly maintenance fees for the upkeep of the buildings and surrounding gardens are about $65. Altogether, the average cost, according to Olsen, is between $200 and $300 a month for mortgage and maintenance. "Obviously," he said, "these people have more than just a Social Security check to live on, and some have substantially more."

Leisure World, however, is not even for everyone who can afford it, as Olsen readily admits. "We don't pretend to be all things to all people," he said. "Some find it's not for them and sell out." Those who leave often say candidly that they grew tired of constantly seeing and being around older adults. One feisty 71-year-old man said that retirement communities like Leisure World are "warehouses for undertakers." He said, "They smell of death." But such people are a minority. Olsen is able to admit frankly that some are dissatisfied with Leisure World because of its resounding success. The Rossmoor Corporation easily sells condominiums that will not be ready for occupancy for another year. They are already assured of their projected population of 26,000.

RETIREMENT COMMUNITY RESIDENTS

If Leisure World is not for people living on Social Security or for older adults suffering from gerontophobia, for whom is it? Who are the people who pack the sales office?

They are mostly upper middle income whites who have chosen to retire among their own. There are no blacks or Mexican Americans, although these minorities are heavily represented in southern California. And there are few Orientals, although they, too, comprise a substantial per cent of the population in the area. Residents are generally well educated. The median level of education is 12 years of schooling, which is considerably above the educational level of older adults as a whole. Before they retired, they were usually professionals, white collar workers, or businessmen. Only 12 per cent were blue collar workers. In short, they are the kind of people who are apt to be members of the country club set in small towns in California and the Midwest.

They are people who are happy with their lives in middle age and moved to Leisure World to preserve it as they grow older, according to a study by Dr. James Peterson and Aili Larson.[4]

------

[4]James A. Petersen and Aili E. Larson, "Social and Psychological Factors in Selecting Retirement Housing," in *Patterns of Living and Housing of Middle-Aged and Older People* (Washington, D.C.,: U.S. Government Printing Office, 1965) p. 129–43.

As these people grew older, Peterson and Larson found, their once full lives started to shrink. Some 15 per cent of the retirees said they missed their work. They felt they no longer had things to do that gave a sense of self-satisfaction. And they said they missed their coworkers and the social contacts that work provided. Almost 40 per cent, including both retirees and housewives who had never been employed, said to their chagrin that they had fewer friends now than they had 20 years before.

Moreover, 41 per cent of the older adults said that they moved to Leisure World because it offered an opportunity to be active again. They liked belonging to a variety of organizations and having an active social life. They were reluctant to give up such a life, and they felt that by moving to Leisure World, they could retain it. "It would seem," wrote Peterson and Larson, "that these are individuals who looked forward to a country club type of living with a major emphasis on social activities and recreation in their own backyard. There seems little doubt that the effort of the builders to make leisure attractive and easily available motivated a large number of in-movers."

Leisure World, and retirement communities like it, are doubly attractive to a certain group of older adults. These people want to escape the pervasive ageism in the community at large that prevents them from living their formerly satisfying lives as soon as they turn 65. Leisure World offers an opportunity to do so. These older adults also want to find new friends and activities to replace the ones that they valued in their youth. Leisure World provides such a chance.

These older adults *like* people of their own age. One 74-year-old man, who was discouraged from moving to a retirement community by family and friends, said, "When people ask me what I'm doing with all these old folks, I tell them I'm running like hell to keep up." And they genuinely prefer the company of older adults. They are emphatically against the age-old tradition of elderly parents moving in with their married children. Although they love their children and grandchildren, they favor intimacy at a distance. One woman said, "I love to see my children and grandchildren, and I love to see them go. I just can't take the confusion of youngsters all the time."

Dr. James Birren offers a blunt explanation for this. "The older you get, the more you want to be with people like yourselves," he said. "You want, to be honest, to die with your own."[5]

Isolated from the rest of society, residents of retirement communities are creating a leisure-oriented life-style. Many new residents are admittedly uneasy with their unaccustomed leisure at first. "The Puritan ethic is deeply embedded in these people," said Olsen. "They've worked hard all their lives and they don't know what to do if they don't work. We've tried to solve that problem by making leisure acceptable." Most adjust after a while, encouraged by the indulgent attitude of the developers and the community. Those who are still troubled by their Puritan conscience set aside a few hours a week for charity work. Forty women regularly attend the weekly Red Cross sewing group at Leisure World, whipping up kimonos, slippers, and other garments for children, with expert speed. "I couldn't live here," said one member, "in all this good life and luxury, which it is for us, without giving of myself to something."

NEW LIFE-STYLES

This leisure-oriented life-style gives older adults a chance to be someone again. The real problem of aging in American society is increasingly not age at all, but a lack of status. Growing numbers of older adults are not bothered by

---

[5]Personal interview.

the infirmities of age, but by their lack of status. Our status system, based largely on occupation and the money and prestige that accompany it, is often irrelevant after retirement. For the majority, just who and what they are and where they belong in the social system become puzzling. Occupation, which confers the most social status in society, no longer applies. Except for individuals of wealth, retirement exerts a leveling effect on income, reducing the differences in income that exist among the employed. Achievements turn into legend or fade and are forgotten. Thus an older person must either accept diminished status in the community or find a new status system. Retirement communities offer the best way.

Residents of retirement communities are strangers, and being strangers, they are more or less equal. When they move in, they begin, as the ads say, "a whole new way of living" where the past matters less than the present. What people were is less important than what they are. "No one cares about the past here," said a 62-year-old retired manufacturing engineer in one community. "The banker can live next door to his teller and be friends."

New identities emerge as strangers become friends. The former architect is begged for the secret of his flourishing roses. The retired banker is the neighborhood fix-it-man, the only one on the block who knows what to do about a leaky faucet or a blown television tube. The grandmotherly housewife is famous for her snappy fox-trot at the Saturday night dances. Retirement communities offer so many activities that almost everyone can find something to excel at and be known for. Older adults acquire through them the feeling once again of being useful, needed, and important. Mental and physical health and the ability to participate in a variety of social activities are the basis of the status system in retirement communities.

SENIOR CITIZEN CENTERS

Health and participation are important, too, at senior citizen centers, which are rapidly emerging as the focus for the leisure-oriented life-style outside the retirement communities. In fact, a former Commissioner of Aging, John B. Martin, said, "The senior citizen center is going to play the same kind of central role in the lives of older people that school plays in the lives of children."[6] The parallel is apt. Senior citizen centers are places for older adults to gather with friends and make new ones, attend adult education classes, have lunch and sometime dinner, and participate in social activities.

Some centers are built and funded by the community, others by churches, and still others by older adults themselves. They range from walk-in store fronts, open a few days a week, to elaborate ultramodern complexes that hum with activity 15 hours a day. They share a common concern for the special emotional needs of older adults. And they try to help both older adults and the community to cope with the problems of aging.

In St. Petersburg, Florida, a long-favored retirement mecca, the senior citizen center is located on the edge of Tampa Bay overlooking the sailboats and yachts bobbing in the municipal marina. The center, planned and built by older adults, is a second home to its 3,000 members. The $6 annual dues entitle members to unlimited use of the center's facilities. There are cards, billiard and music rooms, shuffleboard courts, and a cafeteria that sells sandwiches and soft drinks for a nominal price.

---

[6]Ibid.

The center bustles with activity from morning to night. Dance lessons fill the morning hours, bingo games the afternoons, and several nights a week there are eagerly awaited dances—the high points for most members.

Over 200 elegantly dressed men and women attended a dance one sultry night in July. The men wore dinner jackets, and the women wore cocktail dresses and white gloves. Some brought mink stoles despite the heat. The women outnumbered the men, and the women who were not dancing sat on bridge chairs around the floor, watching and waiting.

On the dance floor, 90 couples did lively fox-trots, cha chas, and rhumbas to the tunes that were popular in the late 1920s or early 1930s. Multicolored lights revolved over the heads of the crowds as the band belted out such old favorites as "I'm Forever Blowing Bubbles" and "If You Knew Susie." And an occasional ladies' choice dance helped to even up the imbalance between the unattached men and women.

Standing on the edge of the dance floor, tapping his foot and ogling the women, a man said, "*This* is the way to live."

Except for the signs on the walls warning "Dance At Your Own Risk," it was difficult to remember that these lively men and women were so-called senior citizens.

The members of this center are fanatically loyal. One 67-year-old retiree looked up from the pool table and said repeatedly, "For $6 a year, you can't beat it or tie it. I come here every day." Some members are waiting at the door when the center opens in the morning. "Some come at 9 a.m. and stay until we close," said one of the center's managers. More than one romance has blossomed over the bingo tables, and several members have met and married—and still come regularly.

The Metropolitan Senior Center in Miami, Florida, is a little different. It is one of 12 centers, located in low-cost housing projects, operated by the Senior Centers of Dade

County, Inc., a nonprofit organization funded by the county, state, and federal governments. These are one-stop service centers for recreation, nutrition, education, and health care.

During my visit, the Metropolitan Senior Center was operating in its usual happy chaos as telephones jangled endlessly and older adults rushed in and out. Some 400 rodeo tickets had been donated to the center, and the residents and staff were trying to locate transportation.

Older adults were making silver jewelry in a workshop, conjugating Spanish verbs with a teacher from the county's adult education department, and attending a meeting of the coffee committee. The center actively recruits older adults to serve on a variety of committees. The director, Cliff McCloud, believes that the professional staff should offer loose supervision and guidance when necessary, but the older adults should make the day-to-day decisions and run the center. They plan eventually to expand from five to seven days a week. "Some of these people never leave their apartments from Friday night to Monday morning," said one resident. "We want to reach these people."

The centers offer more than recreation. It serves 1,000 low-cost meals daily, gives 20,000 free immunization shots annually, screens residents for diabetes and glaucoma, and provides both individual and group psychological counseling. It is planning a homemaker service that would pay older women who live in the housing project for helping invalids with their daily chores.

Retirement villages and senior citizen centers reflect the growing age consciousness of older adults. And as they begin to come together, their age consciousness will be intensified. We will look at some consequences of the emerging subculture of the aging in Chapter X.

WHAT IT COSTS SOCIETY
TO HIDE
OLDER ADULTS

CHAPTER SIX

Old age is not cheap. It is expensive for older adults and for society.

Older adults can be divided in general into two basic groups—the poor who grow old and the old who grow poor. They share a common fate. In a society that fears old age and scorns the old as redundant, they must struggle to provide themselves with the basic necessities of life. Such seemingly simple things as food to eat, a place to sleep, and the ability to get from place to place—things taken for granted by the young—are problems for older adults. Limited funds often force older adults to choose between food and medicine, as we shall see later.

Society also pays, and pays dearly, for its lack of concern for older adults. Lack of concern for their needs and wants is extracting a heavy price. We cheat ourselves when we shut out the special wisdom and point of view that older adults are capable of offering. This loss cannot be calculated. Other losses can be measured in dollars and cents. Our paychecks offer weekly reminders that the Social Security tax is taking a larger and larger chunk out of take-home pay. More and more of our income tax dollars are being used to finance social welfare programs for older adults. We are supporting older people who are not permitted or who are not able to work.

Adequate income in retirement is a new social problem that has been created by the combination of longer life expectancy and a shorter working life. At the start of this century, people generally lived only a few years after they stopped working. At the end of the 1970s, the time between retirement and anticipated death is substantially and steadily increasing. A man who retires at the age of 65 can anticipate another 15 years of life. He will spend 20 per cent of his life in retirement. A man who retires at the age of 58, the average retirement age for federal employees, can look forward to an additional 22 years of life. He will spend 35 per cent of his life in retirement. These changes force older adults to spread their retirement income over several decades instead of a few years.

A few generations ago, older adults tended to live out their lives in the homes of relatives. The relatives contributed to their financial support and, with their own modest but usually adequate savings, older adults were able to manage.

Three-generation households are increasingly rare today. Even the least demanding, most well-intentioned relative is an intruder in the kind of houses that have been built in this country since the end of World War II.

Emotional ties between older adults and their children have also weakened. Children are increasingly reluctant to support their parents as they adopt an urban, secular-oriented life-style.[1] Older adults, in turn, sense this unwillingness on the part of their children to be of assistance. Older people believe they are losing status within their own families. They are no longer sure of their place in the lives of their children. They no longer trust their families to take care of them when they cease to be able to support themselves.[2]

Those who are still in the work force find that it is difficult, if not impossible, today to save money for their own retirement. Inflation cuts into the ability of all workers to pay current bills, much less save for retirement. After the bills are paid, most people are lucky to have enough money left to put some aside for next summer's vacation or a child's education. Very few can afford to invest in their own uncertain future. Those who try must remember to compensate for inflation as they save, since rising prices increase the amount of money that will be needed in the future. In fact, economist Joseph Spengler has estimated that a person who plans to retire on the income from savings must invest between two and two and a half times as much as his grandparents did. The impact of inflation also can be expressed in another way. A worker who now estimates that he could retire comfortably on $1,000 a month would need $1,338 a month in five years if the annual rate of inflation were six per cent, slightly below

---

[1] See R. M. Dinkel, "Attitudes of Children Toward Supporting Aged Parents," *American Sociological Review*, (1944), 370–79.

[2] See Margaret Clark and Barbara Gallatin Anderson, *Culture and Aging* (Springfield, Ill.: Charles C. Thomas, 1967).

the inflation rate of 1976. After 10 years, he would need $1,791 a month. In 20 years, the figure would be $3,207 a month, and 30 years later, it would require $5,743 a month to maintain the same standard of living. This level of savings is beyond the capability of most.

For all these reasons, most older adults can no longer support themselves or depend on financial help from their relatives in retirement. They are increasingly looking elsewhere for financial assistance. Government programs, such as Social Security, Supplemental Security Income, Medicare, and Medicaid, are becoming the main source of income and financial assistance during retirement. They can be expected to assume increasing importance in the future.

We as a society have yet to face up to the problem of maintaining an adequate income during the retirement years, much less find a solution. Dr. Juanita Kreps, Secretary of Commerce in the Carter administration, said, "Recognition of retirement as a relatively new life stage, which requires its own financial arrangements, is obviously necessary and just as obviously lacking. The implications of this life stage for public policy have not been fully accepted."[3] We have fumbled along, passing a new program here, adjusting an old program there. This piecemeal, halfhearted approach to the fundamental problem of increased life expectancy and earlier retirement has created a system that spends billions for Social Security, which does not give economic security; for Supplemental Security Income, which institutionalizes poverty; and for Medicare and Medicaid, which provide partial care at best. It fails to come to grips with the fact that if older adults are not permitted to work to support themselves, then someone else must assume that burden. The burden falls on the working people between the ages of 20 and 64.

---

[3]Personal interview.

RETIREMENT ECONOMICS

Let's begin to look at the economics of retirement.

In general, older adults receive at least some income from a variety of public and private sources. Their own savings still account for some of that income, although an increasingly declining proportion. Private pension plans were instituted at the turn of the century and vastly expanded during the 1950s. The federal government intervened in 1935 when the Social Security Act, the best-known and most common source of income in retirement, was passed. Congress in 1965 passed Medicare to provide health insurance for those over 65 and Medicaid to help the states to provide medical care for the poor of all ages, including older adults who have incomes below the federal poverty level. The Supplemental Security Income program went into effect in 1974 when the federal government assumed responsibility for old age assistance programs, which until then had been administered by the states.

Statistics on the amount of money that these sources contribute to the support of older adults are scarce, and statistics on the number of older adults who receive income from these sources are sketchy. The Social Security Administration, however, has looked at the distribution of the income of thousands of Social Security recipients. Its survey is useful since the findings are expressed in percentages rather than in absolute numbers. Time will not alter the findings unless there are important, and unanticipated, changes in the sources and distribution of income in retirement.

Table 2 shows the financial arrangements of married couples between the ages of 65 and 72.

Table 2

Source of Income	*Percentage of Couples With This Source*	*Percentage of Total Income from This Source*
Social Security	100	37
Interests, dividends, and rental income	64	17
Earnings	53	25
Private pensions	22	6
Veteran's benefits	20	5
Public retirement benefits other than Social Security (military, civil service, etc.)	9	55
Public assistance	5	1
Private group annuities	4	Unknown
Contributions by relatives	1	Unknown
Others	Unknown	3

These figures reveal several interesting facts about the economics of retirement:

1. Older adults derive income from a variety of sources, but most sources contribute relatively little to their total income. No source of income is sufficient by itself to provide an adequate income in retirement. Older adults must rely on makeshift arrangements, some money here and some money there, to get by.

2. Although over half of the older adults earned some income, this represented only a fourth of their total income. Older adults are penalized by reductions in their Social Security benefits if they earn more than the so-called retirement test allows each year. The retirement test was

$3,000 a year in January 1977. After they have earned $3,000, one dollar is subtracted from their Social Security check for every dollar that is earned. The number who already receive some income from their earnings means that employment could be a substantial source of retirement income if jobs were available and older adults were permitted to work.

3. Private pension plans are relatively unimportant sources of retirement income. Although many workers are covered by pension plans at some point during their working years, very few have actually collected in retirement. Arcane rules and regulations have added Catch 22's to most pension plans. Many who thought they were covered by a pension plan have found, to their surprise, that they could not collect after retiring because of a loophole or obscure requirement. Although Congress passed a pension reform act in 1974 to safeguard retirement benefits, this legislation does not help those who are already retired. Those who do collect often find benefits to be less than expected.

4. Older adults now rely on public rather than private sources of income. Only one per cent receive financial help from relatives. Five times that many receive public assistance. Although the majority have some savings or investments, less than a fifth of their total income is derived from that source.

All of us have a strong stake and considerable self-interest in how older adults finance retirement. Let's take a closer look at these arrangements. In this chapter we will look at the way such arrangements affect the taxpayer. In the next chapter we will see how older adults are managing on our tax dollars. We will find that the end result is hardship to both the young and the old. Those who are still in the work force are being severely taxed to support those over 65, most of whom are still unable to maintain a decent standard of living. Those under 65 are growing poorer as a result of supporting those over 65, while those over 65 are still struggling to provide for the necessities of life.

THE SOCIAL SECURITY SYSTEM

Congressional intentions in passing the Social Security Act in 1935 were modest. Congress wanted to help unemployed older workers by replacing some of the income that was lost when they lost their jobs in the Depression. Congress envisioned a relatively limited program, and Social Security, in fact, started off slowly. Employees and employers each contributed a maximum of $30 into the Social Security trust fund during the first year. An estimated total of $576 million was collected by the federal government. The program even then was part social insurance and part welfare, but the welfare aspects were submerged as the government vigorously promoted Social Security as a social insurance scheme, sort of a federally sponsored pension plan.

Over the years two things have happened to Social Security. First, the program increased in size, taking in ever more tax dollars and expending increasingly more in benefits. Coverage has been expanded until the program now touches the lives of almost every American. Second, the federal government has perpetuated the belief that Social Security represents income insurance for workers, with its premiums taking the form of taxes on wages and its annuities taking the form of benefits after retirement.

The program's growth during its relative short history has been overwhelming. An estimated 32 million people received $76 billion in Social Security benefits in 1976.[4] Nearly one out of every seven Americans received retire-

---

[4]Testimony of James B. Cardwell, Commissioner of Social Security, before the Joint Economic Committee, May 26, 1976.

ment, disability, or survivor benefits from Social Security in 1975.[5] The overwhelming majority of these people were over the age of 65.

Tens of thousands of people are employed at the Social Security Administration center in Baltimore, Maryland, to keep track of payments. In many small and medium-sized communities, monthly Social Security checks are the largest single source of income. Approximately 104 million people worked in jobs that were covered by Social Security in 1976. Nine out of 10 paid jobs were covered under Social Security.[6] (The principal exception is Civil Service employment; federal employees have their own retirement system.) These workers paid $72 billion in 1974 in Social Security taxes, which accounted for 40 per cent of all federal taxes on individuals.[7]

Social Security has succeeded so well in becoming a multi-billion-dollar concern because Americans believe overwhelmingly that they are investing in their own future through their Social Security taxes. After a hike in Social Security taxes, syndicated cartoonist Jim Berry drew a cartoon that showed two office workers standing by a water cooler and examining their paychecks. One said to the other, "I've decided to smile about the bigger bite taken by Social Security and fool them by living long enough to get those higher payments."

The idea that each of us has an individual Social Security account somewhere in the federal treasury is encouraged by the Social Security Administration itself. "Insurance

---

[5]"Future Directions in Social Security Unresolved Issues: An Interim Staff Report," prepared for the Special Committee on Aging, United States Senate, (Washington, D.C.: U.S. Government Printing Office, 1975, p. iii.

[6]Testimony of James B. Cardwell.

[7]Robert S. Kaplan, *Financial Crisis in the Social Security System* (Washington, D.C.: American Enterprise Institute for Public Policy Research, 1976), p. 2.

for You and Your Family," a booklet published by the Social Security Administration, says, "Your account number of your Social Security card identifies your old age and survivors insurance account. Your card is the symbol of your insurance policy under the Federal Social Security law." Another booklet, published by the Department of Health, Education, and Welfare, describes the Social Security system in similar terms. It says, "The basic idea of Social Security is a simple one: during working years employees, their employers, and self-employed people pay Social Security contributions, which are pooled in special trust funds. When earnings stop or are reduced because the worker retires, dies or becomes disabled, monthly cash benefits are paid to replace part of the earnings the family has lost."

This belief is crucial to the existence of the entire system. The staff of the Senate Special Committee on Aging took note of this fact in its report on Social Security financing when it wrote:

> . . . (Social Security) must retain one of its most precious assets: the confidence of individual persons, who by paying into the system during their working years, are *entitled* to the many protections offered by the system.
>
> It's not enough for the checks to arrive on time—a common dole could do that.
>
> The people of the United States must also believe—as they have, overwhelmingly, for nearly four decades—that Social Security is *their* program, based on *their* earnings, attuned to *their* changing circumstances.
>
> To a large degree, Social Security has made that belief not only valid, but deeply ingrained. It has the thrust of the public; it adjusts, even while fundamental values and concepts remain fixed.[8]

But the well-hidden truth is quite different. We are *not* contributing to our own Social Security account with

---

[8]*"Future Directions,"* p. iii.

our Social Security taxes. *There is no account* with our Social Security number on it in the federal treasury. We are *not* contributing to our own retirement. We are *not* investing in our own future. The truth is that our Social Security tax dollars go, not for our own support, but for the support of those who are already retired.

Furthermore, what we put into the Social Security system and what we get out of it are two different things. There is only a tenuous relationship between our Social Security taxes during our working years and our benefits once we retire. Benefits depend ultimately not on what we contribute but on what Congress decides our benefits should be. Between January 1965 and June 1975, for example, Congress passed legislation that added up to an 84 per cent increase in Social Security benefits. To put it another way, a couple retiring in 1965 received maximum benefits of $184.50 a month. By 1972 the same couple was receiving $399.30 a month. A respectable increase of $154.80 a month cost them nothing; it was paid for by those who were still working.

The defenders of Social Security describe the relationship between those who are still working and those who are already retired as a moral compact between generations. Those who are working to support those over 65 have nothing to fear because they, in turn, will be supported by other workers. But this moral compact is more accurately described as a chain letter that can be broken at any point. A chain letter is no stronger than its weakest link, and the heavy burden of Social Security taxes on younger and lower income workers means it is weak indeed. Those who are now working to support the retired generation have plenty of reason to fear that the working generation will ultimately rebel and that they will receive little return on their money.

THE INCREASING TAX BURDEN

Workers are already paying a heavy price to support older adults. Increasing Social Security taxes have steadily eroded the ability of workers to save money. In 1942, for example, the average American family had $767 for discretionary expenditures and savings after living expenses and taxes. For every $100 that family could afford to save, Social Security taxes claimed $3.70. Over the years, Social Security taxes have eaten into possible savings. By 1973, 29 years later, the average family had $740 left over, but Social Security taxes claimed $622 of possible savings. As Congressman James Collins of Texas has pointed out, "The opportunity for the average American family to save has been corroded practically to zero."[9]

These figures tell one part of the story, but, by averaging out the cost, they obscure the other part. The support of older adults is borne disportionately by lower and middle income workers.

Unequal taxation. The Social Security tax has been likened to an upside-down income tax. The federal income tax, which is progressive, works on the simple principle that those who earn more should pay more. The Social Security tax does not. It taxes all workers with strict equality and, in doing so, it is grossly unfair to those at the lower income levels. It has been called the poor person's welfare payment to the middle class.

Social Security is a regressive tax, which hits hardest

---

[9]Congressman James Collins, "Review of Social Security Premises Needed," *Congressional Record*, June 21, 1976, p. H6327.

those who are least able to pay. This is because earnings are taxed only up to a certain level. Earnings above that level are not taxed at all. In 1976, for example, Social Security took 5.85 per cent of all earnings up to $15,300. It took nothing from earnings over $15,300. This means that a middle income worker making $10,000 a year contributed 5.85 per cent of his total income to support older adults, while an upper income worker earning $30,000 paid only 3 per cent of his total income for their support. The disparity is even greater than it appears. The Social Security tax is a payroll tax, which applies only to income from wages and self-employment. Income that comes from stock dividends, interest, and similar sources escapes Social Security taxes altogether. The more that a person derives of his total income from these sources, the less that person pays proportionately for Social Security.

Every increase in the Social Security tax takes more from lower income workers than it does from upper income workers. In 1973 the Social Security tax rate went from 5.2 to 5.85 per cent. For lower income families, this represented a substantial porportion of their income. The tax increase represented nine per cent of the total income of a family of four supported by a single worker earning between $3,000 and $4,000 a year. It took only 3.4 per cent of the income of a similar family earning $10,000 a year. In the upper income brackets, the tax bite was substantially less. It took a mere four-tenths of one per cent of the income of a family earning $50,000 and one-tenth of one per cent of a family earning $100,000 a year.

Because of the regressive nature of the Social Security tax, a family too poor to pay income taxes can be forced to spend substantial amounts of its income to support older adults. An estimated 20 million workers, too poor to pay income taxes, have paid more than $6.5 billion a year in

Social Security taxes. In addition, economist John A. Brittain found that 40 per cent of the people filing income tax returns paid more in Social Security taxes than in income taxes.[10] The Social Security tax bite is enough to drop a family below the poverty level.

Future benefits. This heavy-handedness might be justified if low income workers could count on receiving proportionately more in retirement benefits for their disportionately higher taxes during their working years. But, as we have seen, they cannot. The Social Security system has long since abandoned the actuarial principle that there should be a fixed rate of return for every dollar contributed. There is no guarantee that lower and middle income workers of today will be adequately compensated in the future. Social Security has become a pay-as-you-go system. The trust fund concept is no longer inviolate. Many of the basic premises upon which the system was built have been abandoned. This was symbolized in 1975 when the tax reduction act of that year gave every Social Security recipient a one-time payment of $50 from the general revenues instead of the Social Security trust fund.

Low and middle income workers are not the only ones who have reason to worry. Everyone who is now paying into the system has good reason to question what they will be getting out of it when their turn comes to collect. Older adults have reason to question if they can continue to rely on their monthly Social Security checks as a bulwark of retirement income.

When the Social Security system was put on a pay-as-you-go basis, the system came to rest on flimsy foundations. The continued financial solvency of the system became de-

---

[10]John A. Brittain, *The Payroll Tax for Social Security* (Washington, D.C.: Brookings Institution, 1972).

pendent on several variables that are difficult to project with accuracy. If older adults are to get back more than they have paid in, the system must be buttressed by an expanding work force and increased productivity. Unexpected changes in the number of people who are born and die, unprojected fluctuations in the rates of inflation and unemployment can affect the system adversely. This, in fact, has happened.

The high unemployment of the 1970s, which caused less money to come into the system, and the 1972 Social Security amendments, which created automatic cost of living increases for retirees, have led the system to the brink of bankruptcy. In 1975 the system paid out $1.5 billion more in benefits than it collected in taxes. In 1976 benefits exceeded taxes by $4.3 billion. The Social Security system maintains a trust fund that provides a financial cushion against deficits in the short run. But the system cannot run a deficit indefinitely or the trust fund will be exhausted. The deficit is expected to continue to rise until it reaches an estimated $8.5 billion in 1981. The result is sadly predictable. The trust fund will be exhausted in the near future. The exact date when the system goes bankrupt is unknown. It depends on which set of economic forecasts is assumed. Even by the most optimistic projections, however, the system will have exhausted the trust fund by about 1986, in the opinion of the board of trustees of the Social Security system. By their more pessimistic projections, the trust fund will be exhausted by 1982.

As grim as this forecast is, the long-range outlook is not any better. The system will continue to pay out more than it takes in through the remainder of this century and into the start of the next. The board of trustees of the Social Security system estimates an average deficit of 3 per cent between 1975 and 2050, beginning with a three-tenths of 1 per cent deficit in 1975 and rising to a 5.3 per cent deficit in 2050. A panel of economists and actuaries appointed by the Senate Committee on Finance concluded that the Social Security system was in even worse financial straits. The panel decided that the system would run an average deficit of 6 per cent over the same period, ranging from the same three-tenths of 1 per cent in 1975 to 12 per cent in 2050. Table 3 compares the projections of the board of trustees and the panel of the Senate Committee on Finance.

Table 3
[In per cent]

Calendar year	Combined payroll tax rate	Expenditures as a percentage of taxable payroll	
		1974 Trustees' Report	Panel
1975	9.9	10.2	10.2
1990	9.9	11.0	11.5
2010	9.9	12.7	14.6
2030	11.9	17.6	23.3
2050	11.9	17.2	23.9
Average	10.9	13.9	16.9
Average deficit................................		3.0	6.0

One thing is clear from the table—older adults are going to be an increasing burden on the work force in the years ahead.

IMPACT OF THE OLD

The problems created by the financial insolvency of the Social Security system are complex. The cause of them is quite simple. More people are living into old age and fewer people are being born. The result is that the population of the United States is taking on the shape of an inverted bell jar, with an enormous number of people at the top being supported by a relatively small number at the bottom.

Fertility rates have dropped sharply and dramatically

since the 1950s. When the Social Security system was looking ahead in 1957, it assumed that women would have, on the average 3.77 children. By 1965 the fertility rate, the number of children per woman, had dropped to 2.93. Ten years later, the fertility rate had fallen to 1.8. This figure is below the rate of zero population growth, which means that the population of the United States was no longer replacing itself. Thus older adults of the future will have to count on a substantially shrunken labor force for financial support. When the baby boom generation of the post-World War II era reaches retirement age, there will be fewer people around to contribute to their support.

The impact that the growing number of older adults is having on those who are in the work force can be expressed in other terms. In 1940 there were 77 million people between the ages of 20 and 64 and 9 million people over the age of 65. This gave a ratio of 11.7 older adults to every 100 people of working age. One hundred people were working to support 11.7 people who were retired. By 1973 there were about 118 million people between the ages of 20 and 65 and approximately 22 million people over the age of 65. The ratio of older adults to people in the work force climbed to 18.6. One hundred people were then working to support 18.6 people in retirement. The burden of supporting older adults is expected to increase slightly over the next 27 years. After the beginning of the twenty-first century, however, it increases sharply. The Social Security system projects that in 2030 there will be 50 older adults to every 100 adults of working age. The burden will have vastly escalated.[11]

The increasing dependency ratio is cause for concern in itself. The work force will be forced to support an ever greater number of dependent older adults for the foresee-

---

[11]*Part I: Developments in Aging:* 1975 and January–May 1976, (Washington, D.C.: U.S. Government Printing Office, 1976), p. xx. "Testimony of James B. Cardwell.

able future. While this is happening, however, something else is also occurring that is cause for even further concern.

EFFECTS OF INFLATION

When Congress granted automatic cost of living increases for Social Security recipients, it intended for retirees to be compensated for inflation that was beyond their control. But in doing so, Congress overlooked cost of living increases given to those who are still working. The result is a disaster for an already shaky system. In the future, many retirees will be receiving more in Social Security benefits than they received in wages when they were employed.

This is the way that it happens. Social Security benefits are pegged to a formula that is designed to give retirees a certain percentage of their average monthly salary. For example, if a worker had an average monthly salary of $200, and Social Security benefits are intended to replace 50 per cent of that amount, the worker will receive $100 a month after retirement. The cost of living increases were intended to compensate a retiree so that he would continue to receive benefits that would be equivalent to $100 a month in purchasing power despite inflation. If inflation drove up the cost of goods by 10 per cent, the replacement ratio would increase by 10 per cent. The retiree would then receive 55 per cent of his average monthly salary, or $110 a month.

The kinds of inflation experienced in the 1970s vastly complicates the formula. Workers employed during inflationary periods receive wage increases during their working years to compensate for the rising cost of living. At the same time, retirees are receiving increases in the percentages of their wages that are being replaced so they will be compensated.

Let's see what happens to the worker who earns $200 a month when he is employed during a period of 10 per cent inflation. His wages will have increased from $200 to $220 a month. Retirees will have had their replacement ratio increased from 50 to 55 per cent. The worker's average monthly salary at retirement will then be $210, and he will receive 55 per cent of that for a monthly Social Security benefit of $110 a month. The worker will end up receiving $5.50 more a month than a worker who retired earlier with the same real income.[12]

Because of the increases in the replacement ratio, some workers will end up receiving more money than they earned during their working years, while others will receive almost as much. Table 4 dramatizes the effects of inflation on retirement income for single and married workers in different income brackets.[13]

Table 4
Replacement Ratios at Retirement at
Age 65 in the Year 2050
[In per cent]

	Assumed annual increases in earnings/ Consumer Price Index respectively		
Taxable earnings category	*4 per cent/ 2 per cent*	*5 per cent/ 3 per cent*	*6 per cent/ 4 per cent*
(1) Worker without spouse:			
Maximum	32	38	44
Median	42	52	63
Low	65	86	109
(2) Worker with spouse aged 65:			
Maximum	48	57	66
Median	63	78	95
Low	98	129	164

---

[12]Kaplan, p. 7.

[13]Report of the Panel on Social Security Financing to the Committee on Finance, United States Senate (Washington, D.C.: U.S. Government Printing Office, 1975), p. 16.

Future workers will not only be supporting more older adults proportionately, but they also will be supporting an increased standard of living for them.

OTHER WEAKNESSES

The Social Security system is also being weakened by the withdrawal of state and local employees from the system. State and local governments are not required to provide Social Security coverage for their employees, and in recent years increasing numbers of state and local employees have been withdrawn from the system. The Social Security system is losing their taxes at a time when money is most needed.[14]

Until March 1972, only 133 governments employing 9,900 workers had terminated coverage. By December 1975, the number of governments terminating coverage increased to 321, and the number of workers losing coverage had increased to an estimated 44,700. The state of California terminated coverage for an estimated 24,500 employees in December 1976. Other governments announced intentions of terminating coverage for an additional 33,600 employees. Alaska announced termination for all state employees at the end of 1977. These withdrawals, of course, add to the Social Security system's deficit.

All of these things—increasing dependency ratios, higher replacement ratios, and withdrawals from the system—will take their toll on future workers. The combination means higher Social Security taxes. Experts disagree about the exact magnitude of the increase, but they agree that the tax hike will be hefty. The panel on Social Security financing appointed by the Senate Committee on Finance, for example, estimated that payroll taxes would need to be

---

[14]"Coverage and Termination of Coverage of Government and Non-profit Organization Employees Under the Social Security System," U.S. Government Printing Office, 1976, pp. 7–8.

raised by about 20 per cent over the first half of the next 75 years and to be about doubled during the second half. Other estimates run along similar lines.[15]

ADDITIONAL AID TO OLDER ADULTS

Because of the nature of the Social Security system, the economic impact that retiree benefits have on working individuals is easy to document. But Social Security benefits are only the most obvious way that workers help to support older adults. Taxpayers contribute to the economic and social well-being of older adults through their federal income taxes as well as their Social Security payroll taxes. Although the cost to the individual is less obvious, it is no less real.

Taxpayers spend vast sums every month to augment the Social Security benefits of low income older adults. Social Security contributions represent only a portion of that financial support. Taxpayers were spending approximately $245 million a month in 1975 on Supplemental Security Income checks for individuals over 65 who had incomes below the poverty levels. In 39 states, the benefits from the federal treasury are supplemented by state funds. Taxpayers in those states contributed an additional $1.2 billion that year for the support of older adults.

There are numerous other federal programs for older people that are also supported through tax dollars. During the fiscal year running from July 1975 to July 1976, for example, taxpayers spent $125 million for nutrition programs and $12 million for community service employment programs. They spent $15 million to support state agencies that help older people. And they contributed almost $47 million for volunteer service programs for older adults.

---

[15]See Report of the Panel on Social Security Financing, p. 2; Kaplan, p. 9; and "Future Directions," p. 3.

MEDICARE

Taxpayers paid nearly $17 billion, some of it unnecessarily, in the 1976 fiscal year for a Medicare program that has institutionalized waste and inefficiency in the health care of older adults. Although older people pay premiums for Medicare coverage, their contributions do not begin to cover the cost of the system. Our tax dollars make up the difference. And, unfortunately, they are not always spent in the best possible ways.

The Senate Special Committee on Aging has called the Medicare program a system of noncare. It is basically a remedial program, which means that problems must have escalated to the crisis stage before it will intervene. For example, a doctor ordered visiting nurses and home health aides into an older man's home when his daughter was hospitalized. The doctor believed the nurses and aides were necessary to make sure that the man, who had a history of heart trouble and was frail and forgetful, remembered to take his medicine. According to the doctor, the man might forget without his daughter to remind him, and the nurses and aides would prevent unnecessary institutionalization. Medicare paid the bills for two months and then cancelled further payments, although the doctor said they were still needed. If the man had failed to take his medicine, Medicare would have paid for his hospitalization and nursing home care later without question, but it would not pay to insure that he stayed well.

Taxpayers are billed unnecessarily for such irrational decisions. They are forced to spend a lot for institutionalization when they could spend a little for prevention. Institutionalization is an expensive way of caring for older adults. They are forced into hospitals and nursing homes because Medicare refuses to pay for such things as visiting nurses, home health aides, and homemakers. And since older adults must have been hospitalized before they can be admitted to nursing homes, taxpayers pay the higher hospital costs.

Experimental programs have demonstrated the irrationality of the Medicare program. Pilot projects have proven that with a minimum of help at a minimal cost, many older adults can stay in their own homes instead of being moved into institutions. The savings run into the millions and even billions. The Senior Opportunities and Services program, administered by the Community Services Administration, has prevented the unnecessary institutionalization of thousands of low income older adults by providing home health aides and visiting homemakers. It has offered assistance with home repairs, home delivered meals, and transportation. In a single year it helped 800,000 older adults at an average annual cost of $17 per person. These are the types of older people who would have been forced into institutions at a cost of $5,000 and up annually without Senior Opportunities and Services. By spending about $14 million on the program, taxpayers save almost $4 billion on institutional charges.

These income and social programs are already costly. If they are continued in the future, they will be even more expensive since there will be more older adults to be served. And the declining percentage of working adults means that they will have to pay more both in terms of dollars and proportionately for them.

The failures in our public policy on aging that are exemplified by the problems in the Social Security system and the Medicare program are different in kind but similar in cause. They are the result of a failure to come to grips with the lengthening of the life-span. Dr. Harold Sheppard of the W.E. Upjohn Institute for Employment Research said, "We are witnessing a sort of trained incapacity on the part of the spokesmen of the 1930s to conceive of a new system to meet the new problems of the 1970s and 1980s and the 1990s and the twenty-first century."

Fortunately, there are alternatives. We look at new ways of dealing with increased longevity in a later chapter.

THE HIGH COST
OF GROWING OLD

CHAPTER SEVEN

Despite the amount of money that is spent to help older adults and despite the burden this places on the work force, older adults remain among the most economically deprived groups in our society. Millions of men and women over 65 exist below the official poverty level, and millions more teeter on the brink of poverty. Inflation erodes their previous standards of living, while they look at their dwindling bank accounts with frustration and impotent rage. Hundreds of thousands, perhaps even millions, too proud to acknowledge their need, refuse to accept the help that is available. For most of them, poverty is a new experience. The acceptance of what they consider charity would deny at the end of their lives all of the things that they have been for 65 or 70 years —independent, self-sufficient, and self-reliant. They prefer poverty. Socially, older adults who are poor learn to make do or do without.

Not all older adults are poor, of course. Some of the richest Americans are over 65. Before her death in 1973, Marjorie Merriweather Post, the late grande dame of Palm Beach (Florida) society, was a benevolent ruler who exercised power gently from her lush Mar-a-Lago estate. For the kind of palace that a Spanish duke might have fantasized, she paid $50,000 a year in property taxes. There is also Charles Munn, dubbed "Mr. Palm Beach" by the local society press, who has spent thousands of dollars to avoid trifling inconveniences. He once chartered a TWA jet to fly him, his wife, and several friends from Paris to Palm Beach at an estimated cost of $21,000. Munn wanted to avoid the necessity of changing planes in New York. Many other retirees, not millionaires but comfortably well-off, own condominiums with ocean views in resort areas, play endless rounds of golf, and take annual trips to Europe. For those with money, good health and motivation, retirement can be the start of the good life. Unfortunately, these older adults are the privileged few.

THE POVERTY CLASS

Too many older Americans, who endured a major Depression, fought two World Wars, and contributed to the rising standard of living among the population as a whole, are forced to reconcile themselves to a life of poverty. Frequent across-the-board increases in Social Security benefits since 1970 and periodic cost of living increases, which began in 1975, have simply escalated the level of inadequacy for many. Consider these statistics:

1. Almost 16 per cent of those who are over 65 have incomes below the federal poverty level. Another 10 per cent are considered marginally poor, with incomes that are below

125 per cent of the federal poverty line. They are the near poor who can drop below the poverty level at the merest threat of an unexpected expense.[1]

2. The average retired person received $200 a month in Social Security benefits in July 1975. This put his annual income at $2,352, a mere $48 a year above the poverty threshold. A retired worker, receiving the minimum Social Security benefit, had an annual income of $1,212 in 1975. That put his annual income $1,140 below the poverty line.[2]

3. A new generation of older adults with incomes at the poverty level is in the making. Poverty among persons 45 to 54 years old increased by 200,000 from 2.4 to 2.6 million, during the year that ended in August 1975.[3]

These overall figures obscure the special hardships that are suffered by particular groups of older adults. Blacks and women, who have long been discriminated against in the employment market, lose out once again when they reach old age. Because of their low incomes during their working years, older blacks are nearly three times as likely to be poor as older whites,[4] and older women are nearly two times as likely to be poor as older men.[5] Over half of the blacks over 65, close to 53 per cent, are classified as poor or near poor.[6] Over 18 percent of the women over 65 live in poverty.[7] When the handicaps of race and sex are compounded, the hardships are multiplied. Older black women who live alone are among the most severely disadvantaged groups in society. More than 7 out of 10, 70.8 per cent, live in poverty.[8]

---

[1]*Part I: Developments in Aging:* 1975 and January–May 1976 (Washington, D.C.: U.S. Government Printing Office, 1976), p. 64.

[2]Ibid., p. 62.

[3]Ibid., p. 145.

[4]Ibid., p. 64.

[5]Ibid., p. 70.

[6]Ibid., p. 64.

[7]Ibid., p. 70.

[8]Ibid., p. 64.

These figures are alarming, but they are at best rough estimates of the extent of poverty among older adults. Experts believe that there are unknown and uncounted numbers of older adults living in poverty who hide, out of fear and ignorance, from the prying eyes of the census takers. These older people would swell the poverty rolls if they came to the attention of the proper authorities. The extent of hidden poverty among older adults is indicated by the difference between the projected and actual participation in the Supplemental Security Income program, which provides benefits to the aged, blind, and disabled who are below the poverty level. Before the program was implemented, officials at the Department of Health, Education, and Welfare estimated that 6.2 million people would be eligible for benefits. By the end of 1975, two years after the program went into effect, only 4.6 million people were receiving benefits.[9]

Some older adults are confused by the bureaucratic shuffling and red tape that accompany applications for assistance. Others simply do not know they are eligible. Many are prevented by pride from applying for assistance. In some cases, it is a combination of all three reasons. In a concerned effort to ferret out some of the hidden poor, Jewish welfare agencies turned up 800,000 Jews across the country, the vast majority of them over 65, living below the federal poverty levels. These Jews, many of them immigrants who settled in Jewish neighborhoods in the major cities, were left behind when their more affluent relatives moved to the suburbs. Isolated in now decaying neighborhoods of inner cities, they have been overlooked and neglected by most antipoverty programs. S. Elly Rosen, a social worker in New York City, said, "Most of the Jewish poor don't even know they are eligible for public assistance. They think any kind of welfare is demeaning, and they need guidance to get the help they so desperately need." But Jewish older adults are not the only ones who shun public assistance programs. Dr. Jean Mayer,

---

[9]Ibid., p. 72.

professor of nutrition at Harvard University, has said that "quite a few" older adults in New England had quietly starved because they were unwilling to accept food through welfare programs. They would rather starve than let their neighbors know they were accepting welfare.

Most of the older adults who are below the poverty level did not expect to live out their lives in poverty. It just happened.

The Wolfes live in a public housing project. When they met and married in New York City some 45 years ago, they had good jobs. She was a registered nurse; he was a mechanical engineer. They earned good incomes, and in their forties and fifties they had every reason to believe that they would be protected against the unexpected in old age. But Mr. Wolfe suffered a stroke, which left him partially paralyzed, unable to talk, and confined to a wheelchair. Medical bills wiped out their savings. They are still in debt from the hospital expenses.

Instead of living out their lives in relative comfort, they and their possessions, accumulated throughout their married life, are crammed into a small, two-room apartment. Instead of old age being a reward for a life of hard work, it is an almost unsufferable burden, a cruel and unexpected hoax played on two people who worked and saved to enjoy their retirement years.

Their entire income is a $271 check from Social Security once a month. On the day the check arrives, Mrs. Wolfe lists the amount in her small, spidery handwriting on the top line of a loose-leaf notebook. She writes very small to save space because when the notebook is filled, there may not be enough money to buy a new one. As the month passes, she subtracts their expenditures—$35 for rent at the public housing project, $6 on her husband's outstanding hospital bills, varied amounts for medicine, food, and bus fare. They are eligible for a drug allowance from the county welfare department, but by scrimping they are able to get by without it. They feel a sense of pride that they are able to do so. "I figure as long as we can manage without it we will," said Mrs. Wolfe. "There may be someone who needs it more than we do." At the end of the month if they are fortunate, the income and their expenditures tally. If Mrs. Wolfe is very careful and lucky, there may even be a little left over. She said, "I don't know how sometimes, but we always get by."

Getting by has become a way of life for them. Mrs. Wolfe economizes in every way that she knows. She makes her own clothes and those of her husband. She starts making Christmas cards and presents to send to relatives and friends in July. The presents are usually things like dish towels and aprons trimmed with braid and ribbons. She wishes often that she could get to a certain store in town which sells fabric at discount prices. "I could save so much money, I know, if I could just get there," she said. She can't because her city, like so many, lacks adequate public transportation. The alternative is to ask the few people in the housing project who own cars for rides. But she dislikes, and resists as much as she can, such dependency.

Poverty traps the Wolfes in the narrow world of the housing project and the few blocks around it, a small island of the poor and old surrounded by the young and affluent. In their pinched budget, there is no money for even simple pleasures such as an ice cream cone on a hot summer night. Poverty has diminished their wants to conform to their means. During one of my visits, Mrs. Wolfe's sole desire was to find a person who could play their old, badly yellowed, and out-of-tune piano. Although she cannot play, her husband did and composed music before his stroke. "He would like so much to hear his music again," she said.

CONTINUING POVERTY

Not all older adults who are poor have been reduced to poverty in old age. The experience of being without money, of lacking sufficient food, and of foregoing material comforts is not new for large numbers of the disabled, the unskilled, the poorly educated, and members of minority groups. They have lived without these things all of their lives. Yet their despair and hopelessness acquires a new poignancy with age. They realize that their situation will never change. They resign themselves to a life of poverty until they die.

In the basement of a shabby frame house on the fringes of the black ghetto lived such a person. The man was old and black and poor. Before his eyes grew faint and useless, he was a day laborer, never making very much, not even in good months. But he managed to provide himself with the necessities. He had hope, too. Tomorrow, the day after, next month or year might be better. Now his hope was gone, and he was beginning to accept, with an air of resigned inevitability, a life of poverty.

He seemed surprised one humid afternoon when my voice penetrated the murky gloom of the basement corridor. His head bobbed in the direction of my voice, and his sightless, slightly jaundiced eyes turned toward me. With its heavy jowls and slack skin, his face sagged until it looked as if it would drop into his lap. His blindness was in a sense a blessing. It kept him from seeing the flaking paint on his iron bedstead and the newspaper pasted over the broken windows. But it also kept him at the mercy of the fleas that hopped on his arms from the mangy dog that lay, tongue out and panting, at his feet. He swatted at the fleas, but missed more than he hit. When he spoke, his voice sounded like a tool grown rusty with lack of use, creaking and breaking and starting up again.

His only human contact was with the owner of the house. She collected his rent, cashed his welfare checks, claiming a percentage for doing so, and brought his food. He could not remember how long he had been living there, but he guessed it had been many years. He could not really remember another home. He spent most of his days sitting on a wooden footstool in the dark, dank basement corridor, dreaming and waiting for something he could not quite define. He thought that he would be grateful for anything to break the monotony. When he thought about it, which was rarely, he figured that he would most likely die in the corridor. He said it was simply a matter of time before he got through with the business of living.

Recently he had heard a rumor from the owner that he, along with the other tenants, would have to move. The government, he had been told, was condemning the building to make room for a new post office complex. He was afraid that he would lose his home. Although it was bleak and dismal, it was still home. Blind and handicapped, he had no way to look for a new place to live. Even if he could get out to hunt for a new room, it would be difficult to find a place he could afford. He said, as much out of despair as hope, "I guess the Lord will provide for me because He surely knows that I can't provide for myself."

THE MONEY SQUEEZE

Older adults are caught in the squeeze between rising prices and a fixed income. The double-digit inflation of the first half of the 1970s hit older adults especially hard. Inflation in general diminished the value of their money, carefully set aside and saved over the years for their retirement. At the same time, the cost of goods and services that consume the greatest proportion of their budgets has risen particularly fast. Older adults must spend about $8 out of every $10 for housing, food, medical care, and transportation. The rate of increase for these items exceeded the rise in prices for all other items in the Consumer Price Index by 42 to 29 per cent between 1973 and 1974 alone.[10]

---

[10]*Developments in Aging:* 1974 and January–April 1975 (Washington, D.C.: U.S. Government Printing Office, 1975), p. 16.

Although rising prices reduce the buying power of all of us, inflation is worse for older adults with fixed incomes. Quite simply, they have less to lose. They have few ways of adding to their income. Their Social Security benefits are reduced if their earnings exceed a minimal amount. Their fixed incomes offer little hope of improving their financial situation. Almost all older adults feel the impact of inflation. It is not limited to those who fall below the official poverty level. Social Security increases have not kept pace with inflation. The Consumer Price Index, for example, jumped by 23 per cent between October 1972 and December 1974. During this same period, Social Security benefits were boosted by a mere 11 per cent. The automatic cost of living adjustments are raising a level of benefits that lagged behind the rise in prices in the past.[11]

A fixed income demands unaccustomed and painful cutbacks in the budgets of lower, middle, and upper middle income older adults. With few exceptions, older adults must resign themselves to an increasingly impoverished standard of living.

I spent a morning talking with a retired manufacturing engineer in his comfortable, three-bedroom ranch house on the outskirts of a small town in the South. The house, the way it was furnished, and the late model car parked in the driveway indicated an upper middle income lifestyle. Once that was true. It is no longer. When Bob Harmuth was working, he and his wife rarely worried about money. Although they had few real luxuries, they had more than enough to take care of their necessities and provide for a few extras. Six years ago, when he retired on his doctor's orders, his savings, along with a small pension and Social Security, seemed adequate for their needs. Now they are not

---

[11]Ibid., p. 14.

so sure. They are fighting the rising cost of living, but they fear it may be a losing battle.

"The savings are beginning to look pretty puny," he said, worry flickering across his face. "Inflation has cut drastically into our retirement funds. We have gradually curtailed our activities. We rarely go out to dinner these days, for example. We are trying to be increasingly conservative in our spending habits. We eat more hamburger now than steak. And when it comes to a choice between spending money now or trying to hold off a little longer, the choice has got to be holding off. Right now the car needs a new set of tires. Usually I've bought the best because I believe it is the best value in the long run. I put off purchases for as long as I can now, and when I've got to buy things, I look for cheaper items on sale."

People like the Harmuths have discovered for the first time in their lives after retirement that lack of money means lack of choice. They face a world of steadily narrowing alternatives. They stop asking themselves "What do I want to do?" and start asking themselves "What can I afford to do?" It is a question that pervades their entire existence.

Since older adults generally are unable to increase their means, they must reduce their wants. After housing, food, transportation, and medical care are paid, they have $2 out of every $10 left over. That money must cover such expenses as clothing, insurance, personal maintenance, upkeep of household appliances, gifts, books, magazines, and entertainment. The goal becomes sheer survival.

BUDGETS FOR OLD AGE

The Bureau of Labor Statistics and others have drawn up hypothetical budgets, based on the Consumer

Price Index, for older adults. They are frugal at best. A budget prepared by the Planned Protective Services, Inc. of Los Angeles points up the difficulty of getting by.[12] The monthly budget for a single person, based on the 1975 cost-of-living indices in the Los Angeles area is shown in Table 5.

Table 5
Apartment costs (1 bedroom in an older section of the city, water and trash paid)

Rent:	$130
Utilities (gas, electric, phone):	$ 35
Housekeeper:	$ 40
Medical costs:	$ 45
Food:	$100

Total expenses for food, shelter, and health: $350

This modest budget was already beyond the reach of the average retired worker on Social Security, who, in July 1975, received $200 a month in benefits. It also exceeded by $70 the amount of income needed to maintain an intermediate level of existence based on Bureau of Labor Statistics estimates. A budget prepared by the Institute of Aging at Portland (Oregon) State University for Supplemental Security Income recipients in the area was even more spartan.[13] The average SSI recipient had a monthly income of $248, a mere $6 above the poverty level. Based on the cost of living in the Portland area, the recipient would spend:

Housing:	$ 84
Utilities:	32
Food:	65
Medical:	36
Transportation:	2
Other:	29
Total:	$248

---

[12]*Part I: Developments in Aging:* 1975 and January–May 1975, p. 23.
[13]Ibid., p. 25.

Before double-digit inflation took its toll, the Bureau of Labor Statistics estimated that a couple over 65 living in an urban area would need $4,489 a year to maintain a moderate standard of living. The Bureau's definition of a "moderate living standard" is modest indeed. By one calculation, the modest budget would enable a retired couple to afford one wool dress for the wife every three years, an overcoat for the husband every 10 years, a new vacuum cleaner every 25 years, and a dollar a month for books, magazines, and other recreational items. Even then, approximately two-thirds of retired couples were unable to afford that budget.

When older adults look at their income, they see a hard choice between necessities. Often they must gamble between food now and medical care later. Let's see how they manage.

ASSETS AND TAXES

For most older adults, their home is their chief asset. Two-thirds of older adults own their own homes, and 80 per cent of the homes are free of mortgages. The houses represent a lifetime of savings. Yet, in a very real sense, older adults are house poor. Owning a home, many discover in later years, is a deceptively cheap form of housing. The maintenance, repairs, and furnishing of a house can consume 34 per cent of the budget of a middle income older adult. Moreover, soaring property taxes are financially paralyzing homeowners in many parts of the country. Some older adults are paying 20 to 40 per cent of their income in property taxes, which are inherently regressive. As a result, older homeowners with limited incomes pay a disproportionately larger percentage of total income for property taxes. Wisconsin found that more than 8,000 retired homeowners in the state with incomes of less than $1,000 a year paid approximately 20 per cent of their income in property taxes. Homeowners living in abject poverty with an average total income of $300 a year were paying 58 per cent of income in property taxes.

Property taxes are going up, not down, around the country. Older adults fear that rising property taxes will tax them right out of their homes. In Bergenfield, New Jersey, for example, a couple bought a modest six-room house on a 50' by 100' plot in 1931 for less than $8,000. They are now watching the rising taxes in panic. At the present rate of increase, they figure that they will be paying more in property taxes in 1988 than they originally paid for the house. With one eye on their bank balance and the other on the calendar, they are hoping that they will die before that point is reached. "If we are fortunate enough to live another 15 to 20 years, will we be forced to sell our house and wind up on relief?" the man asked in desperation. "This is something I have worked and sacrificed all my life to prevent."

Older adults looking for an escape from rising property taxes can rent. This, too, is costly even if an apartment can be found, and frequently it cannot be. Waiting lists at housing projects for low income older adults are frequently three to four years long. In New York City, when 96 apartments were opened up, 5,000 older adults applied. In Los Angeles, applicants at federal housing projects for older adults have been told that there are waiting lists of 3,000 to 6,000 applicants. In New Jersey, state officials estimated a need for 70,000 additional apartments in low and moderate income housing projects to accommodate the number of eligible older adults by 1980. At the same time, they had no hope of meeting this goal. During the administration of Richard Nixon, funds for such projects were frozen, guaranteeing a three- to four-year backlog in housing even if the original funding had been adequate, which it was not. Meanwhile, millions of older adults are living in old-age ghettoes or watching rising housing costs nibble away at their already depleted bank accounts.

Older people end up resigning themselves to their lack of alternatives. A 68-year-old woman, still employed, said, "I just don't know what I will do. I can't work much longer and I don't know how I will keep up the mortgage payments then." After 20 years of owning her three-bedroom tract house, she pays only $50 a month to the mortgage company. Assessments for new sewer lines, repairs, and the occasional need to pay someone to trim the trees and haul away debris, however, eat into her small income, which will be further reduced when she stops working. Although she has considered selling her house, she knew she could not find a livable apartment in her city for $50 a month. Looking out her living room window at the shadows of palm trees that inched their way across the small front yard, she sighed in frustration. "I guess I'll have to take in boarders, rent out a room or something," she said. "I never thought I would be forced to do such a thing."

FOOD

Older adults also need well-balanced, low-cost meals. Because of rising food costs and lack of education about proper diets, malnutrition among older adults is increasingly common in this, the richest country in the history of the world. Dr. Donald Watkins, an expert on nutrition and a leader of the 1971 White House Conference on Aging, has said that improper eating habits have been reaching the proportions of a national emergency among older Americans. Although some malnutrition may be the result of ignorance, most of it is caused by the inability of older adults to afford to eat properly.

The income crunch has forced many older adults to resort to eating pet food or to shoplifting. An official with a nonprofit group in Washington, D.C., that helps older adults said, "You see them in the supermarkets buying more cat food than you know they have cats to feed, and you know that they are eating it themselves." Shoplifting among older adults has approached the proportions of a local crisis in South Miami Beach, Florida, according to local shopkeepers.

South Miami Beach is an enclave of older adults who are predominantly Jewish. They live in decaying rooming houses and old efficiency apartments not far from the luxury hotels of Miami Beach. Some 37,000 older people are crowded into a one-square-mile area. Most of the retirees living on fixed incomes came to South Miami Beach seeking camaraderie in their old age and a sunny refuge from the problems of modern life in the large cities of the North. Increasingly, their retirement dreams of sun and fun, clung to through decades of harsh northern winters and made possible by the careful setting aside of many one-dollar bills, are being destroyed. Many can afford only two meals a day. Others can afford only one. A shockingly large number turn to shoplifting food and vitamins to survive.

In the shadow of hotel rooms that rent from upward of $50 a day even in the sluggish summer season, a supermarket manager said that a large proportion of the apprehended shoplifters are older adults. His supermarket, like many in the South Miami Beach area, have been the target of shoplifters over 65 who crave a steak or pear that they cannot afford. The number of older people who are caught shoplifting has increased in recent years. "Before, they might try to put an item under their clothing," he said. "Now they're coming in with shopping bags. They take small expensive items—cans of shrimp and tuna. Things that let them put a lot in one bag." A manager at another supermarket in the area said, "Some of the older women put little packages of meat in their bras. They steal what they need at the time—vitamins or cans of tuna fish."

The supermarkets admit they are in a quandary over the handling of the elderly shoplifters. Although they are reluctant to prosecute, they are equally reluctant to encourage the shoplifting by repeatedly letting the shoplifters go with just a warning. "We treat them like you would mom or dad," said a security chief at one supermarket. "Some feel because they gave the store their business in better days, they are entitled to whatever they want to take." Some are prosecuted, however, and the Congress of Senior Citizens, an association of some 100,000 older adults in the area, has been kept busy helping with the legal defense of those who have been caught shoplifting. Although sympathizing with their strained budgets, the chairman of the Congress of Senior Citizens, Max Friedson, deplores the shoplifting. "We should set an example to the young," he said. "We should be elder statesmen. There should be other ways to make ends meet than shoplifting."

Some communities are helping older adults to cut food costs by initiating "meals on wheels" programs for those who are unable to shop or cook their own meals. Older adults who have low incomes and are housebound can be assured of at least one hot meal a day at minimal cost. Other communities have taken over school auditoriums or church halls for group lunches. But such programs do not reach all of the older adults who need them. In a Methodist church in Miami, a lucky few can buy a 50-cent lunch of baked chicken, string beans, potato salad, and fresh tomatoes, but the hot lunch program does not begin to meet the needs of the thousands of low income older adults in the area, as the number of shoplifters in Miami Beach proves. Furthermore, inflation has cut drastically into the ability of existing programs to help these people. In Alameda County (San Francisco), California, for example, the local senior citizens council originally requested funds for 1,400 meals a day. They received funds for 800 meals a day, an inadequate grant to begin with. Inflation then forced them to eliminate 150 meals.

TRANSPORTATION

Like most of the pressing problems of older adults, hunger cannot be solved by itself. It is directly related to the need for inexpensive and efficient public transportation. Even if the hot lunch program were large enough to provide for all of San Francisco's older adults, most would still need a way of getting to the center. Since few of them have a driver's license or a car, the lack of public transportation enormously complicates their ability to provide adequately for themselves. The lack of readily available public transportation also reduces their purchasing power. Since taxis are a luxury, older adults usually shop at neighborhood grocery or convenience stores, which are generally more expensive than the chain supermarkets. Without transportation, older people are literally imprisoned in their homes, unable to go anywhere or to do anything. In a large city that has almost no public transportation, a 70-year-old woman talked of the hardships. "You can't go out to the shopping mall or downtown to shop or to a movie in the evening or to the city auditorium," she said. "In fact, you can't do anything. I don't know anyone anymore because I don't go out to meet anyone. Even if I did have friends, I wouldn't be able to get to their houses. All you can do is to watch television and go to bed at 9 p.m."

HEALTH COSTS

Older adults are plagued by rising health costs and a steady decline in the help offered by Medicare and Medicaid.

Most of them believe that Medicare will take care of them if they get sick, but they have found with increasing frequency that their trust has been misplaced. A man said, "Medicare is a wonderful thing, but Medicare to us is like a leaking umbrella. You go outside when it is raining and think that you have protection, and you open it up and the rain comes right through it." Supplemental health insurance is expensive for those who can get it. Many don't know, until too late, that it is necessary.

A complete analysis of the failings of Medicare and Medicaid, which is the state version of Medicare for those below the poverty line, requires a book of its own. Nevertheless, it is important to take even a cursory look at some of the problems, because health expenditures and income maintenance are interrelated. Social workers have said that high medical expenses are the most frequent cause of poverty among older adults. Hospital and doctor bills from a single illness can wipe out a lifetime of savings.

The problems are twofold: medical costs have gone up, and the proportion of medical bills paid by Medicare has gone down. The result is a whopping medical bill for older adults. Their health expenditures are staggering. The per capita health expenditure by persons over 65 is almost seven times that of persons under 19 and nearly three times that of persons aged 19 to 64.[14] Even with Medicare, the average older adult spent $415 in 1975 out of his own pocket for medical bills.[15] In fact, older people were spending more than they did in 1966, the year before the Medicare act was passed.

During the 1970s, several factors contributed to this rise in out-of-pocket expenditures. The average length of hospital stays declined. This increased the amount of the deductible that older adults must pay before Medicare begins

---

[14]Ibid., p. 94.
[15]Ibid., p. 79.

to cover costs. The cost of outpatient treatment and diagnostic services increased, but Medicare reimburses for these expenses at a lower rate than it does for inpatient hospital stays. Premiums have gone up, and other changes in the Medicare program have forced older adults to shoulder more of the cost for medical care. Doctors have refused with increasing frequency to participate. Only about 52 per cent of the doctors in the United States participated during the 1975 fiscal year.[16] All in all, Medicare covered a mere 38 per cent of the medical costs for older adults in 1976.[17]

Although Medicare has reduced the anxiety created by failing health for many, others have found that their limited resources are still being drained by the high cost of health care. A 68-year-old man, troubled by a variety of complaints that require frequent visits to the doctor, pointed out, for example, that Medicare only partially covers doctor's visits. A typical bill still cost him $9.60 after Medicare payments were subtracted.

And some older adults simply cannot afford the Medicare premiums on their limited incomes. One 76-year-old woman lives in a public housing project with her totally blind and disabled husband. Her choice is simple—food now or medical care later. Her Social Security check cannot cover both. She can only hope and pray that she won't need medical care. She hopes that she can forestall illness by this simple act of faith before she is released from the constant worry about possible illness by death. "I don't know what would happen if I got sick because I can't afford a doctor," she said. "I just pray I'll never need one."

Medicare does not cover the seemingly simple problems that lead to an increasingly impoverished quality of life for older adults. Although it will pay millions for extended

---

[16]Ibid., p. 79.
[17]Ibid., p. 94.

care in nursing homes, it will pay nothing for health items such as eyeglasses and hearing aids. Because of inability to pay for them, older adults find themselves forced into premature isolation from the rest of society. In a self-perpetuating, debilitating cycle, simple problems lead to exclusion. Loneliness aggravates previously existing chronic ailments, which leads, in turn, to further withdrawal.

Finally, because of the intricacies of the Medicare regulations, many who need help most desperately are denied it. In many ways, the Campbells were like other older adults who needed help but can't find it. Elisha Campbell needed an around-the-clock nurse for his 81-year-old wife, Emma, who was bedridden with diabetes and the flu. For years Campbell had taken care of Emma himself, but passing time had sapped his strength. His money, too, was exhausted by the continual rise in the cost of medicine. And money was the problem now. There simply was not enough of it left to pay for the kind of nursing care that Emma Campbell needed. Campbell tried to get Medicare to pay at least part of the bills, but Medicare would not pay for a nurse because Mrs. Campbell had not been hospitalized previously, a prerequisite for that kind of financial help under the program.

One sultry summer evening, Campbell called a family conference on his front porch. Somewhat desperately, he explained to family and friends the futility he felt about their situation, about not having enough money, about seeing his wife in pain and being unable to stop it even for a little while. The others promised to help out, although none of them could undertake the 24-hour-a-day nursing that was needed. Campbell said angrily, "I can't afford 80 damn dollars a day for the nurse. I would rather see Mom dead than suffer like this." Campbell went into the house, and the family and friends left.

A little later the neighbors heard two shots. According to police reports, Campbell walked into their small bedroom, loaded and aimed a .32 caliber revolver, and fired twice. One shot took his wife's life; the other took his own. Emma Campbell no longer suffered, and Elisha Campbell no longer endured the pain of watching that suffering.

When Congress passed, with much fanfare, the Older Americans Act of 1965, older citizens were promised "an adequate income in retirement in accordance with the American standard of living." This promise obviously has not been kept. As we have seen, older adults cannot afford the standard of living that people under 65 often take for granted. They often cannot afford even the necessities. Moreover, the gap between the young "haves" and the old "have nots" is widening in many instances. Although changes in the Social Security Act will help the financial plight of older adults to a certain extent, the underlying causes of inadequate income in retirement have not been dealt with. The basic problem is to devise a means of proportioning work and income evenly and equitably over the course of a lifetime. We will consider solutions to that problem in Chapter 9.

GROWING OLDER TODAY

CHAPTER EIGHT

Her face had been chiseled by age so that her features looked like deft sculptor strokes and her skin had a translucent pallor. But, despite that, she did not look 89-years-old. It was easy to see that she had once been a beautiful woman. She held her head, haloed by a wispy cloud of white hair, high as she talked about her life, what was left of it. Some days it did not seem like much. On bad days, her life seemed to be unraveling like a tattered sweater, leaving nothing in her shriveled hands but formless threads. The good days seemed outnumbered by the bad as she grew older, and on such days she wondered why she kept living.

"I don't see that I have any reason to live," she said. "I would just as soon be dead. I can't understand why God lets me live, but I suppose He has a reason and I just hope He will supply me with the strength to go on until I can get this business of living over with."

In a voice that crackled like dry leaves in an autumn windstorm, she talked about her "terrible sick spell" and her precarious struggle to live on $150 a month from Social Security, her only source of income. But mostly she talked about the loneliness. She recalled her husband who died 12 years ago in the three-room apartment where she continues to live. Her children and friends are all dead, too, she said. Tears started to trickle down the parchment-thin skin, but her head stayed erect. "There's not a soul left of my own," she said. Alone and lonely, too sick to seek help and too proud to accept it if it were offered, she lived on like the sturdy flowers that manage to return year after year to bloom and flourish in the dry ground beneath her windows.

Her bleak life is a mirror that old age holds up to the young, and the reflection of youth's future is ugly. Telling her about the so-called golden years is subtle mockery, a way to quiet older adults with soothing words of reassurance that degrades speaker and listener alike. She knows such talk is a way for the young to forget the aging without guilt.

Her loneliness, depression, and boredom are shared by thousands of men and women over 65. Many older adults become unwanted masses of human flesh who long for death as an alternative to the kind of existence they experience. As it is, their lives are a form of social death, lived out in isolation without meaningful relationships to others or the community.

This woman, and the thousands of others like her, are excellent reasons for paying attention to the combined effects of ageism, earlier retirement, and our country's nonpolicy on aging. The possibility of long life and youthful vigor, the combination of prolonged life with prolonged youth that has eluded us since the first person noticed the first wrinkle, is now present. In Greek mythology, the gods forced Tithonous to choose between eternal youth and immortality.

He chose immortality, but, granted life without youth, he grew sicker and sicker until he cried out to the gods to be released from the curse of such a life. The gods, taking pity on him, granted his wish, and he was allowed to die. Our scientists are promising us life and youth beyond the powers of the Greek gods.

Research proceeds on the assumption that a longer life and youth are desirable. The assumption has never been questioned. It is time, now to ask a few, belated questions. For example, what are we saving people for? A few more decades of idleness, boredom, and loneliness? Or a creative, fulfilling period of life that provides the opportunity for leisure to be used productively and for meaningful contributions to others and to the surrounding community?

Before we can begin to answer these questions, we need to understand what life is like *now* for millions of older adults.

LIFE IN OLD AGE TODAY

Old age begins, before most of us even notice it, in middle age during those years that are called, paradoxically enough, the "prime of life." The years between 45 and 55 are the turning point for many. Bernice Neugarten, a sociologist at the University of Chicago who has studied the life cycle, suggests that 40 is the old age of youth, while 50 is the youth of old age. That would explain the subtle shifting from looking toward the future to looking at the present and past that occurs during those years. At some point in midlife, our perspective shifts, and we stop counting the years after birth and start numbering the years before death. Old friends die or move into retirement communities, and new friendships are increasingly difficult to form. Jobs, too, are difficult to find or keep. The changes produce a kind of mental bookkeeping that begins to tally up the assets and debits, and if the minuses seem to outweigh the pluses, the result can be the adoption of a "last fling" attitude. In the midst of a divorce from his "old" wife and subsequent marriage to his "new" wife, a man in his midforties said, "If I don't do it now, I never will."

Retirement makes these changes, so private and intensely personal, public. Dr. George Maddox, director of the Duke Center for the Study of Aging and Human Development, points out that retirement is a social as well as an economic event in the life of an individual. He writes, "For better or worse retirement is a rite of passage, usually an informal one, between productive maturity and nonproductive old age."[1] Retirement does not occur in a social and emotional vacuum, and the drop in income that accompanies it is only one of the losses that retirement brings. It also has profound social and emotional consequences, entailing the loss of professional associates and friends who have shared similar work experiences. It causes a loss of routine, the ordering and structuring of the day around a job. It forces an altering of one's self-image, the redefining of self in a way that does not include a work role.

Sociologists believe that retirement is easier to adjust to, in general, when we are able to arrange our retirement years so that they closely resemble our working lives. One sociologist has given the phrase "consistency of life-style" to this similarity. What it means is that we continue to pursue many of the same activities after retirement that we engaged in before, with the exception, of course, of working.

Personality as a Factor. Certain personality types appear to adjust more readily than others. Three patterns of successful adjustment—the mature, the armored, and the "rocking chair" styles of retirement—have been identified by

---

[1]George L. Maddox, "Retirement as a Social Event in the United States," in *Middle Age and Aging,* 2nd impression, ed. Bernice S. Neugarten (Chicago: The University of Chicago Press, 1970), p. 357.

psychologists Suzanne Reichard, Florine Livson, and Paul G. Petersen.[2] *Mature* people are able to grow old with little regret for the past or sense of loss in the present. Although work may have been central to their lives, they have interests and hobbies apart from their jobs. They are not forced to resort to basket weaving and shuffleboard to fill up the empty hours. They are realistic and relatively free of neurotic conflicts, able to accept themselves and old age. *Armored* people also keep busy, but their activity is a way of exorcising their fear of aging. Afraid of passivity and helplessness, they maintain a steady whirl of activities to keep their fears at bay. These people fit naturally and readily into retirement villages with their structured activities. *Rocking chair* people may find retirement easiest of all. Basically passive by nature, they are secretly relieved to be free of their responsibilities and to escape from social pressure to compete in the working world. They welcome the opportunity to substitute rocking chairs for desk chairs.

Although no one knows which style predominates, Dr. Adriaan Verwoerdt, a psychiatrist who specializes in aging, said that he suspects there are more rocking chair people than we might like to believe. Even in old age, society insists on a certain amount of activity. Public approval goes to the person who, as we are apt to say, "certainly doesn't act like he's 60 or 70 or 80," or who, we might say later, "worked right up to the end." Those who are idle even though retired are scorned. "No one really knows what the old want because they have never had the money or opportunity to do what they really want," said Verwoerdt. "I suspect that a goodly number would like to sit in the sun and do nothing."

Those people who cannot adjust to retirement are a source of unhappiness to their families as well as to themselves. Life with a responsible adult who has suddenly lost his

---

[2]Suzanne Reichard, Florine Livson, and Paul G. Peterson, "Adjustment to Retirement," in *Middle Age and Aging*, pp. 178–80.

responsibilities can be trying for those who live with him. Wives who have raised their families and may be looking forward to their own "retirement" are unexpectedly forced to cope with the problems of their newly retired husbands.

One woman wrote in desperation to a syndicated advice column for help with her husband. Not knowing how to occupy his time after retiring, he took up gourmet cooking. Not only was he spending large amounts of their limited retirement income on exotic ingredients, but also he was barring his wife from the kitchen. She resented this unwanted intrusion into what she considered her own private domestic domain. Having no responsibilities, he was trying to take over what had been hers, and she was resisting.

Another woman who was having problems with her newly retired husband summed up the wife's dilemma in a similar letter, "I married him for dinner, not for lunch," she wrote.

Studies of retirement have focused exclusively on the impact on men. No studies so far have shown the way that working women react to retirement. They seem to adjust easily when their children leave home, according to sociologist Gordon Streib, and for many of them, raising their children has been, in effect, their life's work, and career. After studying older women whose children had left home, Streib concluded the so-called empty-nest syndrome is largely a myth. These women were not depressed or distraught because their children were grown and their child-rearing days were over. They had not regrets, no sense of loss, no longing for their absent children. But seeing children leave home and retiring from the work force may not be emotional equivalents. Children, after all, come home for visits, but there are few opportunities to go back to work. As more middle-aged women enter the work force and more women work throughout their lives, their reactions will be important to watch. These women work for the same reasons that men do—security, comforts, prestige, a sense of fulfillment, rewarding professional relationships, a feeling of being part of the community. The chances are good that retirement will turn into a wrenching experience for career women, too.

SOCIETY'S IMPACT

We are not prepared for retirement and old age. We are educated to earn a living, not to use leisure constructively. We are raised to be good citizens, good parents, good husbands or wives. We are provided with examples to follow in learning these roles. But we are given no models of good older adults to emulate. We are shown no examples of successful aging. The very words "successful aging" sound strange to our ears.

Society does not make growing old with grace easy. Our culture, our customs, and our values frequently demand the impossible of older adults. Our culture celebrates the do-it-yourselfer, the maverick, the hero against the world, the ambitious Horatio Alger. We believe that life should have a happy ending as in an old MGM movie and that the beautiful coach will never revert to a pumpkin at the stroke of midnight. Self-reliance and independence are prized as if we were still living in the middle of a hostile forest. Ugly names such as moocher and leech are often reserved for those who can't get along by themselves. Yet the meager resources and failing health of many older adults make it inevitable that they will need help at some point. Caught between the reality of old age and the values of society, older people are subjected to unbelievable stress. Many crack under the pressure of aging in America. The increase in the incidence of psychological problems among those over 65 is startling. When the National Institute of Mental Health looked at the number of new cases of psychopathology by age groups, it found the incidence per 100,000 population leaped after the age of 65. There were 2.3 cases for those under 15; 76.3 cases of those 25 to 34; 93.0 cases for those 35 to 54; and 231.1 cases for those over 65.

MENTAL PROBLEMS

Our culture fails older adults. The customs and values of youth are inappropriate for old age, and older adults who cling to them are likely candidates for mental breakdowns.

Anthropologists Margaret Clark and Barbara Gallatin Anderson studied 435 older adults at length. Some of them had a history of recent psychiatric treatment; others did not. When the anthropologists compared the two groups, they found a striking difference. The group that had suffered from mental illness still judged themselves by the standards of their youth. They were driven by ambition and to compete and achieve to prove their self-worth. Productivity was at the top of their list of satisfactions in life. They were perfectionists with high standards of excellence. They saw time as their adversary as they realized that the time left for further achievement was dwindling. A typical member of the group said, "There haven't been many bad things in my life except disappointment in not being able to accomplish more."

The group that had no history of mental illness was not driven by a compulsive need to achieve. These people were happier in "being" than in "doing," content with the present, and they had a lively interest in the affairs of others. They put cooperation and concern for others ahead of control over others. They accepted themselves as they were and were content with what live had brought. At the top of their list of life satisfactions were "entertainment and diversions." A typical member of the group said, "I have no reason to be jealous of anyone now. I'm not a burden upon anyone, and I'm still alive. What else can anyone my age ask for?"

Commenting on their study, Clark and Anderson wrote, "We are struck by the fact that the value orientations which seem to be maladaptive for the aged in this sample are strikingly similar to values found to be characteristic of American culture generally by a number of observers. It seems to us that the major orientation of American culture then, while they may be eugenic enough for a young population, probably aggravate the particular problems which confront the aged in our society."[3] In short, typically American values of productivity, achievement, success, independence, and self-reliance, of making one's own way and being on one's own—the very things we are taught from youth on to strive for—are psychologically harmful when they are carried over into old age. Older adults who try encounter trouble.

GROWING OLD ALONE

Without successful models of good aging, without help in exchanging old values for new ones that are more appropriate now, without social, emotional, or financial support, we stumble into old age, doing the best we can. We grow old alone.

For the least fortunate, old age brings social death. It begins in isolation and segregation. To be socially dead means also to be invisible. Like the physically dead, the socially dead are whisked out of the sight of the rest of society. The troublesome are kept away from those who might be troubled. Over one million older adults are living out their years in hospitals, nursing homes, and mental hospitals. According to the best estimates of gerontologists, between 25 to 50 per cent of these people do not need to be in institutions.

---

[3] Margaret Clark and Barbara Gallatin Anderson, *Culture and Aging* (Springfield, Ill.: Charles C. Thomas, 1967), p. 208.

They could remain in their own homes if they had homes or if they had a little help with routine housekeeping and homemaking chores. They could live with relatives with some assistance from visiting nurses if such help were available. Such supports are unavailable to those who are institutionalized needlessly. Dr. Leonard Gottesman, professor of psychology at the University of Michigan, found that institutionalized older adults were more likely to be poor, uneducated, single, and only marginally employed throughout their lives than those who were living in the community. In short, they were to a great extent society's losers, without family, friends, or personal resources to fall back on in old age. "Institutions are primarily a place to live for people with nowhere else to go," he said.

Lacking resources of their own, these older adults are left to vegetate behind the walls of institutions until they are discharged by death certificates. While they are there, they are frequently treated with unbelievable callousness. Their cries are ignored. They are talked about in the third person. It is as if they had neither eyes nor ears nor feelings, as if, in fact, they were already dead. In the presence of his patients, one nursing home administrator whom I was interviewing pointed at a ward and said, "This is death row. The next stop for most of them is the cemetery."

South Florida State Mental Hospital in Hollywood, Florida, is a typical state institution. It serves several counties in South Florida that have one of the highest proportion of people over 65 in the country. At first glance, it is an attractive hospital. The tree-shaded buildings are scattered over broad grounds, and both the buildings and grounds are well kept. But it does not take long to realize that the geriatric buildings are warehouses where the "patients," who are not treated but merely attended, wait to die.

The day passes slowly for the 365 men and women over 65. It begins at 6:00 A.M. and ends at 9:00 P.M. when the lights are turned off for another 9 hours. The day is punctuated by three meals, five doses of tranquillizers, and one doctor's perfunctory visit.

The time between waking and sleeping is passed in a locked dayroom, a spare dull space, painted a dreary institutional green, without pictures or bright spots of colors to relieve the sterility and add a note of cheer. In their state-supplied green uniforms, the men and women blend into the walls. The uniforms guarantee anonymity and stamp "mental patient" on all of them. Everything is designed to turn the individual into an inmate. There are no games or magazines or books in the dayroom. There is little to do and nothing to talk about. Mostly, they sit in rows of plastic chairs keeping vigil in front of an out-of-focus television set. They slump in their chairs, nodding in and out of the heavy, sweet oblivion of drugs. It is literally a death watch, for only death will end the wait for many. Death can take a long time to come, however. The average geriatric stay is 1,374 days, almost four years.

Not far from the hospital, another group of frail older adults are living out their lives in wheelchairs and on stretchers amid the turmoil of an emergency ward in a Miami, Florida, hospital. They have been abandoned there like automobiles that have served their purpose and been junked. Some were left on the hospital's doorstep with "Do not return" notes pinned to their clothes. Others have been found wandering dazed and helpless through the streets. They were brought to the hospital by the police or concerned citizens who don't know what else to do. The exact number of older adults, called boarders by hospital personnel, varied from 11 to 40. Lewis Didomenico, the administrator of Jackson Memorial Hospital, said, "The problem is always the same. They're too sick to live alone, but not sick enough to be admitted to the hospital. And it's nearly always a case of money. Either the relatives can't afford to keep them any more or the nursing homes won't take them because Dade County doesn't pay enough. And if a nursing home does take them, it will dump them out the minute they're no longer profitable." Most are old, broke, ill, and helpless. They need supervision and someone to make sure that they take the right medications and eat decent meals, but they don't require hospitalization.

During the day, the boarders sit in wheelchairs or on the benches in the emergency ward waiting room. "At night when things quiet down, we kind of fit them in on any stretcher or bed we can find," said Didomenico.

Although the hospital tries to find places in institutions for the boarders, it is rarely successful. After much urging, one nursing home agreed to accept a 61-year-old man as long as he did not have another asthma attack. A few days after moving into the nursing home, he was stricken with a severe attack. The nursing home left him at the entrance to the emergency ward with a "Do not return" note pinned to his hospital gown. Now he spends his days sitting in a wheelchair and staring into space. Several boarders have died while waiting for placement, and their deaths have gone unnoticed for hours.

LONELINESS

For those who escape such a cruel fate, the common foe is loneliness. Even in the communal life of an old age home or nursing home, there is little relief from it. It does not matter how they say it, the meaning is always the same—"I'm lonely." In one nursing home, a woman blinked back tears as she said, "There is nobody to come to see us. There is nothing but eat, sleep, and look at television." There are few distractions. Birthday parties once a month, a visit by a minister's wife on Sunday, and every now and than a bingo game as a special treat are the limited entertainments. "We'd love to have something to do," the woman added. The other women nodded their heads in agreement. Their heads bobbed like flowers, slightly gone to seed, but still pretty in their own way. For them, the world begins and ends at the barbed wire fence that separates the nursing home from the busy street that runs beside it. Without an attendant, they cannot leave the grounds. In the stillness of the home, the ticking of a grandfather clock, keeping track of the passing hours, sounded large. Hearing it, a 72-year-old woman said, "We are waiting for the end. Life is really over."

An older woman, driven by searing loneliness, sat down at a small table in her cramped, one-bedroom apartment and wrote with fingers crippled by arthritis, a letter to the *Los Angeles Times*. "I'm so lonely I could die. So alone. My hands and fingers pain me, pain me," she wrote. "I see no human beings. My phone never rings. I'm so very old, so very lonely. I hear from no one . . . way past 80 years. Should I die? . . . Did you ever feel sure the world ended? I'm the only one on earth. How else can I feel. All alone. Here no one. Oh dear God, help me. Am of sound mind. So lonely, very very much. I don't know what to do." She enclosed a dollar to pay for a telephone call if someone would call her and six stamps to pay for postage if someone would write her. A *Los Angeles Times* reporter phoned her, and she broke into tears at the sound of a human voice.

She told him, "If you are alone, you die every day. I can't do anyone any good. I can't do myself any good. I'd like to meet people and whatever they like, I'd like, too. I just eat and sleep. Sometimes I just dread to see myself wake up in the morning. Isn't anyone else lonely like me?"

Unfortunately, there are a lot like her. Doctors and nurses who work in public health clinics know that many older adults are painfully lonely. They see older people, who are not sick but in need of human contact, filling up the clinics, drawing the time and attention of medical personnel away from the physically ill. Health experts say that hypochondria is a frequent consequence of loneliness. Illness, even if it is feigned, is one of the few acceptable ways for older adults in our society to demand attention. The sick are among the very few who are permitted to be dependent and who can admit to being dependent and continue to maintain self-respect. At one clinic, a public health nurse said that a visit was almost like a social event for many older adults, who arrive with their lunches in brown paper bags and spend the day there. "The treatment process, seeing the tests run, meeting the doctor gives them a sense of personal concern," she said. "It revives their sense of self-worth. It re-establishes a personal relationship for them." Furthermore, Dr. Ewald Busse, chairman of the department of psychiatry at Duke University Medical Center, says hypochondria is a way of gaining society's support. He says it is an easy, socially acceptable way of being a "nonachiever," of escaping in a socially approved way from social and financial requirements that, in the case of older adults, can no longer be met.

Early one morning, I met a sprightly 73-year-old woman moving quickly and with swift, sure gestures through the packaging area of a branch of Goodwill Industries. Her superiors said that she was among their best workers, although as she held up her hands, I could see they were swollen with arthritis. She said that when she started working two years ago, she was taking six aspirins a day for the constant pain. Now, she said, she had ceased to notice it. The pain started after her husband died and life seemed to lose its meaning. For several years she stayed at home, rarely going out, spending most of the day watching television. She was ready to spend her remaining years as a shut-in and chronic invalid when her son, concerned about her deteriorating condition, urged her to go out and find new friends and activities. She applied by chance for a job at Goodwill Industries and was accepted. "This is the best thing that ever happened to me," she said. "It makes life worth living again. I didn't have anything to look forward to before, so I sat and felt bad. Now I go home and work in my yard for a while, then I eat dinner and go to bed early so I will be fresh for work in the morning." This woman was lucky. She was saved from social death by a sympathetic son and the good fortune of finding a meaningful activity. Others are not so fortunate. Their later years are a burden to themselves and a tragic waste for society.

In the midst of the losses that accompany old age, one thing that does not diminish or grow old is the need for love and affection. These desires do not change. Only the ability to satisfy them gets harder. Afraid of being rejected or rebuffed, people struggle to develop the courage to reach out to others. Both single men and women feel something like white elephants at a church rummage sale, unwanted but really too good to be thrown away. They feel equally rejected by a social world that is dominated by married couples. An attractive woman in her early sixties whom I met at a senior citizens club complained that the women outnumbered the men at the group get-togethers. "Not enough men come to these meetings," she said. "The married women won't bring their husbands because they're afraid we'd try to take them away. As if we'd want them!" Similar feelings are experienced by single men. A man, widowed twice in 16 years, said, "I, too, am persona non grata in all social gatherings of married couples. The insecure males think I am a menace to their precarious positions because I can converse, dance, hum or sing, although not well. I assure you I have no designs on any of their wives."

Single men and women share an identical loneliness in a paired off, Noah's ark type of world. When they are alone in the night, minor pains seem like forerunners of death, expected for sure before dawn. They worry about dying and not being discovered for days, or, worse, lying for days on the floor after a fall, waiting for help that never seems to arrive. One of the most gregarious men I have known, a lively 73-year-old widower who is involved in many community activities admitted, "To live alone is a rough thing. You do get lonesome. I have emphysema, and there are times when I wake up at night that I would like to know someone was there. It would help to have a woman friend."

LOVE AND SEX

Passion and romance are not the exclusive desires of the young. Older adults also are capable of reacting violently when threatened by the loss of a loved one. Examples often appear in newspapers in cities with a high proportion of older adults. In one instance, a frantic husband whose 70-year-old wife ran off with a new love, hunted her down, shot her, and then himself. He intended to kill both of them, but his aim was shaky and both recovered. The man was 75. In another instance, a frustrated lover hurled a Molotov cocktail concocted from a prune juice bottle filled with kerosene through the window at his girl friend. His addiction to prune juice was well known in his neighborhood and led to his arrest on a first degree arson charge. He was 78. In still another instance, a jealous husband caught his unfaithful 65-year-old wife in bed with another man and blasted her lover with a shotgun. The husband was 81.

Despite the existence of such desires, older adults find fulfillment difficult, partly because of lack of opportunity and partly because of the disapproving attitude of society. It is a way that society forces older adults into infantilism. Older people need and deserve a sexual bill of rights.

Fearing ridicule by prospective partners or society itself, older adults lapse into an unwanted sexual abstinence. Their fear is entirely reasonable. The aging lover and his fading physical prowess is a frequent target of stag jokes. The phase "dirty old man," with its obscene and vulgar connotations, is part of our language. What is virility at 25 may become lechery or debauchery at 65. As Dr. Stanley Dean, professor of psychiatry at the University of Miami School of

Medicine, points out, "Society does not take well to grandparents cavorting in bed."

Even if they are able to conquer this fear within themselves, they may lack available partners. Older women in particular are sexually disadvantaged. After menopause, many
women are more desirous of sexual activity than ever before,
but it is at precisely this time that their husbands, who are
often older, may begin to show signs of impotence.

If older women are single, which statistically they are
likely to be, their problems are multiplied. It is relatively easy
for an older man to attract a younger woman. Even quite old
men are capable of attracting desirable women 10 or even 20
years younger. Supreme Court Justice William O. Douglas
and his wife Cathy and Jacqueline Kennedy Onassis and her
late husband, Aristotle, are two well-known examples of
May-December marriages. Although an older woman finds a
scarcity of eligible men her own age, a liaison with a younger
man is unthinkable from society's biased viewpoint. The plot
of "Harold and Maude," a cult movie that first appeared in
the early 1970s, dramatizes the problems of a relationship
between an older woman and younger man. In the movie, a
17-year-old boy and a 81-year-old woman meet at a
stranger's funeral and fall in love. The relationship seems
credible because of the off-beat personalities of the characters. But when Harold asks a priest to marry him and Maude,
the priest recoils in horror. He talks about Maude's wrinkled
flesh, the skin that is no longer firm and is covered with liver
spots. He says that he can't imagine Harold's young flesh
pressed against Maude's old skin. The priest says that the
relationship fills him with revulsion, and he dismisses the
marriage as unworkable and impossible.

Unfortunately, there is little that women can do, at
present to change their situation. Despite the feminist
movement, most older women lack the aggressiveness to
pursue their desires as a man would. They resign themselves

to denial while inwardly rebelling. "Many elderly women, Dean said, "secretly envy the aging movie queen who, because of her money and position, can surround herself with young studs."

A solution, of course, is to reverse the long-standing pattern of women marrying men older than themselves. Women could be encouraged to marry younger men in their youth. One of Dean's patients proposed setting up a society to fight for reversal of the older husband-younger wife pattern. It would be known as the Society for the Chronological Role-Reversal of Emancipated Womanhood, the acronym of which is SCREW. Such a solution requires a long time. It offers no help to the frustrated older woman of today.

Although retirement is difficult for men, old age in general is rougher for women, who suffer from the dual handicaps of age and sex. The lack of sexual opportunities in old age is but one of the special problems that confront older women. With their greater longevity, women are left to grow old alone without financial or emotional support. Even this is not all of the problem. It cannot be solved by increasing widow's benefits from Social Security or supplying, if it were possible, women with male companions in old age.

Instead, the real problem is related to what it means to be a woman in the United States in the late twentieth century. Older women have lost the two things that society prizes most in its women—youth and beauty. The truth is that men are considered attractive for longer periods of time than are women, and women are well aware of it. A still attractive woman in her early seventies said, "How can I go out of my house when I am so old and look it?" Except for occasional trips to the doctor and the store, she never left her house, afraid she would see her loss of early beauty reflected in the face of everyone she met. She is a captive of society's dual standard of aging.

This double standard of aging shows up in our jokes and the cartoons published in our magazines. Assuming that jokes and cartoons are a reflection of society's attitudes, Dr. Erdman Palmore analyzed 264 of them to discover their attitude toward older adults. He found about 50 per cent contained negative attitudes about aging. However, he also found that they were more critical of women than men. "There may be a double standard of aging," he said, "whereby aging among women is viewed more negatively than aging among men."

So, many women cling tenaciously to the little that is left. They have lost so much—husbands, lovers, friends, beauty, children—that their fear is understandable. More than anything, they cling to their homes. The home is a link to the past. Abandoning their homes is an admission of failure that they are unwilling to make. Without their own homes, their lives are controlled by the whims of others. They are no longer capable of doing things in the way and at the time they want. Their privacy, the ability to lock the door and shut out the world, is gone. Moving into an institution or the home of relatives forces older women to renounce the qualities of self-control and competency that have given their lives a sense of meaning.

I know such a woman. She lived alone except for a big fluff of an orange and white cat. She and the cat were a lot alike. They took care of their own needs and seldom asked for help from others. Her eyesight was failing, but as she liked to point out, she didn't need it. She knew the nooks and crannies of her house. In one corner was her dead husband's lounge chair, which she patted affectionately as she passed. One spare bedroom had stuffed animals on the shelves. They had been her children's and then her grandchildren's. She was saving them for her great-grandchildren. Her window overlooked the playground of a school across the street, and she liked to watch the children growing up. "I just hope I can get by somehow," she often said. "I've lived a full life and I'm not afraid to die." Instead of losing her life, she lost her independence, and it was worse for her. Worried about her failing health, her children forced her to sell the house. She moved in with her daughter and son-in-law. I don't see her very much anymore, but she calls quite often, usually when her daughter is out of the house. She knows her children acted out of kindness, but she just wishes it didn't hurt so much. Always she asks, as if she were inquiring about a long-ago friend, "How are they taking care of my little red house?"

THE GOOD LIFE

Old age is not inevitably a time of remorse and loss. For those with money, good health, and the incentive to stay active, old age offers opportunities that were not available during the child-rearing, working years. These lucky few can find old age fulfilling. Some discover time to travel, pursue hobbies, and volunteer their services to the community. One retiree, active in community and senior citizen groups, said, "While I was working, I was mainly interested in my family and job. I was selfish I know. Since I retired, I found out there were other people in the world. I began a love affair with life, and I'm getting more out of it than I'm putting in."

One of the best examples of an energetic and fulfilled old age is Florida Scott-Maxwell, an American born psychologist who made her home in England. At 50, her children grown and on their own, she embarked on a second career. Mrs. Scott-Maxwell moved to Zurich, Switzerland, and began training in analytic psychology under one of the pioneering psychoanalysts, Carl Jung. She practiced in psychology clinics in Scotland and England. At the age of 84, she launched a third career with the publication of *The Measure of My Days*. The book, a classic among people interested in aging, is a kind of an interior monologue, a knitting together of stray perceptions into a total view of life. She writes, "Age puzzles me. I thought it was a serene time. My seventies were interesting and fairly serene, but my eighties are passionate. I grow more intense as I age. To my own surprise, I burst out with hot convictions. Only a few years ago I enjoyed my tranquility, now I am so disturbed by the outer world and by human quality in general that I want to put things right as though I still owed a debt to life." She admits that luck is partially responsible for her pleasures in old age. Her passionate attempt to consume life in her final years is made possible by her independence. Only a person who is free to meet life on his own terms could write as she did: "My kitchen linoleum is so black and shiny that I waltz while I wait for the kettle to boil. This pleasure is for the old who live alone. The others must vanish into their expected roles."

Her writing provides a glimpse of what old age could and should be like for everyone, not just the privileged or lucky few. To make the later years of life into something other than a dreaded period of constantly accumulating losses, we need to change the rest of life. The horrors of old age are the inevitable result of society's notion about the appropriate time for work and leisure—first we work, then we do nothing. We need to make our entire lives more open, more free, more a matter of individual choice. Out of the aimlessness of old age, gerontologists, sociologists, and economists are already talking about a revolution in life-styles.

A NEW WAY
OF WORK AND LEISURE

CHAPTER NINE

All too often our lives are regimented by society. In general, we must spend our childhood and adolescence in school, our middle years at work, and our final decades in the forced leisure of retirement. There is a "right" time to be educated, to work, and to play. In the socially decreed scheme of things, personal preferences matter little or not at all.

For the majority, the time sequence is fixed and inflexible, and, for the most part, people are left with little control over their own lives. Those who dare to rebel, to break out of the socially ordered lockstep, to march to a different drumbeat do so at their own risk. In youth, a person who chooses to leave high school or college to work for a while is tagged with the label of dropout. His chances of being re-admitted may be hurt, and his ability to secure scholarships or educational loans that make advanced education possible for many may be permanently injured. In the middle years, a person who returns to school, takes time to travel or simply to re-evaluate his life goals, risks career advancement. At the end of life, a person who continues to work is denied the full Social Security benefits that have accrued to him.

Although the timestep of work now, play later imposes a certain comforting social order, the cost is high. The individual pays heavily in missed opportunities for personal growth. Society, in turn, pays in the form of job malaise, reduced productivity, and diminished creativity from people who have outgrown their lives.

Once this ordering of education, work, and leisure made social sense. There was work to be done, and only so many were available to do it. Workers had to be trained in youth because society needed skilled people during their most productive middle years. Those who survived were only too happy to sit and do nothing for their few remaining years. Retirement, as we think of it today, was virtually unknown at the turn of the century. The difference between life expectancy and work expectancy was a scant three years.[1]

With increased life expectancy, the system has become senseless. The rigid pattern of work and play is neither desirable nor functional from the viewpoints of both the individual and society. Our method of financing retirement is clearly unworkable. It places heavy financial burdens on workers and forces many retirees to live out their lives in poverty. It forces workers into a deadening 9 A.M. to 5 P.M. routine and requires retirees, who have ordered most of their lives around a time clock, to suddenly cope with 10 or 20 years of leisure.

---

[1]Manpower Report No. 8, "The Length of Working Life for Males, 1900–60." U.S. Department of Labor (July 1963), pp. 7–8.

THE FLEXIBLE LIFE-STYLE

We need a radical reshuffling of education, work, and leisure throughout our lives. We need a break with the highly structured pattern of education, work, leisure. We need a flexible life-style, a life of "simultaneity" that discards the notion that life is a succession of stages corresponding to physical growth and deterioration. The flexible life-style has been aptly described by R.N. Iyer in *Looking Forward: The Abundant Society.* "In place of the succession principle," he says, "I recommend the principle of simultaneity of pursuit of education, work and leisure during the whole of a man's life in the new society . . . work would become voluntary, training for and enjoyment of leisure a continuous activity linked with a philosophy of life-long education."[2] In the flexible life-style, we will lose some of the certainty, but we will gain variety. We will have more choices. For the first time the average person will be able to choose, especially in his twenties and later in his fifties and sixties, between education and work and between work and leisure. We also will be forced to make more choices to take advantage of the changing opportunities and demands throughout our lives.

In the flexible life-style, work and leisure will be rearranged so that we can enjoy weeks, months, even years without the pressure of work. Work and leisure will gradually blur together as both paid and voluntary activities are considered worthy and valid uses of time. Leisure will be spent for the mutual benefit of oneself and one's community, so that older adults will be valued and productive members of society instead of outdated machinery, tossed aside after

---

[2]R. N. Iyer, "The Social Structure of the Future," in *Looking Forward: The Abundant Society* (Santa Barbara, Calif.: Center for the Study of Democratic Institutions, 1966), p. 23.

their usefulness has ended. Education will teach us to enjoy leisure as well as prepare us to work.

REVERSING WORK AND LEISURE

The flexible life-style reverses the separation of work and leisure that has evolved since the Middle Ages. In earlier times, and in primitive societies still, everyone lived close to nature, working and playing in a natural rhythm. When there was work to be done, all participated. The men hunted or fished; the women raised the children, cooked, and helped to tend the crops. When the work was finished, everyone played, gathering around the campfire to dance and sing and retell the ancient legends. Leisure, like work, was shared equally by the tribe.

As civilization developed, this natural rhythm was broken. Leisure became the property of the few, and work was the curse of the many. In Western Europe, for example, nobles accumulated wealth through the ownership of land, extracting taxes from the peasants who toiled on their estates.

Eighteenth-century France, during the height of the Old Regime, strikingly illustrates the difference between the few and the many. In the stylized court of Louis XIV, nobles fought over the privilege to hold the right sleeve of the king's nightgown when he dressed. Several decades later, Marie Antoinette and her friends at court adopted the dress of shepherds and shepherdesses in an attempt to capture the idealized pleasures of rural life in the shadow of Versailles. Meanwhile, the peasants, who comprised between 75 and 90 per cent of the French population in the late 1700s, lived a far from idyllic life in the countryside. They struggled to eke out a bare subsistence by farming the land of the nobles. Despite their ceaseless toil, they were often unable to afford the price of bread. The nobles played at court and escaped taxes; the peasants worked from sunrise to sunset, paid heavy taxes, and frequently starved.

The Industrial Revolution, which began around 1800 in Great Britain and then spread to Western Europe and the United States, strengthened the separation of the working and leisure classes. Peasants became millhands, spending 14 hours a day in dreary, sunless factories. Their lives were regimented by the factory or business that employed them. They ate when the company told them they could, relaxed when their superiors ordered them to, and retired when the personnel department said they must. Their bosses amassed large fortunes, built extravagant houses in Newport and Palm Beach, and in general pursued a life of devotion to conspicuous consumption.

This separation still exists, but it is being reversed.

Modern technology enables workers to provide for their needs with fewer and fewer hours of work over the course of a lifetime. By our grandfather's schedule, we are given the equivalent of a four-month, paid holiday annually. We work fewer hours a week and receive more time off in the form of paid holidays, paid vacations, and paid sick leave. Since 1890, the work week has shrunk from an average of 61.9 hours to 40.7 hours. At the same time, we have gained four days a year in paid holidays, six days in paid vacations, and a week in paid sick leave. Altogether, we work on the average of 1,200 fewer hours a year than our grandfathers. Moreover, we have more years when we don't work at all. We spend a total of nine more years in school and retirement.[3] In short, workers are being forced to learn to play.

Leisure time has increased for the average worker, but there is no evidence that it has increased for those work-

---

[3]Juanita Kreps and Joseph Spengler, "Future Options for More Free Time," in *The Future of Work*, ed. Fred Best (Englewood Cliffs, N.J.: Prentice-Hall, Inc., 1973), pp. 87–92.

ers who occupy the upper echelons of business and govern-ment. Henry Ford II spends more hours a week at his desk than a worker in the Ford plant in Detroit spends on the assembly line. The President of the United States works more hours a week than a clerk-typist at the White House. In fact, research on the life-styles of self-made millionaires found that 100-hour work weeks were not uncommon. Many barely managed to squeeze in a few hours a week for their families, and a round of golf or a drink after work with friends was a rare occurrence for these work-possessed men.

The educated elite, which once enjoyed unlimited leisure, now savors the privilege of working. Their work is a privilege because we as a society have not yet learned to play. The elite is not confronted with the necessity, as the average worker is, of finding meaningful, rewarding ways to spend leisure. Furthermore, the growth in free time for the average worker is not true leisure. It provides time off from work, but it is time that is still structured by a time clock. The opportunities for personal growth are still missing. It is not flexible time. As a result, the elite uses what could be its leisure time to work, while the rest of society works at finding ways of filling up its leisure.

The solution is not beyond our reach. It requires more imagination than anything else. Since society does not require all of its members to spend all of their productive years at a full-time job, people should not be forced to do so. Work should alternate with leisure throughout our lifetime, restoring the natural rhythm of our days and creating more opportunities for employment and for play for people of all ages.

Economists Juanita Kreps and Joseph Spengler have pointed out that our current patterns of consumption of work and leisure are not the only possible ones. They have provided vivid examples of the various ways we might choose to use our growing leisure time. In their hypothetical examples, they assumed that our per capita income remains at $3,181 a year from 1960 to 1985. Technological progress would enable this level to be maintained with fewer hours of work over the years. As a consequence, we could choose 25 years later under our present pattern to work only 22 hours a week, or 27 weeks a year, or to retire at the age of 38. But this leisure also could be channeled into manpower training or adult education, for two examples. If leisure were used for training, half of the work force could be in training at any time, acquiring new job skills. If leisure were used for education, the economists predict that the amount of time available for education might exceed our capacity for learning.[4]

Individually, we might set up hour banks, similar to savings accounts, that would enable us to save hours of work and withdraw hours of leisure. We could put in and take out hours as we please, withdrawing hours and the money when we are able. The average person today works 2,000 hours a year if he works 40 hours a week and takes a two-week vacation. With an hour bank, a person could put in 80 hours one week and take the next week off. He could control his time and life to work half a day, half a week, or half a year as long as the hours of work and the hours of leisure balanced. The person who enters the labor force at 25 and retires at 65 works 307,200 hours a lifetime. Through deposits and withdrawals in an hour bank, a person could spend some of those working years in leisure and some of the retirement years at work. A person of 70 might be working, therefore, to repay the hours borrowed when he was 45-years-old.[5]

---

[4]Ibid.

[5]Several specialists in work and leisure have proposed hour banks. Dr. Max Kaplan, director of the Center for Leisure Studies at the University of South Florida, is one. See also Joseph C. Spengler, "The Aging of Individuals and Populations, Its Macroeconomic Aspects," in *Aging and Social Policy*, eds. John C. McKinney and Frank J. DeVyver (New York: Appleton-Century-Crofts, 1966).

Such proposals are not as farfetched as they might seem. In many parts of the country, people are already experimenting with new mixes of work, leisure, and education. Alternative work patterns, such as shortened work weeks, staggered work hours, and flexible working hours, known as flexitime, are being tried with beneficial results for both employees and employers. They prove that the lockstep of education, work, and leisure can be broken. These people are pioneering the future. What is the life-style of some of us today may be the life-style of all of us tomorrow. Let's look at some of these arrangements.

The 40-hour, five-day work week is not sacred. It is simply a convenient way of organizing the work week, and it is a fairly recent phenomenon, first appearing in the United States around 1908. Only five per cent of the American labor force was on this schedule by 1929. Since then, however, it has become such an established norm that any deviation appears radical. Although the 40-hour, five-day work week is convenient, it is certainly not the only way of arranging working hours. Companies in places as different as Lowell, Massachusetts; Littleton, Colorado; and Gastonia, North Carolina are experimenting with three- and four-day work weeks with varying numbers of total hours. In 1976, an estimated 10,000 corporations with approximately one million employees were on a four-day work week.[6] Estimates of the number of companies on the more recent and innovative three-day work week are scarce and suspect. But Mrs. Riva Poor, a management consultant who edited *4 Days, 40 Hours,* a book that has become the definitive reference work in the field, suggests that as many as 100 companies may be experimenting with the three-days-on, four-days-off schedule. Other employers, including the federal government, are trying flexible working hours that enable employees to choose

_____

[6]*New York Times*, August 20, 1976, sec. D, p. 1.

within certain broad limits the hours they will start and finish work. An estimated 45 firms are experimenting with flexitime, and about 28,000 federal government workers, roughly one per cent of all federal employees, are under the flexitime system.[7]

Like many innovations, the experiments in shortened work weeks and flexible working hours were born of necessity. Under the regulation 40-hour, five-day work week, job malaise often shows in chronic absenteeism, declining productivity, and frequent turnover in personnel. Many businesses discovered that traditional ways of keeping workers happy and on the job, such as incentive pay raises or bonuses, no longer worked when workers were rebelling against the regulation of their lives by a time clock. They wanted more leisure, not more money, and the control over their lives that leisure provides.

The experience of the Wales Manufacturing Company, a knitting mill in Gastonia, North Carolina, is a typical example. With local unemployment running at one-half of one per cent, employees did not need to worry that they would be replaced if they took the day off. According to Walter Talley, a partner in the firm, absenteeism was so bad that "I carried 100 people on the payroll simply to get 75 in for work every day." The offer of a 20-cent hourly bonus for those who completed a full 40-hour week failed to cut absenteeism.

Talley and his partner, Lester Cutler, hit on the idea of offering a bonus in leisure time instead of money. They asked employees to work 12 hours a day, three days a week for the same amount of pay as they received under an 8-hour day, five days a week. Although initially the workers resisted, vetoing the plan in a polling of the plant, the partners went ahead, instituting a four-day week as a transitional device. When the three-day work week was finally adopted, there were few complaints.

---

[7]*Washington Post*, August 3, 1976, p. 1.

Although the three-day work week might not be feasible for all companies, it is working well at Wales Manufacturing, which now employs two separate labor forces to keep the mill operating six days a week. Employees are particularly enthusiastic about an extra bonus built into the system. Once a month, employees who have been working Monday, Tuesday, and Wednesday change places with those who have been working Thursday, Friday, and Saturday. Because of the changeover, one group works six straight days while the other gets an entire week off. In effect, employees are getting six additional weeks of vacation a year.

With such incentives, mill production has risen by a minimum of four per cent and absenteeism has virtually ceased. During the first four weeks of the new schedule, only one employee was absent, and then for only one day. Mrs. Rachel Falls, a knitting machine operator, said, "I like this better. After you get used to it, it's just about like an eight-hour shift."

Another textile mill in the South, the Handley mill in Roanoke, Alabama, saw the three-day work week as a way of solving two interrelated problems—the demands of younger employees for more leisure time and educational opportunity, and the need of management to insure a steady labor force and high productivity.

Employees of the Handley mill, like workers at the Wales mill, work a 12-hour shift, arriving at 7:30 a.m. and leaving at 7:30 p.m. Incentive pay, roughly equivalent to four hours of work, is added to the paychecks of workers who complete their 36-hour-a-week shift. Every eight weeks, the Monday through Wednesday work force switches with the Tuesday through Saturday shift, giving most Handley workers an extra week off.

The three-day work week is benefiting both employers and employees. James R. Eichelberger, the production vice-president, said that the new schedule has not hurt productivity, while turnover and absenteeism are "about the same as always."

For employees, the biggest advantage of the three-day week is the opportunity to attend nearby Southern Union State Junior College. The college has arranged its class schedule to accommodate employees on the three-day work week, a vivid example of the blurring of lines between work and education, and education and leisure in the flexible life-style. Among those combining work with education in their free time is Mrs. Mary Cofield, a 20-year-old high school graduate. Mrs. Cofield works 36 hours a week while attending Southern Union State full time. She eventually hopes to get a degree in nursing, but without the three-day work week her hope would have remained an impossible dream. Under the traditional five-day week, she doubts she would have been able to afford the time or money to go to college, although it costs only $67.50 a quarter, or about $202.50 a year.

In the future, Thomas E. Brumbloe, president of Handley's parent corporation, Canton Textile Mills, Inc., envisions a similar combination of work and education for high school students. Through cooperative arrangements between the local high school and the mill, students would be able to start work at the mill when they are 16-years-old, while they continue to attend high school classes. By combining work and education in this manner, many teen-agers who lack the financial resources for higher education would be able to attend college. "Eventually," Brumbloe said, "we hope to offer a full six-year work and study opportunity to take participants through college." Auburn University is within commuting distance of the Handley mill in Roanoke.

The shorter work week offers many possibilities for combining work and advanced education. In Thorndike, Maine, the school district, which comprises 1,700 students in 11 rural communities, is experimenting with a four-day school week for students with in-service training for teachers. Students attend school Monday through Thursday; Fridays are reserved for training teachers in modern methods of teaching.

Although some local residents complained that teachers were being paid more for teaching less, test scores show that students have benefited. Students from grade school through high school were given standardized tests before and after the introduction to the four-day week. When the scores were compared, the students were found to score higher in 31 categories, lower in 26, and the same in three. David Day, special projects coordinator for the district, said, "It wasn't dramatically better, but at least it was better, indicating that it isn't how long the kids are in school but the quality of education they receive while they are there that makes the difference."

School superintendent Albert J. Brewster proposed the four-day week when the school budget was cut three consecutive years. He figured, correctly, that the four-day week would cut the cost of transportation, janitorial services, and school lunches. The result was a $19,000 saving during the first year. At the same time that the school system faced budget cuts, it was embarking on an ambitious program of individual instruction under a $10,000 federal grant. Day said, "Immediately we thought that we could not only save money, but we could provide teachers with some really prime time in-service training on Friday." So far, the four-day week is working beneficially for the students, teachers, and the school system itself.

Predictably, workers use their new leisure time differently. While some pursue higher education, others use their time in more mundane ways. A woman who works for Interstate, Inc., a manufacturer of paint rollers in New York City, said that she uses her Fridays for washing and ironing so she can be totally free to enjoy the weekends with her husband. Other women say that they appreciate the extra time with their children. And a government worker, employed under the flexitime schedule, said that he uses the hours that would have been spent in traffic snarls to buy materials for his weekend projects around the house. What workers do with their leisure is not as important as the freedom it gives to create a satisfying personal life.

The concept of flexible working hours has aroused the interest and support of a growing number of members of Congress. During the 94th Congress bills were introduced in both the House and Senate to encourage flexible working hours by promoting the employment of permanent part-time workers. Congressman Barber Conable of New York sponsored a bill to stimulate such employment in the private sector by providing a tax credit to participating employers. Employers would receive a credit for a certain percentage of the expense of employing part-timers such as recruiting and training. Former Senator John Tunney and Congresswoman Yvonne Burke, both of California, sponsored a bill to create 200,000 permanent part-time positions in the federal government over a five-year period. Moreover, Senator Gaylord Nelson of Wisconsin, chairman of the Subcommittee on Employment, chaired a series of hearings in 1976 on "Changing Patterns of Work in America" which probed the pros and cons of flexible working hours and permanent part-time employment.

The growing popularity of the shorter work week is one way to break the rigid separation of work and leisure in our society. Other ways are also possible. Older workers could extend their vacations, gradually diminishing the number of hours worked during the year, so that retirement occurs gradually over a 10- or 20-year period. After the age of about 50, workers might receive two additional weeks of vacation a year until they retire. By the age of 65, they already would be spending 30 weeks a year in retirement. Similarly, after the age of 50, workers might cut back the number of hours they work each week. They would retire, then, by stages, working 75 per cent, 50 per cent, or 25 per cent of their present working hours, to the age of 70 or even 75 depending on their desires and abilities.

Sabbaticals offer still another way of carving leisure out of our working years. Many teachers and college professors regularly take one year out of every seven years to go back to school, write, travel, or think. The concept of sabbaticals could be extended to other occupations so that leave time might be earned through employment. All of us, and society as a result, would benefit if we had a chance to renew ourselves occasionally. Such sabbaticals need not be "constructive" in the usual sense. We might benefit most when we spend our time in the least "productive" ways. A radical change in our customary life-style can be exhilarating, as Dr. John R. Coleman, the 51-year-old president of suburban Philadelphia's Haverford College, discovered when he temporarily abandoned his academic position for the life of an itinerant laborer.

A firm believer in getting away from it all, Coleman, a boyishly handsome authority on economics and labor, exchanged his cap and gown for work clothes during a two-month stint of physical labor. He trained for his new life by working 13 hours a day on a friend's dairy farm in Canada. After cleaning cow barns, he dug ditches for sewers in Atlanta for $2.75 an hour, washed dishes in Boston, and collected garbage in Silver Spring, Maryland. "I just wanted to get away from the intellectual life for a while," he said afterward. "I wanted to relearn things I had forgotten." Among other things, Coleman, who is listed in *Who's Who in America*, learned what it is like to be fired and experienced the loss of confidence that comes from being unemployed. He was fired as a dishwasher after a day and spent three depressing days looking for work before he was hired as a substitute sandwich-and-salad man at Boston's Union Oyster House. On that job he had trouble remembering orders that were shouted at him by waiters. "I need the written word," he conceded.[8]

Unbroken leisure of the kind offered by sabbaticals has become a bargaining issue for labor unions as contracts come up for renewal. Unions have found that many of their members, especially the young ones, would rather have more leisure than more money. They are willing to accept smaller raises in exchange for more time off. The United Auto Workers Union considered demanding, although later rejected, minisabbaticals in 1973. Under one proposal, tossed out as "food for thought" by a spokesman, workers would receive four hours of leisure time credit for every 40 hours a week they worked. Thus a worker would be entitled to a little over two weeks off every six months.

Three years later, the United Auto Workers struck the Ford Motor Company when negotiators failed to agree on how to reduce the standard 40-hour week. The union wanted workers to be guaranteed a specific number of days off each year, preferably one day a month, with the extra time rotated through the work force on a regular schedule. The company countered with a proposal of setting up a time bank that would enable workers with high seniority to earn up to five extra days off a year. Thus the relative amounts of work and leisure, once simply a private concern, are becoming a public issue.

Although workers demand more leisure, they also resist the spiritual death caused by an early and forced retirement. Surveys have found repeatedly that people, when asked to choose, prefer work over retirement. Fully 90 per cent of the men and 82 per cent of the women between the ages of 46 and 71 said in one survey that they would continue to work whether or not they needed to financially. Nevertheless, a sizable majority of the men and women in their forties and fifties complained about their lack of free time. After the

---

[8]"Through the Looking Glass," *Newsweek*, June 25, 1973, p. 77.

age of retirement, however, both men and women were even more likely to choose to work. Ninety-seven per cent of the men and 86 per cent of the women said that they would still work even if they did not have to.[9] The desire of workers for leisure and retirees for work are interrelated problems. They will be solved together or not at all. Retirement is simply the final stage of a life that has gone wrong from the beginning.

A NEW PERSPECTIVE

The first signs that something is wrong begin showing up in middle age.

By the age of 40, many workers are trapped in routine, boring jobs that offer little personal satisfaction and almost no chance of advancement. Others find that their careers, launched enthusiastically in their twenties, are engaging less and less of their best efforts. Many would like to change, seeking new, challenging jobs that would make the alarm clock something to be welcomed again. A survey by the W.E. Upjohn Institute for Employment Research found that nearly 40 per cent of the workers over 40 thought seriously about changing occupations and would enter an educational program to acquire new skills if they could receive a reasonable living allowance.[10]

But for most workers, changing occupations is difficult if not impossible. New career skills are difficult to obtain. Few universities are sensitive to the needs of the older student, and many middle-aged men and women, envisioning themselves in a classroom of 18 year olds, reject the idea as ludicrous. Training programs, including ones run by the federal government, are reluctant to accept older workers.

---

[9]Eric Pfeiffer and Glenn C. Davis, "The Use of Leisure Time in Middle Life," *The Gerontologist* (Autumn 1971), Part 1, pp. 187–93.

[10]*Work in America,* (Boston: M.I.T. Press, 1973).

Even if midcareer training were readily available, few workers could afford to take advantage of it without financial help. After paying for household expenses, few workers can set aside money to pay for job retraining.

We need late starts as well as head starts, second chances as well as first chances. In many cases, they are necessary since rapid technological developments make job skills learned in the twenties obsolete by the fifties. But with longer lives, second careers become possibilities for all. If the life-span is extended by 10 years, a person who now retires at 65 would be able to devote an additional two decades to a second career. Businesses that are presently reluctant to hire new employees over the age of 40 could afford to hire those who change careers in midlife because these workers could offer many more productive years.

Although the idea of millions of middle-aged workers handing in their resignations to return to school or launch new careers sounds radical, it is common for many occupational groups. Military officers often trade their uniforms for business suits in their midforties, retiring from the armed services to start new careers as civilians. Take the case of Colonel Albert E. Paul, a retired Marine who lives in Tampa, Florida. In his seventies, Paul is still spry, carrying himself with the erect bearing of a former military man. His dark hair, now flecked with silver, is just beginning to recede from an unlined forehead. "Retired? Who is retired?" he said. "I'm on my third career."

After retiring from the Marines in 1962, he served a 10-year stint as director of the Tampa-Hillsborough Civil Defense. Paul then started teaching classes in oil painting for the city recreational department. He is a serious painter who has exhibited at shows in Florida and Georgia. During his 32 years in the Marines, he sketched as a hobby and, while stationed in China, studied Chinese art and culture. Now he is turning his hobby into a career that brings pleasure to himself and others. "Pictures are to be enjoyed," he said. "We go out into the woods and mountains, and if we can capture some of that beauty on canvas, we hang it on the wall for pleasure."

Along with an appreciation of art, his pupils absorb some of his vitality and intensity for life that continues to drive Paul. "There are so many things in this world to do, the word 'retired' is obnoxious to me," he said. "I hear so many people say, 'pretty soon I can retire. I am looking forward to it—just taking a long rest.' But in most cases, if they rest too long, they vegetate!"

Although the idea of retraining middle-aged workers is new to the United States, it is taken for granted in other industrial countries. Over 250,000 Germans return to school annually to increase their productivity, their effectiveness, and, as a consequence, their job satisfaction. Sweden operates an extensive educational program for adults that enables one per cent of the population to be in continual retraining to gain new industrial skills. French workers can receive vocational training at almost 100 centers throughout France.

Recognizing a spreading epidemic of job "blahs" among blue and white collar workers, the Department of Health, Education, and Welfare commissioned the W.E. Upjohn Institute for Employment Research to study the nature of work in the United States. After a year-long examination of the social consequences of work, the task force concluded that we *must* redesign dull, repetitive jobs that blunt our autonomy and initiative. They recommended that work be restructured by combining retraining programs and sabbaticals in the form of worker self-renewal programs.

Under this proposal, two types of worker self-renewal programs would be created. The first would enroll workers who are trapped in stagnant industries. They would be trained for jobs in growing industries. A coal miner, for example, might be taught keypunching. The second, called the Universal Self-Renewal Program, would support workers financially for six months to a year while they engage in a variety of educational pursuits, anything from upgrading job skills to attending college, which would enable them to escape dead-end jobs. Workers could take six months off after working for seven years or a year off after working for 14 years. During this time, they would receive a living allowance that would equal 70 per cent of their regular salary.[11]

Robert Morris, professor of social planning at Brandeis University, has suggested that the length of the sabbatical be based on the number of unemployed workers in the country. If five per cent of the work force was unemployed, for example, a worker could earn a year's leave after 20 years of work. If 10 per cent of the work force were unemployed, a worker could earn a year's sabbatical after 10 years of work.

Naturally, this would be expensive. The task force estimated that the cost would be about $22 billion a year if their projections of three million workers a year in training were realized. However, the cost might be offset by the use of funds that are now being spent on higher education, welfare, manpower training, and vocational education. The task force suggested tapping business for additional funds, since they would benefit by reduced training costs. Money also might be raised by a nonregressive tax on the salaries of workers who would benefit by increased earning power after their sabbatical.

Both programs, but particularly the Universal Worker Self-Renewal Program, would provide opportunities for life-long education. We could leave college and return later to earn a degree. We might enter the work force after high school, deferring college until our job goals are more clearly defined. If we felt trapped in jobs that were stifling, that no longer interested us or offered little prospect of advancement, we could risk a change.

In implementing the task force report, the government should consider establishing counseling centers to help

---

[11]Eleanor G. Berman, "Do You Want to Change Your Career?" *Parade*, April 15, 1973, pp. 14–16.

people switch careers. After all, since we already support family counseling centers and mental health clinics, there is no reason that we should not help people who are suffering from midcareer crisis. A model for such centers already exists in New York City.

Mainstream Associates, a company founded by Carl Beilby, who himself switched from the ministry to family and marriage counseling and then to career counseling, helps people to find a more satisfying way of life with as little drop in salary as possible. The company is not an employment agency; the actual job hunting is left up to the individual. Instead, it helps people who are dissatisfied with their jobs to examine their personalities and capabilities, to find out what they would like to do and are capable of doing. "Almost everyone has unused skills, untapped potentials for growing and learning," said Beilby. "Career switching is an ideal way to make use of these abilities and make life satisfying." The average client, who falls in the 32 to 42 age bracket, spends two months reassessing his careers and relocating in a new job. The steady stream of clients is varied, ranging from a 53-year-old former monk who is now a $30,000-a-year educational sales consultant, to an ex-police officer who now teaches at a community college. Although the service is valuable, it is also expensive. Mainstream charges between $800 to $1,000 for its services.[12] Federal funds would enable such counseling centers to be opened throughout the country, extending midcareer guidance to people who live outside of New York City or who are unable to afford such fees.

The obvious question is: Can it work? Can we break the lockstep of education, work, and leisure? Are we capable of making such a radical change in our social structure? Are we willing to accept the uncertainty of the flexible life-style? Are we willing to pay for sabbaticals such as self-renewal programs?

---

[12]Sidney P. Marland, Jr., "Education for More than One Career," *World,* July 18, 1972, pp. 46–49.

Dr. Sidney P. Marland, former U.S. Commissioner of Education, believes that we not only can, but that we must. "At a time when life expectancy is moving into the seventies," he wrote in *World* magazine, "the notion that a person should be trained for a single vocation or profession is costly and obsolete. Nothing is more wasteful than human energies and talents—regardless of the age of the person involved—that are not being utilized."[13]

As proof, he cites the case of Anthony Morley, who spent 15 years in an inner city ministry before beginning full-time graduate work in school administration at the City University of New York.

"In my ministry, I felt I was nibbling away at the fringes of social problems," Morley said. "Given my particular interests and abilities, I felt I could do more and enjoy it more inside the educational system. It reaches every child."

At the university, he has been searching for new ways to use the computer in the classroom. He also has been exploring ways of reforming school finances. After graduation, he hopes to work in a state department of education, because he believes that the responsibility for reform in our schools lies at the state level.

Morley is among a small group of people, successful in other fields, who were prepared for new careers in education with financial help from the U.S. Office of Education. They have included a vice-president of a large pharmaceutical laboratory, an army lieutenant colonel, the president of a management consulting firm, and the executive assistant to a former mayor of New York City. Like Morley, most of the people in the program took a hard look at their lives around the age of 40 and decided that some changes were in order.

The Educational Leadership Program, which was responsible for the training of Morley and the others, was a small step in the right direction. But if the flexible life-style is

---

[13]Pamela Swift, "Never Too Late," *Parade,* June 4, 1972.

to become a reality, we need broad-based education for careers, the kind of career education that will enable us to move easily in and out of different careers over the course of our lifetime.

Career education is very different from vocational education, which prepares a student for a specific job, say, as a welder or bookkeeper. Career education would teach children from kindergarten through sixth grade about the working world through "career awareness" studies. They would explore broad job clusters. If they were studying manufacturing, for example, they would visit factories, talk to assembly line workers and corporation presidents, perhaps set up a small factory to make potholders or Christmas decorations in the classroom. During grade school, students would select jobs that interest them in two or three of the job clusters to be explored in depth in junior high school. Career education would continue through high school and college, although less thought has been given to designing programs to meet the needs of older students. Marland said, "The student would be equipped occupationally, academically, and emotionally to spin off from the system at whatever age he chooses—whether at age 16 as a craftsman apprentice or age 30 as a surgeon or age 60 as a newly trained practical nurse." Career education would help to keep a middle-aged worker in the midst of a midcareer crisis from floundering. Instead of wondering what it would be like to be a lawyer or teacher or construction worker, he would know. The person would have some hard facts on which to base a decision to switch occupations.

Since Marland first coined the phrase "career education," it has caught hold in many areas of the country. Endorsements have poured in from such organizations as the U.S. Chamber of Commerce, the National Alliance of Businessmen and the National Association for the Advancement of Colored People. It has also won the support of a number of corporations including General Motors, General

Electric, and American Telephone & Telegraph. General Motors, in fact, has career-education coordinators in most of its 117 plants. By 1976 some 9,000 of the country's 17,000 school districts had launched programs.

The real impetus has come from federal and state legislation. Congress provided $64.5 million between 1969 and 1976 for 248 pilot projects. It also set up in 1974 the U.S. Office of Career Education with a four-year authorization of $15 million. At least four states—Michigan, Iowa, Louisiana, and Kentucky—require their school systems to set up such programs. Eight others have appropriated money. These states are Arkansas, Colorado, Florida, Kansas, Ohio, Vermont and Washington.

Serial careers will put new demands on colleges and universities. With the spread of education over the life-span, universities will no longer be communities inhabited exclusively by the young. In fact, today middle-aged and older adults make up a growing minority on campuses across the country. At the University of California at Los Angeles, for example, the student body as a whole is growing older—37 per cent of graduate students are now over 30 and 41.5 per cent of undergraduates are over 21. The percentage of entering freshman over the age of 21 has increased from 1.6 to 5.5 per cent.[14]

At nearby University of Southern California, Dr. James Birren says he predicts the trend toward an older student body will increase as universities awaken to their responsibilities to the older student. "Colleges and universities have neglected their responsibilities to the entire community," he said. "They have overlooked the middle-aged and the old. But this is changing. In the future, we will see a steadily increasing number of older students on campus."

---

[14]John G. Rogers, "Happy Schoolmates," *Parade*, September 10, 1972.

ters around the country, like the one at Sarah Lawrence College in Bronxville, New York.

Sarah Lawrence offers unstructured, continuing education with emphasis on independent study. Applicants are not required to have taken specific courses such as math and science, and they are not subjected to scholastic aptitude or achievement tests. Students attend weekly seminars that last two hours, and they meet twice a month with a professor to discuss individual study projects.

The emphasis is on liberal education, not vocational preparation. Mrs. Sally Levene, who interviews applicants, said, "If she has a precise aim, such as becoming a teacher, and only wants to attend classes in order to get a teaching certificate, then Sarah Lawrence really isn't for her." A typical student, Mrs. Muriel Green, says, "I had no vocation in mind. I just wanted to explore knowledge."

These who *do* want a teaching certificate or specific vocational preparation might enroll in the experimental "Universities Without Walls," sponsored by the U.S. Office of Education. The University Without Walls program believes that adults with varied backgrounds and career interests learn best in untraditional, innovative settings. The classrooms may be located in a downtown store front or a high rise office building, although the programs are affiliated with accredited colleges that grant the actual degrees. In the program, a person who wanted to be a teacher might alternate between taking education courses at a nearby college and working as a teacher's aide in a classroom. At the same time, the student might undertake individual study projects, say, a report on the impact of the state educational funding formula based on personal interviews with legislators, administrators in the state department of education, school superintendents, and teachers. Students create individual course packets with the help of an advisor, and they proceed at their own pace.

Both middle-aged and older adults need more educational opportunities, but for different reasons. The middle-aged generally need education for careers. Older adults in general need education for personal growth. Although colleges are beginning to meet the educational needs of the middle-aged through continuing education centers, they have yet to become sensitive to the needs of older adults for education for living. There are signs, however, that their attitudes are changing. Birren said, "In the years after World War II, universities concentrated on meeting the educational needs of the young and neglected their responsibilities to the rest of the communities. As the college enrollment of young people drops, colleges will have to respond by soliciting new students. We can expect to see a different mix on campus." Another educator, Dr. Karen Weiss, director of The Second Wind program at The University of Maryland, said, "Colleges have to start thinking about the returning student, that's where they're going to find their tuitions in the next decade."

North Hennepin State Junior College in Brooklyn Park, Minnesota, is a school that reassessed its responsibilities to older adults with gratifying results. As a result older people comprise a substantial number of students during the regular school year. During the summer session, older students outnumber the college-age students.

The junior college took a new look at its responsibilities to older adults after a seminar on services for the elderly. Although the seminar was aimed at social workers and nursing home directors, older adults also turned out in large numbers. Up to that point, the junior college felt that it was fulfilling its responsibilities to older adults by offering free movies and concerts. But, at the seminar, the older adults were so interested in the school and its students and so distressed by their own lack of educational opportunities that the college decided to explore the possibility of opening college courses to them. The first meeting on the subject drew 400 older adults. When they were asked what they wanted, one replied, "Educational opportunities, just like everybody else." A 73-year-old widow said, "I had to quit school in the sixth grade. Now I've got time to improve myself, but I need help, somewhere to go."

The junior college began modestly with a tuition-free program of senior students' classes. Most of the classes were for personal enrichment. But, almost immediately, the older adults asked to be admitted and were accepted in courses for college credit.

Opening up colleges and universities has a beneficial by-product. The younger and older generations are reintroduced. Although the young and old share many similar attitudes, they rarely have a chance to discover the similarities.

Both the younger and older students at North Hennepin agree that the warm friendships and intergenerational communication are enrichening their college years. Periodic talk sessions give both a chance to sit around a table and share their feelings. Loretta Sundquist, who takes public speaking courses along with her husband, says that she tries to help students to see another viewpoint when they complain about their parents' materialism. "One girl was particularly upset about this," said Mrs. Sundquist. "Well, my husband and I have worked all our lives, and I asked the girl, 'Why do you suppose your family has such a nice home and two cars and you can easily afford to be in college? Those advantages don't just happen by magic. Somebody has to work for them.' I tried to get her to see that whether your aim is realistic or materialistic, you have to work for it. That girl and I have become good friends."

Mike Nagell, a 20-year-old sophomore, says, "We do a lot of arguing, but we never get sore at each other. None of them, for instance, likes the idea of a guy and a gal living together before marriage. Overall, we find that you can learn things from these old people. They've already been through things."[15]

Wherever colleges have opened their doors to older

---

[15]*New York Times,* August 13, 1976, n.p.

students, they have soon found a line of older adults waiting to be admitted. The best programs, such as the Institute for Retired Professionals at the New School for Social Research in New York City, try to meet the special needs of older adults without isolating them from younger students.

The Institute for Retired Professionals was set up by and for older adults. Hyman Hirsch, the director, who is retired himself, said, "The Institute is for the retiree who doesn't want to get into the ceramic ashtray syndrome. It uses the skills and experience of retirees in a university setting to allow them to function as learners and leaders."

Students are required to take one course a semester in the regular school curriculum. They also take courses at the Institute that are taught by retirees. Some 80 retirees, many of whom have never taught, lead courses in history, current events, literature, and poetry. Retirees also plan the curriculum and administer the Institute.

Hirsch said, "The hobbies, the golf games, the concerts that filled the nonworking hours before retirement are forms of recreation that simply are not enough after retirement. The Institute for Retired Professionals provides a way of life which retirees can look to for intellectual stimulation and emotional sustenance."

The most exciting and rapidly growing of the new programs is the Elderhostel movement, which offers older adults a week of attending courses, lectures, discussions, and films at a college campus. It started in 1975 as a summer experiment at the University of New Hampshire. By the end of the first year, 21 colleges and universities in New England participated, and over 1,000 older adults were enrolled. Older adults have taken courses ranging from White Mountain geography at New Hampshire's Plymouth State College to early American music at Wesleyan University to Shakespeare at the University of Bridgeport. The cost is deliberately kept low. The Elderhostel at the University of

Bridgeport, for example, charges $60 a week for room and board, with other expenses covered by government funds for those on Social Security or over 65. The response of older adults has been overwhelmingly enthusiastic. The program has received 9,000 inquiries and has a waiting list of 600 applicants. "It's been fantastic," said Sally Sylk of Havertown, Pennsylvania. "I'm on Social Security, and where could I ever get a vacation like this?" Pauline Lipsher of West Palm Beach, Florida, added, "We stayed another week instead of going to a resort. After this, the resort would have been an anticlimax, in fact, dull."

Living in the dormitories with coffee and snacks available 24 hours a day, the older adults have found informal socializing easy. Elderhostel, however, is more than a cheap vacation or a way of making new friends. There is an intellectual exchange and a shared spiritual experience. Robert Fuessle, director of Elderhostel at the University of Bridgeport, said, "There was almost an evangelical fervor, the feeling that we'd given them something new in life."[16]

THE FLEXIBLE LEISURE-STYLE

The flexible life-style will create unprecedented leisure. Although sabbaticals, vocational retraining programs, and educational pursuits will help to stretch out work, we will still have more leisure than our grandparents ever dreamed of. Ten years of retirement equals 45,000 hours of leisure, the equivalent of 20 years of work days. If we continue to believe that work as represented by a weekly paycheck is the sole measure of a person's worth, we will have difficulty coping with the future. Instead, we must think of paid employment as only one form of work that has as its ultimate goal the creation of a good community where all of us can grow and enjoy life. It would help if we discarded the word "work" entirely and substituted in its place a word such as "commit-ment." We would then pursue life-long commitments, some-times for money and sometimes for joy, as Paul, the ex-Marine, pursued painting first as a hobby and then as a career.

As the middle-aged find more leisure during their working years, older adults should find more opportunities for work in retirement. Such opportunities have long been sought by retirees who detest the idleness of enforced re-tirement. The Gallup poll has reported that 60 per cent of those over 60 were willing to spend at least four hours a week in volunteer activities, but they lacked the opportunity. As our communities grow aware of the untapped resources of older adults, such opportunities should develop.

Many older adults are already working in their com-munities. They are planting flowers, building lakes, and cleaning up the countryside under one federally funded program. Others are scouting the community for low income older adults, going from door to door in the old-age ghettos and steering the needy older people to the proper commun-ity agency for help. Many work with children in institutions for the retarded, in classrooms as teachers' aides and in day care centers for low income children. Some, not content with working in their own communities, pack their suitcases and take off for remote corners of the world as Peace Corps volunteers.

Halfway around the world, Peace Corps volunteer, 67-year-old Dora Roach of Madison, Wisconsin, has found unexpectedly rich rewards teaching freshman English at Middle East Technical University in Ankara, Turkey. A self-admitted campus character, the strikingly attractive American quickly established a close rapport with her stu-dents, who were not accustomed to teachers taking a per-sonal interest in them. After her first year of teaching, she was amazed that her former students made a special point of dropping by her office when classes resumed in the fall.

Many became regular visitors. One student confided that she was the first teacher to give him confidence in himself. "They can't get over the fact that I can call each and every one by name," she said. "It wasn't easy, believe me, but I worked at it and it certainly paid off." Instead of being considered out-of-date and passé, she finds her age an asset in a country that automatically accords older adults respect. "I've found that even here in the big city, the 'problems' that young [Peace Corps volunteers] have aren't even problems to me," she said. "I don't seem to have problems, and I lay that to what I hope I can call maturity."

In this country, several thousand older men are improving our parks, fixing up recreational areas, and restoring historical sites. They are employed under the Senior Community Service Employment Program administered by the Department of Labor. Although the average worker is in his sixties, the men do hard physical labor and love it. John Crosby, a 72-year-old resident of Wheatland, Pennsylvania, spent three years on a Green Thumb project at Sandy Lake, some 60 miles from the Ohio-Pennsylvania border. His Green Thumb team fixed the dam at the lake and cut down trees between the lake and highway so that it would be visible to passing motorists, and they started to raise fish to stock the pond for fishermen. "By being on Green Thumb, that gave me a big hand (financially) and I was able to help some people out of that," he said. "I am age 72, and I feel like I could do just about as much as I did when I was 42."

In Newton County, Tennessee, Green Thumb workers have revived the slowly dying community of 4,800. Newton County was so rural that mail was delivered on horseback and so poor that the main sources of income were Social Security and welfare. Without public transportation or a doctor and with a total county budget of a mere $160,000, the county was almost dead when four Green Thumb organizers moved in. They recruited a team of workers, hoping to fix up the road and build roadside parks so the area could draw tourists. Before anyone was fully aware of what was happening, Al Capp bought some land and created Dog Patch, U.S.A., a major tourist attraction for the county. Now Dog Patch, U.S.A. and Green Thumb have the largest payrolls in an increasingly prosperous community.

Not surprisingly, older adults have a special skill for communicating with others of their own age and with children. They work with children in a variety of programs, but their work with other older adults is paid for through the Senior Community Service Employment Program. Some 5,000 men and women over the age of 55 are employed at the average rate of $2 an hour for a 20-hour week. They do an amazing variety of work. They visit elderly shut-ins in the inner city, do clerical work in senior citizen centers, serve as key aides to social workers and psychiatric specialists, and help to prepare and deliver low cost meals to the elderly.

At the mammoth Dade County Senior Centers, the senior aides do a little bit of everything, but their most important work is helping to find "lost" older adults who need help but haven't come to the attention of the social service agencies. The senior aides soothe their fears, explain how the agencies operate, and give them the self-confidence and assurance to ask for the help they need. Mrs. Melissa Harris, a heavy set woman in her middle sixties, is the sole link between five of these older adults and the outside world. "Without aides, these would be isolated," she explained. "Two are in wheelchairs, two are blind, and one doesn't talk. I take them to and fro for medicine and bring them down to the center. We make them happy, and they make us happy."

Of all federally funded employment programs for older adults, the most successful is probably the Foster Grandparent program. It employs 13,627 older adults who work with approximately 34,000 children a day. According to estimates by one private consulting service, the program generates from $1 to $4 million more in benefits than costs in a single year. First, the program helps a number of older adults to escape welfare. Second, many Foster Grandparents work in institutions for the retarded, handicapped, and emotionally disturbed. They speed the progress of the youngsters, enabling many to go home earlier than predicted. Thus the Foster Grandparents ease the patient loads at state-supported facilities.

Not all benefits can be measured in dollars and cents. That is obvious every morning when a candy-striped red and white bus, known as "The Granny Special," rolls to a stop at the Dr. Joseph H. Ladd School for the retarded in Exeter, Rhode Island. Some youngsters greet the grandmothers at the door, but the children who need the grandmothers the most can't come to the bus. These severely retarded and handicapped youngsters spend the days lying on the floor. A few scream continuously or stare blankly at the walls.

As the grandmothers enter the room, the children begin to respond. The blank stares focus on the women, and they seem to recognize them. Some children try to move toward the women. The grandmothers go to their children, greeting them with hugs, kisses, and reassuring words. Many of the children have seldom, if ever, known these things.

The relationships between the children and grandmothers are deep and lasting. Mary Warnock gave a big hug to a semi-paralyzed girl in a wheelchair as she said, "Three years ago this girl was not able to talk at all. She hung her head all day. Now she tries to tell and show me things. She saw a bird the other day and pointed it out to me."

These federally sponsored programs show the range of things that older adults are capable of doing in their communities. They show the kinds of jobs that older adults may fill when employment opportunities are opened to them in the private sector.

Although many low income adults participate in the federally funded programs because they need to, other older adults work because they love to. Paid or unpaid, they are performing a valuable service, and our communities are better for it. Ideally, we might come to view retirement as a promotion, permitting older adults to do more of the valuable and human kinds of work and less of the drudgery.

In the future, which may be closer than we think, there will come a day when parents will not worry if their children don't want to start college after high school. A college president who spends two months at hard labor will not make the front page of *The New York Times*. And no eyebrows will be raised if a 70-year-old retiree goes back to school to earn a Ph.D. or starts a third career. On that day we will know that the flexible life-style has arrived.

SENIOR CITIZENS
ON THE MARCH

CHAPTER TEN

In Boston, Massachusetts, 5,000 older adults turned out for a tumultuous, hand-clapping, foot-stamping rally to voice their support for a proposed 25 per cent increase in Social Security benefits. The rally drew a number of politicians, too, who were eager to champion the cause of older adults. Among those who showed up were U.S. Senators Edward Brooke and Edward Kennedy.

In New Orleans, Louisiana, several hundred members of the Oldies But Goodies Organization marched through the twisting streets of the historic French Quarter to protest what they said were inadequate Social Security benefits. They marched to city hall and on to Louisiana State University, where the U.S. Commissioner of Aging, was speaking.

In Pontiac, Michigan, older adults, tired of unfulfilled promises by city officials to install traffic lights at busy intersections, staged sit-ins that snarled traffic for miles. Embarrassed by the demonstrating senior citizens and swamped by complaints from angry motorists, the city leaders quickly installed the much-needed traffic lights.

These seemingly random happenings are clues to our political future. A new political pressure group, composed of outraged older adults, is emerging. Across the country, older people are forming political action groups. It is a nationwide, spontaneous movement nourished by impatience, frustration, and fear. And it is tackling the problems of older adults at the local and national levels. The little old lady of today is apt to be wearing combat boots instead of tennis shoes.

Willingly or unwillingly, we—the rest of society—will be forced to respond. In our political system where, paradoxically enough, stability depends on a constantly shifting balance of power, older adults can get more only if the rest of society is willing to accept less. We will have to decide how much should be spent on senior citizen centers and how much on day care centers for children. We will have to choose between highways for those who drive and mass transit for the 60 per cent of older adults who have neither cars nor driver's licenses. Conflict is inevitable between older adults who want more goods and services and younger people who will have to pay for them.

POLITICAL ACTION GROUPS

Older adults are becoming one of the most politically organized groups in the country. They have started to form and join organizations seeking to improve the lives of people over 65 through political actions. Some of these groups are purely local organizations, and they work at the city and state levels. Three groups are based in Washington, D.C., have a national staff, a nationwide membership, and a network of local affiliates across the country. They have a legislative affairs staff to maintain contact with Congress, testify at Congressional hearings on behalf of senior citizens, and publish newsletters to keep members informed on developments in Washington.

The smallest and oldest of the three groups is the National Association of Retired Federal Employees which was formed in the 1920s, and grew to over 250,000 members by 1976, most of them concentrated in the Washington, D.C., area. Its political activity is aimed primarily at improving pension benefits for retired federal employees. The larger two groups are the National Council of Senior Citizens, with over 3.5 million members, and the American Association of Retired Persons and the National Retired Teachers Association (AARP/NRTA), with close to 10 million members in 1976.

The National Council of Senior Citizens was organized by members of the 1961 White House Conference on Aging. It received strong initial support from labor leader Walter Reuther, who was an early proponent of Medicare, and in its early days the Council concentrated its political efforts on passage of the Medicare Act. Since then, its focus has broadened, but it still has strong ties to organized labor and, although it claims to be nonpartisan, to the Democratic party.

The AARP/NRTA also received its initial impetus from the need of older adults for low cost health insurance. When Ethel Percy Andrus organized the National Retired Teachers Association in 1946, one of her objectives was a national health insurance program for retired teachers. Her efforts paid off in 1955 when the Continental Casualty Insurance Company agreed to a group insurance program for NRTA members. The American Association of Retired Persons was organized in 1958 to provide similar benefits to older adults who were not teachers. The two groups retain

separate identities, but they share offices and staff. The
AARP/NRTA has also broadened its focus from its early
days.

Both of these groups are growing rapidly. The National Council of Senior Citizens claims that 20 new affiliates
are being formed every month, while the AARP/NRTA reports that 2,000 older adults are mailing in their membership
forms to the national office each day. The growth of local
groups that are not affiliated with the national organizations is
equally spectacular. In Iowa, not usually considered a hotbed
of political activism, for example, the number of senior citizen groups rose from 275 to 654 in just one year. The Dade
County (Florida) Congress of Senior Citizens claims over
6,000 members, while in New York City the Congress of
Senior Citizens claims some 500,000 members, about half of
the older adults in the city.

Such growth reflects the rising political consciousness
of older adults. Max Friedson, the peppery 72-year-old president of the Dade County Congress of Senior Citizens, said,
"We're not kooks or militants, but we're getting very, very
politically minded because that is the only way we can get
what we need." Looking at the growing political activism of
older adults from a slightly different perspective, Dr. James
Petersen, a sociologist who acts as the liaison between the
AARP and the Ethel Percy Andrus Gerontology Center at
the University of Southern California, says that older adults
are turning into the most politically minded group in the
country. "This is an undercurrent that hasn't been recognized yet," he said. "But I know because many of the new
members of AARP are asking for the names of local chapters
so they can get politically active on the local level. The political potential of the old is about to be felt in this country."

Most politicians are sensitive to the political demands
of older adults. The mere thought of a demonstration by
aging grandmothers and grandfathers, leaning on their
canes as they picket in the street, is enough to make most
politicians cringe. Older adults have the potential of making

an officeholder look like a cold-blooded ogre, especially to voters who may be just a few years away from collecting Social Security themselves. Such voters are certain to remember the officeholders' actions, or lack of them, when they come up for re-election.

Because of this potential for embarrassment, senior power to date has rested largely on the implied threat of what older adults might do if their wishes are ignored. Up to now most political activity has been confined to writing, calling, or sending telegrams to elected officials. But the tactics are shifting. Older adults are growing adamant.

Older people in various parts of the country have adopted forceful, sometimes dramatic, tactics. In Ohio, members of senior citizen groups converged on the state capitol to support a bill requiring sprinkling systems to be installed in nursing homes, which they referred to as death traps. They wrote and visited their state legislators, and as the bill came up for a final vote, they did more. They filed into the visitor's galleries and knelt for a pray-in. With their older adult constituents watching and praying above them, the legislators voted the bill into law. In Boston, Massachusetts, older adults went even further. They stormed the office of a state legislator who had refused to let several bills out of his committee that would have benefited older people. The older adults barricaded the state legislator into his office, knowing that he would have to leave to take medication at a certain time. Sitting in front of his office door, they refused to let him leave until he promised to let the bills they wanted out of his committee. Only after he did so was he permitted to leave his office.

SENIOR POWER—THE VOTE

Ultimately, of course, older adults possess the power of the vote. If they cannot get concessions from current officeholders, they can always vote them out of office and elect new officials who will be more responsive. William Hutton, director of the National Council of Senior Citizens, says that he means "the vote," not marches, sit-ins, or picketing, when he talks about "senior power." He points out that there are 22 million people over 65 and another 20 million between 55 and 65 in the country, almost all of whom are eligible to vote. "That's a lot of levers being pulled in a lot of voting booths," he said.

Politicians who have ignored the senior citizen vote have done so at their own peril. Older adults have retaliated in the voting booth. Senator Barry Goldwater of Arizona, the Republican presidential nominee in 1964, was spurned by older adults when he spoke out against compulsory Social Security. Older people interpreted his remarks as a threat to their own Social Security benefits. In that presidential election, older adults voted overwhelmingly for Lyndon Johnson, the combined result of Goldwater's statement on Social Security and Johnson's avowed determination to push for passage of the Medicare Act. In *A Sacred Trust*, an account of the passage of Medicare, Richard Harris concludes that Johnson's stand contributed substantially to his landslide victory.[1] According to the author's analysis of the election returns, people over the age of 60 accounted for 22 per cent of the votes cast, and most of them went for Johnson. Moreover, two million voters over the age of 60, who would normally have voted Republican, switched their votes in favor of Johnson. Although seven out of the 10 states with the highest percentage of older voters are normally in the Republican column, the Democrats captured all 10 of them. In that crucial election, older adults were a significant force.

Another politician who learned too late the power of the senior citizen vote was former Congressman John G. Schmitz of Orange County, California. Schmitz was elected

------

[1]Richard Harris, *A Sacred Trust* (New York: New American Library, 1966).

initially with the overwhelming support of the Republicans in Leisure World. Over 69 per cent of them voted for Schmitz in his first bid. Two years later, when Schmitz was up for re-election, he lost the older adult vote and the Republican primary. The second time around, he drew only 27.6 per cent of the Leisure World vote. His loss was attributed to an off-hand remark at a press conference that year. In response to a question, Schmitz said that he favored President Richard Nixon's trip to the People's Republic of China, but not his return. The Congressman intended his remark to be funny, and although the newspaper reporters laughed, they also wrote the story. In print, the remark did not seem so humorous. The Orange County Republicans, who were staunch supporters of Nixon at the time, never forgave Schmitz.

Basically, older adults are asking for simple things. They want adequate incomes in retirement, decent housing, readily available and cheap transportation, and nourishing meals. They want property tax relief, so they can keep the homes they have worked so long to pay for. They seek assurances that one serious illness will not bankrupt them.

Older adults have already won significant victories in many places. They have been particularly successful in winning lower fares on public transportation and property tax relief.

More than 50 cities have reduced fares for older adults on public transportation, usually during nonrusn hours, although Boston and Philadelphia, where the lobbying by senior citizen groups was heavy, offer cut rate fares around the clock. Special senior citizen fares are not limited to cities with a high percentage of older adults in their populations. Bus fares have been lowered for older people in such places as Cincinnati, Ohio; Richmond, Virginia; Long Beach, California; and Kansas City, Kansas. In St. Petersburg, Florida, authorities have gone one step further. They have designed special bus routes, called the Sunshine Special, for older adults. The Sunshine Special passes the senior citizen center, the hospital, city hall, the library, and medical complex.

Forty-eight states have extended some form of property tax relief to older adults, many of whom are terrified that they will be taxed out of their homes. Recognizing that regressive property taxes put a heavy burden on those least able to pay, state legislatures have passed a variety of relief measures. Such programs disbursed almost $2 billion in tax relief to 10 million older adults by 1974. Illinois has enacted a whopping $16 million-a-year program to help an estimated 300,000 elderly and handicapped homeowners. The grants are based on the amount of income and the real estate taxes owed. South Carolina approved a $5,000 homestead exemption; Kentucky voters approved a $6,500 homestead exemption for those over 65 in a special referendum. The homestead exemptions are deducted from the assessed value of the house before the property tax is computed, thus lowering the value of the house for taxing purposes. Wisconsin goes even further, extending help to older adults who rent rather than own their homes. They are given credits against their state income taxes for a certain portion of the rent they pay.

Older adults have demonstrated a willingness to keep pressing for more exemptions and for more liberalized benefits once their initial victory has been won. California began by giving rebates to homeowners over 65 with yearly incomes of less than $3,350. Three years later, after intensive lobbying by senior citizen groups, relief was extended to homeowners over 62 with incomes up to $10,000 a year.

Some of these laws were written by older adults themselves. Many senior citizen groups have begun writing their own special interest legislation instead of waiting for a sympathetic lawmaker to do so. The National Council of Senior Citizens has compiled some 40 model statutes to guide state legislators. The statutes cover the gamut of concerns of older adults, from the regulation of hearing aid dealers to the reduction of public utility rates for those over 65. The Illinois State Council of Senior Citizens Organization adopted a hard-hitting legislation program calling for exemptions from the state income tax and the state sales tax on food, clothing, fuel, and medicine for older adults. At a rally in Trenton, New Jersey, more than 1,000 older adults, who were members of the New Jersey Council of Senior Citizens, submitted a packet of proposals to legislative leaders that demanded reduced fares on public transportation and lower property taxes.

LOBBYING BY OLDER ADULTS

These happenings illustrate the increasing political consciousness of older adults. One of the best examples of their emerging political clout was the lobbying in the early 1970's on behalf of a proposed 20 per cent increase in Social Security benefits. The National Council of Senior Citizens mounted an extensive and sustained lobbying effort.

Not long after the increase was first proposed, the council's monthly newsletter, the *Senior Citizen News*, ran a front-page story under the headline, "Social Security Could Rise 20% Without Tax Boost, Experts Say." Inside was a story urging members to "flood lawmakers with letters of support." The article offered advice on the best way to write a member of Congress along with sample letters from those who had already written in support of the increase.

Throughout the spring and into the early summer, the newsletter reported the action taken—or not taken—on the increase. Names of members of Congress who had or had not announced their support were printed, and the three million readers were again and again encouraged to write their representatives. They did. Senator Russell Long of Louisiana, chairman of the Senate Finance Committee, said it was the most mail he had received on one subject since Medicare was passed in 1965.

By the time several thousand members began heading to Washington, D.C., for the annual convention that summer, the lobbying was already intense. It intensified as convention delegates headed for Capitol Hill upon arrival. Delegates, armed with lists of members of Congress and their positions for or against the increase, prowled the halls of Congress, buttonholing their representatives with the elan of professional lobbyists. Back home again, they wrote more letters.

The lobbying paid off in October when Congress completed work on the bill and sent it to the President for his signature. It paid off again the following January when the 20 per cent increase showed up in Social Security checks.

The clout of older adults was demonstrated again in 1977 when reform-minded Senators tried to eliminate the Senate Special Committee on Aging as part of an overall reorganization of the Senate committee system. The reformers, led by Senator Adlai Stevenson of Illinois, said that the aging committee, which had been created in 1961 to undertake a one-year study of the problems of the elderly, had outlived its usefulness. They said the senior citizens would be better served by merging the aging committee into the Senate Committee on Human Resources which, unlike the aging committee, has legislative authority. Senator Frank Church of Idaho, chairman of the aging committee, took the fight to save his committee to the Senate floor. "Today," he said, "the need for the special committee is greater than ever before. The number of older Americans stands at an unprecedented but ever-growing number. Surely, if the veterans were thought to be entitled to a special committee of their own and small business was thought to be so entitled, then the senior citizens of this country deserve at least as much consideration."

Meanwhile, the committee staff organized and directed a campaign by older ,adults to preserve the aging committee. It included "seniorgrams" from thousands of older adults, telegrams from state and local officials and a box score in the Senior Citizens News listing those Senators who were most helpful in urging retention of the committee. The box score helped to rally some Senators who otherwise would have voted against the committee. The Special Committee on Aging survived by a lopsided 90 to 4 vote.

Although older adults have just begun to exercise their political potential, they are already inspiring a backlash against them. Former Secretary of Health, Education, and Welfare Robert Finch once complained, "We are spending too great a share of federal funds for persons over 60." In Florida, with its heavy concentration of older adults, a state legislator confronted the distribution of resources issue head on during a debate on increasing old-age assistance. "We are faced with a problem of philosophy and politics," he said. "Given the choice of deciding between the 80-year-old who is dying, maimed, and blind and the eight-month-old infant who can starve to death, who are we going to support and who is the federal government going to support? What is the logic of saying that we're going to give money to the group that is most expensive to support?"

Aid for older adults also has been challenged on the grounds that it violates the Fourteenth Amendment's guarantee of equal protection under the law. The Civil Aeronautics Board scuttled a request by domestic airlines to reduce fares for older adults on such grounds. The city commission of Coral Gables, Florida, vetoed a proposal to exempt older adults from an increase in garbage rates when the city attorney warned that an exemption might be considered discrimination against people under 65. Rather than risk a court test, the commission dropped the proposal.

The relief that goes to older adults in the form of reduced bus fares or help with property taxes comes out of the pockets of the young and middle-aged to pay taxes. Our economic resources are not unlimited. The economic pie can be divided into only so many portions. If older adults are to receive more, other groups must receive less or taxpayers must be prepared to accept higher taxes. The rest of society is unlikely to greet the political demands of older adults for a larger share of our economic resources with a generosity of spirit. A middle-class, middle-aged housewife, complaining about the senior citizen discounts offered by local movie theaters, bluntly voiced her resentment. "I don't see why they should get special rates," she said. "A lot of them have more money than I do. And if they can't afford the price of a ticket, they can do what I do. They can stay home."

The influx of retirees to The Springs on the East End of Long Island, New York, for instance, has divided the community into bitter camps of "us" and "them."[2] The local chapters of the American Association of Retired Persons, 35,000 strong and including 10 per cent of the entire population over 55, have become a political force to be reckoned with in the opinion of local politicians. Under New York law, local tax districts are permitted to exempt those over 65 with incomes under $6,000 from 50 per cent of their real estate taxes. The law, which itself is a product of heavy lobbying by senior citizen groups, has been implemented on Long Island as the result of vigorous prodding by older adults. James Black, president of The Springs chapter of the AARP, said, "They [the politicians] think money grows on trees. We just have to remind them it doesn't." The older adults feel their exemptions are justified because of their fixed incomes and because they do not use many of the municipal services such as the schools. The younger taxpayers, particularly in the middle-income sections where the median income of residents with school-age children is not much more than the average retiree's income, feel that older adults are receiving special treatment they don't deserve. "They cry poverty all the time," said a South Fork school administrator. "Yet just a fraction of them are even eligible for tax exemptions. We've

---

[2]*New York Times*, May 20, 1973, n.p.

got families of five and six living on less than two retirees live on—and paying their full tax share."

A backlash is predictable. As John Martin, the former Commissioner on Aging, points out, "Any group that develops a voice that can be heard also develops a backlash, especially when money is involved." The backlash will grow as the government assumes a larger share of society's support for older adults and as workers feel the tax bite of supporting the aging, nonproductive sector of the population. In an age-segregated society, the burden of support for older adults is steadily shifted from the family to the government. The young will no longer contribute directly to the support of their parents. Instead, they will give their tax dollars to an impersonal government to be revolved through a variety of assistance programs for the support of unknown masses of older adults. The resentment will intensify as the level of support increases. In another 10 years, instead of being divided by race, society may very well be split into hostile camps of different generations.

INFLUENCES THROUGH THE YEARS

Before we explore the potential political clout of older adults in the future, let's look at the past. Twice before, older adults have banded together to force economic concessions from society. They succeeded at a time when older people comprised a much smaller proportion of the population than they do now. Thus their successes are all the more remarkable.

In the early 1930s, Dr. Francis Townsend of Long Beach, California, a retired doctor with the ability to stir the imagination of older adults, proposed a plan that would give a pension of $200 a month to people over 60—the equivalent of $600 a month in 1970 dollars. The recipients would be required to spend the $200 within 30 days. This, supporters argued, would stimulate the economy and benefit the population at large.

The Townsend Plan, proposed when the country was still suffering through the dark night of the Depression, was received enthusiastically. The proposal caught on quickly. In 1935 a state legislator, elected because of his advocacy of the Townsend Plan platform, introduced a bill incorporating the basics of the plan into the California legislature. The following year, the U.S. House of Representatives began holding hearings on the proposal. By the summer of 1936, new recruits swelled membership in the Townsend society to 5,000,000. When the Townsendites gathered in Cleveland, Ohio, that summer for their national convention, over 12,000 delegates marched through the sweltering streets, singing—to the tune of "Onward Christian Soldiers" —"Onward pension soldiers marching onto war/With the plan of Townsend going on before." Pinned to their shirts, they wore buttons that said "Youth for Work— Age for Leisure."

Eventually Congress, which had already passed the Social Security Act, defeated a form of the Townsend plan, and the Townsend movement died abruptly. Some Townsendites tried to regroup into the National Annuity League, but the impetus, the feeling of a surging mass movement overwhelming obstacles by sheer momentum, was lost —except in Colorado.

In the late 1930s, the National Annuity League succeeded in winning approval of its pension plan in Colorado. Through the dedicated organizing efforts of a group of young men, the League won support of its old-age pension plan in a statewide referendum by a margin of almost 2 to 1. The old-age assistance act provided benefits of $45 a month for people over 65, at the time the highest of any state in the country.

At its peak, the National Annuity League claimed 38,000 members, 66 per cent of the older adults in the state.

Still, it needed all the help it could get to defeat three well-financed attempts to repeal the old-age assistance act. The last, most aggressive, and nearly successful repeal drive came in 1948. The fight was a struggle, the first of many to come, between the rights of the young and old. In this case, the right of the young to get an education was pitted against the right of the old to live decently in retirement. The Colorado Education Association and the state Parent Teachers' Association launched the repeal drive. They won the support of the powerful *Denver Post,* which waged a vigorous editorial campaign on behalf of repeal. In an editorial entitled "No Accent on Youth," the *Post* said, "The state of Colorado in 1947 spent $45.11 on each of 200,000 public school children so that one out of five of them may eventually become an old-age pensioner, costing the state $800 a year."

The repeal drive captured the attention of the national press, which in general was biased against the pensioners. One of the reporters who covered the repeal drive, Roscoe Fleming of the *Christian Science Monitor,* accused the National Annuity League of seizing control of the state and the state of surrendering to the demands of the pensioners, who comprised less than four per cent of the state's population. Although Fleming's accusations were an exaggeration, the National Annuity League wielded extraordinary influence at the polls, in the state legislature, and in the governor's mansion as well.

When the votes were counted in the last repeal drive, the National Annuity League's strength was obvious. The opposition, although powerful, was easily defeated.

Summarizing the success of the National Annuity League, Edith Smith wrote, "It became one of the most potent political forces in the state and no legislation against its position was ever able to be passed. It succeeded in obtaining a medical program of $10 million, and a couple of years later an additional $1 million, while at the same time securing the pension at a minimum of $100 per month with a cost of living escalator to guarantee its effectiveness."[3] She concluded that the National Annuity League was able to survive and succeed, even when threatened by powerful, outside forces, through a fortuitous combination of capable leaders and followers who were individuals driven by a sense of great need, a sense of personal inadequacy, and a sense of being economically underprivileged.

These same motivations propelled the followers of George McLain and his California Institute of Social Welfare movement in the early 1950s. The California Institute of Social Welfare was formed by old-age assistance recipients under the leadership of McLain, a charismatic demagogue who used older adults as a political power base in a unsuccessful drive for the governorship.

Between 1951 and 1954, McLain mobilized the scared and frustrated elderly poor into a political movement that almost took him into the state house. Approximately 20 per cent of the old-age assistance beneficiaries, some 65,000 to 70,000 people in all, joined the California Institute of Social Welfare. The group had a fleeting success. They were able to force referendums on revising and liberalizing public assistance programs for the aged in three separate elections. In doing so, they managed to win increased benefits and to liberalize the eligibility requirements. These were later repealed, however, and afterward members began to drift away from the California Institute of Social Welfare. McLain's power base was dispersed.

Political scientists Frank Pinner, Paul Jacobs, and Philip Selznick say that the older adults who looked to McLain for leadership were preoccupied primarily with their low social status as welfare recipients. Although they were ostensibly seeking an increase in welfare benefits, they were

---

[3] Edith Sherman, "An Inquiry into the Nature of the Gerontological Movement in Colorado 1935–1962," unpublished doctoral dissertation, University of Colorado.

driven by emotional, not economic, needs. These older people wished to be respected and respectable above all. They joined the California Institute of Social Welfare because they wished to become, in their own eyes and the eyes of others, something more than welfare clients. They saw McLain's movement as a way of raising their social status and gaining prestige.

Like the old-age assistance recipients who followed George McLain, older adults of today are talking about economics. Yet they, too, are ready for a movement that would enable them to have pride along with steak and artichokes. Another charismatic leader, appealing to their pride as well as their wallets, could rally older adults for a new assault on the political establishment, which would alter the lives of the young and middle-aged as well as the lives of older adults.

Older adults may have found such a new leader in Margaret Kuhn, a 71-year-old Philadelphian who is the organizer of the Gray Panthers, a movement of older adults so-called because of the color of their hair and their assertiveness. Mrs. Kuhn intends to liberate older adults from endless rounds of shuffleboard, the paternalism of old-age homes, and, as she phrases it, their "fuddy-duddy" image. She says that she finds the image of "mellowed, sweet old people" repugnant and the idea of golden age clubs "asinine." She is willing to lead demonstrations, sit-ins, and protests, and take whatever other action is necessary to win new life-styles, freedom, and justice for older adults. "We're finding old people are very responsive to being radicalized," she said. "They are an explosive new force."

Mrs. Kuhn, called Maggie by her colleagues, is no fuddy-duddy herself. Lively and outspoken, she acknowledges her age with good humor and accepts the failings of age with grace. She wears her fashionably long dresses slit up the side to reveal stylish leather boots and sports a friendship ring "from a nice old man." Chuckling, she said, "Sex is beautiful until rigor mortis sets in." She doesn't fight her gray hair, which is tucked into a washerwoman's knot at the nape of her neck, her many wrinkles, and the arthritis in both hands. "I celebrate my freedom from the bureaucratic restraints that once held me," she said.

When she retired in 1972 after 24 years with various Presbyterian welfare agencies, she was determined to liberate other older adults from the same shackles. The result was the Gray Panthers, which in 1976 claimed over 6,000 followers, mostly on the East Coast. Wtih funds provided by the United Presbyterian Church in the U.S.A. and the United Church of Christ, the Gray Panthers have started lobbying in Washington, D.C., for increases in Social Security benefits and legislation that would establish a bill of rights for residents of nursing and old-age homes. Grass roots organizing has also been under way. Maggie Kuhn travels around the country regularly and maintains an active speaking schedule, all aimed at enlarging Gray Panther membership.

In solidarity lies power. Without a sense of group consciousness among older adults, a senior power movement can neither be strong nor lasting. Older adults must first recognize that their problems are not individual concerns but group problems, shared by millions of others like themselves. As Friedson, who likes to refer to himself as the "Ralph Nader of the Social Security set," says, "We've got to learn to stick together. Otherwise, we'll hang separately."

Age segregation fosters a sense of togetherness among older adults. Society has tried to deal with the growth in numbers of older people by isolating them. In doing so, it has created the conditions that are right for molding older adults into a powerful political force that cannot be contained within old-age ghettos. Shunted off by the rest of society and excluded from community life, older adults have steadily turned to senior citizen centers, organizations of retirees, and golden age clubs for friends, social life, and a sense of belonging.

These groups heighten the age consciousness and encourage the political involvement of older adults. Those who are members are more likely to be concerned about social issues and interested in politics. They talk frequently about rising taxes, increasing inflation, the needs of older adults, and other social problems, while older people who are not members discuss these subjects rarely or not at all.[4]

These groups also breed a similarity of perspective. Their members come to view the world through the prism of old age. Other ties to the community—links to professional groups, memberships in fraternal organizations, churches, and unions—lose their hold. As other ties weaken, members have less exposure to the views of other generations. Age is an increasing reference point. A man who might once have seen himself as a businessman, a member of the Presbyterian Church, a Rotarian, and a Boy Scout leader now sees himself as an older adult. Political activity based on age and age alone then becomes acceptable. As James E. Trela writes, "To the degree that they are joining the growing number of senior citizen centers and other groups of aged and confining their associations to age peers, they are shielded from cross-generational viewpoints and may increasingly adopt age as a reference point from which social and political processes can be interpreted."[5]

The rise of senior consciousness is encouraged by the rapid growth of senior citizen centers across the country. Their extraordinary increase makes it impossible to maintain an accurate tally of their numbers. When the senior citizen center movement was starting in 1964, there were 334 centers. By 1974, the last year for which an accounting was avail-

---

[4]Frank A. Pinner, Paul Jacobs, and Philip Selznick, *Old Age and Political Behavior* (Berkeley: University of California Press, 1959).

[5]James E. Trela, "Some Political Consequences of Senior Center and Other Old Age Group Memberships," *The Gerontologist* (Summer 1971), Part I, pp. 118–23.

able, there were over 5,000 senior citizen centers and clubs.[6] More are being organized and built every day. The political impact will follow. The full impact may not be felt immediately, but it is coming. "One of these days," a retiree said during a discussion of senior power, "all of us senior citizens are going to march on Washington. It won't be the fastest march that town's ever seen, but it will be one they will remember."

POLITICAL BEHAVIOR

To understand what all of this will mean, we need to examine the political attitudes and voting behavior of older adults.

Little research has been done on the relationship between age and politics, but what has been done explodes the stereotype of the radical young and the conservative old. There is no evidence that people grow more politically conservative simply because they grow older. After studying the political attitudes and beliefs of all age groups, Angus Campbell concluded that there was no simple relationship between age and political ideology.[7] Data from the Survey Research Center at the University of Michigan showed conservatives among the young and liberals among those over 65. Older adults, for example, were not the biggest supporters of George Wallace's presidential campaign in 1968. Although his law-and-order pitch and his stand against campus protest might be expected to attract older people, they were, in fact, least responsive to him. At the height of the war in Vietnam and the peak of campus protest over American involvement,

---

[6]Conversation with author, the Administration on Aging, October 15, 1976.

[7]Angus Campbell, "Politics Through the Life Cycle," *The Gerontologist* (Summer 1971), Part I, pp. 112–15.

older adults were more opposed to the war and more in favor of pulling out entirely than any other age group. When older people were asked about social welfare issues that split along liberal-conservative lines, such as a guaranteed minimum income and the government as the employer of last resort, they showed the same pattern of responses as those under 65.

Older adults have considerable clout at the polls, an influence that is out of proportion to their numbers. Although they comprise 10 per cent of the population, they made up 20 per cent of the registered voters in the country in 1976.[8] Their strength has not been confined to states that attract large numbers of retirees. They represent over 15 per cent of the registered voters in half of the states. They are particularly strong in Iowa, South Dakota, Nebraska, Arkansas, Missouri, Kansas, and Maine, in addition to Florida. They accounted for over 17 per cent of the registered voters in those states in the 1972 elections.[9]

Their political strength stems from the fact that older adults who are registered to vote actually do so. They vote with greater frequency in presidential and Congressional elections than people under 65. In the 1972 presidential election, 87 per cent of the registered voters over 65 went to the polls. Only 55 per cent of the people under 65 voted.[10] In previous presidential elections, people in their seventies and eighties, despite the frequent handicaps of age, physical infirmities, and ill health, have turned out with greater frequency than people in their early twenties. About 75 per cent of people in their seventies and 66 per cent of people in their eighties have voted in presidential elections. In nonpresiden-

---

[8]Conversation with author, Director of Political Research, Democratic National Committee, October 12, 1976.

[9]"A Look at This Year's Voters," *U.S. News and World Report,* April 17, 1972, p. 27.

[10]Conversation with author, Director of Political Research.

tial election years when the voting turnout usually drops dramatically, older adults continue to go to the polls in large numbers. About 80 per cent of the over-65 registered voters turned out in 1974.[11]

Public officials have begun to court older adults seriously. Former Senator John Tunney of California, for example, won his first Senatorial campaign in 1970 despite the loss of the senior citizen vote. They cast their ballots for his opponent, the conservative and older incumbent George Murphy. The loss of the senior citizen vote was a nasty shock to Tunney, and after the votes were counted, he vowed that he would make sure it did not happen again. "There are two and a half million elderly in California," he said. "I need that vote." In 1976, however, Tunney was defeated for re-election by linguist S. L. Hayakawa, who was in his seventies.

The wooing of the senior citizen vote has been especially intense in Florida, where older adults comprised over 21 per cent of the vote by 1972. The efforts by candidates in that state to secure the support of older adults is a portent of things to come in the rest of the country. Both Governor Reuben Askew and U.S. Senator Lawton Chiles made a strong pitch to older adults in their initial bids for office in 1970. The support of older people was considered the deciding factor in the election of the then political unknowns. During the 1972 Florida primary, viewed as a key contest by political analysts; John Lindsay, then mayor of New York City, devoted considerable time and attention to the older adults in South Miami Beach, an area largely composed of Jewish retirees from New York City. Senator Hubert Humphrey, whose long-standing support of such programs as Medicare and Social Security gave him a natural claim to the senior citizen vote, also hoped that their votes would be decisive in his favor. Campaigning in Florida, his wife, Muriel, said, "We've met so many former friends, so many people

---

[11]Ibid.

who say that they have supported us in the past. We're counting on them now."[12]

Senior citizens will change the lives of the middle-aged particularly. William Ewald, a former fellow at the now defunct Center for the Study of Democratic Institutions, has speculated that a politically powerful coalition of the young and old, both motivated by a desire for social and economic change and perceiving of the establishment as the obstacle to such change, may unite against the middle-aged. "The young may want change and not care about (or understand) the consequences," he said. "The older (generation) may demand change and have nothing to lose. It may well be that the true conservatives are the middle-aged workers deeply commited to the short-term perspective of the system and (who) believe they have much to lose from change." Using projected population figures, Ewald estimated the future strength of such a coalition as follows:

	Progressive Voters in Millions	
	1985	*2000*
20 to 24 year olds	21	21
25 to 34 year olds	41	38
65 year olds and up	25	28
TOTAL	87	87

	Conservative Voters in Millions	
	1985	*2000*
35 to 65 year olds	74	100

By Ewald's projections, the progressive young and old voters would outnumber the conservative middle-aged voters by 1985. They would be strong enough to wrest political concessions from them. Although their numbers would de-

---

[12]Personal interview.

cline by the start of the twenty-first century, they would still be able to rival the power of the middle-aged.

Although projections are speculative, there have been examples of young and older adults meeting across the generation gap.

Eugene Yap, a slight, soft-spoken retired accountant, for example, was elected president of the 5,000-member student body at Honolulu Community College. Yap, whose young daughters urged him to return to school, campaigned on a platform of "Fun, Frolic and Fellowship." He defeated two young opponents in winning his office. Yap attributed his election to a genuine interest in young people. "I always was interested in young people and not afraid to respond to them with friendliness," he said. "I think the students sensed that."

At the Democratic National Convention in 1972, old and young forged a temporary alliance. Before the convention, members of the Youth International Party (Yippies) arrived in Miami to try to create a temporary radical coalition of young and old that would influence the party platform.

The Yippies pitched tents in a people's park in the midst of South Miami Beach, a decaying stretch of cheap hotels and apartment buildings inhabited mainly by Jewish retirees from New York City. Between games of frisbee in the muggy air of hot July nights, they set out to rally the retirees to their cause.

They toured the senior citizen clubs, trying to allay fears of riots by the young, fanned by the well-publicized arrival of the National Guard. They urged older adults to join their fight for a better life for all people.

It seemed incongruous at first, the long-haired, haphazardly dressed young men appealing to the groups of retirees in their bermuda shorts and neat flowered dresses who sat stolidly in the heat, listening. The older adults were skeptical in the beginning, but they listened when they heard the young people telling them, as one did, "We feel the two most oppressed groups in the country are the young and the old. It is the middle-aged that control this country. They are the oppressors. If the young and old joined together, we could control this country." After hearing the speakers, many came to agree.

Two days before the convention officially began, Yippie leader Rennie Davis and Max Serchuk, president of the Dade County Council of Senior Citizens, organized a mass rally of 5,000 young people and older adults to publicize the plight of the old. Davis, whose hair resembles an exploding dandelion, and the stooped, wiry Serchuk made an odd couple as they went from the frisbee games of the kids to the bingo games of the retirees soliciting support for the rally. But somehow it all worked. At the rally the older adults cheered and the young waved signs that said, "Long Hairs, White Hairs Struggle Together" and "Youthful Enthusiasm Joins Elderly Wisdom." Both applauded equally hard when Senators George McGovern of South Dakota and Frank Church of Idaho, chairman of the Senate Special Committee on Aging, called for immediate action on the problems of aging.

Speculation about future possibilities of a young-old coalition does not change the fact that senior power is an emerging reality now. Their movement is growing and will continue to grow. They may not need to seek allies, although they would, of course, welcome them. As their political consciousness is raised, they will gain influence and power. Other political pressure groups may then turn to them enabling older adults to dominate such coalitions with the consequent assurance that their demands will be pressed strongly. As Senator Thomas Eagleton of Missouri commented succinctly, "The old are growing in political sex appeal."

TOWARD A NEW COMMUNITY

CHAPTER ELEVEN

Growing old is inevitable; old age, as we have come to know and think of it in the United States in the 1970s, is not.

As we grow old, few of us are able to escape some mental and physical afflictions. Longer life-spans may postpone the onset of the aging of our minds and bodies, but at some point and usually sooner than we would wish, our minds and bodies begin to fail. No drug or medical technique currently envisioned by our scientists will enable us to stay at our peak mentally and physically until we die. We may accept it with resignation or rebel against it, depending on our natures, but we cannot escape it.

Under the proper social conditions, however, we *can* escape the type of old age that Simone de Beauvoir, the French writer, accurately terms "an absurd parody of our

242

former life." Although our minds and bodies must age, our spirits need not deteriorate. Old age does not have to be an indignity, a curse that society visits on those who no longer conform to its dictates of beauty or who are unable to keep up with its dizzying pace.

THE CHOICES OF OLD AGE

In modern society, however, an older adult has two choices. He can try to keep pace with the young, spending time and energy in an ultimately futile attempt to compete with the young on their own terms. If the older adult fails, he will be mocked and ridiculed, mercilessly exposed to society's contempt. Society will scoff at his attempt to meet socially on terms that are set by the young and middle-aged and biased against the old. Society will mutter, "Look at that old man. Why doesn't he act his age?" If he manages to succeed, often at great physical and psychological cost, the older adult will win a grudging measure of respect and admiration from society, at least temporarily. Young people will say, "He certainly doesn't act 65 or 70 or 80 years old." It is dubious praise, granting respect and admiration to the individual while acknowledging the general low esteem that society accords older adults. Success, however, is only temporary. Eventually, failing in health and energy, the older adult must concede defeat.

If an older adult has neither the energy nor inclination to compete, he must choose to withdraw, living out his life apart from the concerns and activities of the rest of society. The older person may continue to live in his own home. If financial resources are exhausted, he may end up in an old-age ghetto. If the older adult is lucky enough to have money and health, he may move to one of the glamorous retirement communities in California, Florida, or Arizona. In any case, he is apart, labeled "old" by the rest of society and usually forgotten.

Such alternatives, if they can be called such, are the only ones available to us in our old age. Because they are our only choices, grim and harsh as they may be, we rarely question them. We fail to ask if society can do better. At the most, we direct our efforts to alleviating some of the harsher conditions and ranker injustices of old age. We come up with federally funded programs for hot meals, low income public housing, senior citizen centers, and low cost medical care. We raise Social Security benefits and pass pension reforms to insure that people who have contributed to pension plans receive some benefits in retirement. At best we treat the old like helpless children who need our aid to attain the necessities of life. The public attitude toward older adults is tainted by paternalism, and our public policy often seems calculated to reduce older people to infantilism. Indeed, older adults *are* often helpless. They *do* often, because of ill health or low income, need our assistance in providing for their needs. But they *are not* children.

All of our programs, as valuable and important as they may be, ignore the basic problem of old age. That basic problem is the creation of a society that will enable a man to remain a man in old age. Instead of asking how we can solve the economic problems of old age—and the problems such as poor health and malnutrition that stem from lack of money—we should be asking how to build a human society.

As long as men come to the end of life alone and empty-handed, old age will be a condemnation of our entire social system. It will announce our failure to create the kind of country originally envisioned by our founding fathers, a society that recognizes the common humanity of all its citizens and freely encourages the growth of each individual. Historian Arnold Toynbee expressed this thought most eloquently when he wrote, "The moral tone and life-span of a civilization can be measured by the respect and care given its senior citizens."

The answer to the question of whether society can do

better for older adults is that society not only can do better, but society must do better.

A model of old age exists in the U.S.S.R., in the Republic of Abkhasia, a hard and rough land, although beautiful, extending from a subtropical coast along the Black Sea through the populated lowlands and valleys to the main range of the Caucasus Mountains. The Abkhasians have lived there for over 1,000 years, preserving their ancient culture despite numerous raids and domination by Greeks, Turks, and Russians. Once they were herdsmen, but now they are mostly farmers, deriving their living from tilling the crops of tea and tobacco planted in the valleys and foothills. Some 100,000 Abkhasians live in this area, and an amazing number range in age from 80 to 110. In 1954, the last year for which statistics were available, 2.58 per cent of the Abkhasians were over 90. This compares to 0.4 per cent of the population in the United States.

Also surprisingly, the older Abkhasians do not look their age. Although their faces are weathered and lined and their hair is gray, it is difficult to tell if they are 70 or 107. It is as if the physical and mental decline that we regard as natural as we grow older simply stops at a certain age among the Abkhasians. They have good eyesight and hearing. One researcher found that close to 40 per cent of the men and 30 per cent of the women could read without glasses. Over 40 per cent have reasonably good hearing. They stand erect, often walking more than two miles a day, and frequently swim in the cool waters of the streams that trickle down from the Caucasus Mountains. They are a handsome, energetic, and active people.

Moreover, they retain remarkable intellectual powers into advanced age. An exceptionally large number have good memories, recalling recent and not-so-recent events clearly and lucidly. They think logically. They are actively interested in the social and political affairs of their families and tribe. There were no reported cases of mental illness, including senility, in a nine-year study of 123 people over 100-years-old.

Abkhasians have a moderate approach to life. They eschew the American attitude of "eat, drink, and be merry for tomorrow we die." They are rarely overweight, which is considered a symptom of disease. They eat little meat but plenty of fresh vegetables, fruit, and buttermilk. Few smoke, and they drink neither coffee nor tea. They do drink a locally produced dry red wine, which has a low alcohol content, at lunch and dinner in small quantities. They consider sex good and pleasurable when it is private, but that, too, is indulged in moderately. Sexual relations rarely start before the age of 30 when an Abkhasian man traditionally marries. But they compensate for this late onset of sexual activity by remaining sexually active into their eighties, nineties, and in some cases even later. A 104-year-old man explained their view of sex by saying, "A man is a man until he is 100, you know what I mean. After that, well, he's getting old." But some of these proud, handsome men retain their sexual potency and desire even longer. Doctors collected sperm from one man, who had fathered his last child at 100 years of age, when he was 119-years-old. He was still sexually potent.

The Abkhasians also have remarkably different attitudes and expectations about old age, work, and the family than we do. They see life in its entirety, with childhood blending naturally into adulthood and adulthood into old age, although they do not think in these terms. The Abkhasians do not use the word "old" when they speak of people of a certain age. Instead, they refer to "long-living people" for those over 100. They avoid the harsh break with the past and our former selves that we experience when we turn 65 and discover that we have been put into a different category, separate and distinct from all that we were.

Abkhasians never retire. They maintain a consistent life-style alternating between work and rest from childhood through old age. Children do the easiest work, adults the most strenuous, and in old age both men and women do what they are capable of doing, but always contributing in some way to the ongoing life of the community. As they approach 80 and 90, their work load and working hours gradually decline. Shepherds may stop following the herds into the mountains and begin tending the farm animals instead. Farmers may stop plowing and may till less land, but they continue weeding and doing the simpler, less demanding chores. Women may stop working in the fields, but they continue to keep the house. Even the people whom we would consider very old avoid idleness. They may pick up fallen fruit, whittle toys for their grandchildren, and clean the large courtyard, which is the family's central meeting place.

Abkhasian families are large, with complex, extended relationships that are cherished. Because of the large families and intermarriage with other large families, Abkhasians often number their relatives in the thousands. The immediate families are close despite the largeness. Everyone is valued and everyone has a place, including those over 65. Instead of being a burden to their families, older adults play an important role in ceremonial occasions, mediate family disputes, transmit cultural values, and share their knowledge of farming and other kinds of work. Those over 65 do not fear and dread their old age. They know they are needed. One 99-year-old man said, "It isn't time to die yet. I am needed by my children and grandchildren, and it isn't bad in this world—except that I can't turn the earth over and it has become difficult to climb trees."

A number of factors may be responsible for the extraordinarily long life-spans of the Abkhasians, including their diet, their prolonged sex life, and possibly genetic weeding out and selections. One anthropologist who has studied these people, however, believes that their optimism about old age and the remarkable continuity of their life-style are the determining factors. Anthropologist Sula Benet said, "My own view is that Abkhasians live as long as they do because of the extraordinary cultural factors that structure their existence: the uniformity and certainty of both individual and group behavior, the unbroken continuum of life's activities, the same games, the same work, the same food, the same self-imposed and socially perceived needs. And the increasing prestige that comes with increasing age."[1]

Old age is strikingly different in Abkhasia and the United States. The differences are so apparent that they need no elaboration, being almost mirror images.

We have a lot to learn from them, not so we can prolong life—our biologists are already working on that —but so we can add life to our years. We, too, can create a society that will permit old age to be a gentle denouement preserving the tone and harmony of our earlier lives, rather than a harsh catastrophe that mars, while it denies, our youth and middle age.

Abkhasia is still a rural, agrarian society; the United States of the 1970s has already left the post-industrial age, hurtling toward some still unfathomed, yet to be disclosed form of society. Abkhasia resembles nineteenth-century America. That century of small towns and family farms was probably the kindest to older adults in this country. But it is unrealistic, and not necessarily desirable—assuming it were possible—to return to the social structure of the last century. We can, however, take Abkhasia as an example of a good society for older adults and translate the best of that society into twentieth-century American terms. We can create a society that integrates people of all ages in a way that makes age irrelevant. We can do so while recognizing the special needs and talents of older adults. This is the unrecognized challenge of longevity.

LONGEVITY AND MODERN LIFE

We must create such a society if increases in longevity and the changing population are not to place unprecedented

---

[1]Sula Benet, "Why They Live to be 100, Or Even Older, in Abkhasia," *New York Times Magazine*, December 21, 1971, pp. 3–32.

strains on our social structure. As we saw earlier, there have been predictions of outraged yippies, geriatic hippies, causing riots and hurtling their anger against a society that excludes them. Older adults deserve better, and such a future is unworthy of the United States. Obviously this is an extreme view of what is to be. Still, there are all too many reasons for older adults to be angry. They have been the hidden minority. While other minorities have been catered to or courted, they have been ignored. The Democratic Party, to take a glaring example, eagerly solicited the support in 1972 of the young, blacks, and women. These groups were assigned quotas in the state delegations to the national convention to assure their proportional representation. Older adults, however, were overlooked. There was no effort to insure that they were included, although many older adults have been stalwart Democrats since the New Deal, long before the youthful backers of presidential nominee George McGovern had been born.

Although few envision older adults leaving their Leisure World homes to loiter along Sunset Strip, many thoughtful gerontologists and political scientists believe that we are entering a period of protracted struggle over age rights. Modern Western societies passed through a period of struggle over political rights as people fought for an end to suffrage based on the ownership of property. That was followed by a period of struggle for economic rights as people fought for a decent day's pay for an honest day's work. Now older adults are fighting for equality with the middle-aged and the young. Older adults are seeking an end to ageism and gerontophobia, to discrimination and to arbitrary policies, such as mandatory retirement, that make decisions on the basis of age rather than ability. They are seeking the right to be judged on their own merits. They are demanding their fair share of our national resources.

How can we build an age-irrelevant, age-integrated society in the United States in this last part of the twentieth century? The federal government, as the nation's largest single employer, should lead the way by encouraging an end to discrimination against people over 65 in employment. This is the single most glaring example of age consciousness in our society. The federal government can begin by assuring that federal employees are hired on the basis of their ability and merit regardless of their age. The Federal Mortgage Association has hired a number of retirees to take bids over the phone twice a month during its open market operations. But federal agencies in general do no more than private industry does to encourage the employment of persons once they have passed their sixty-fifth birthday. The federal government can also stop asking prospective employees their age. A presidential directive would insure that people over 65 receive equal consideration for the 2.5 million jobs—blue collar, clerical, technical, professional, and executive positions—in the federal bureaucracy.

Manpower training programs and research grants should be open to all. Few older adults, who may need new job skills the most as technological advances eliminate their jobs, have benefited from training programs. Research grants have been restricted by the government in some cases to "younger" scientists under the age of 40. Such discrimination is based on a false cost-benefit concept. The government apparently reasons that a 39-year-old scientist will live longer than a 65-year-old scientist, thereby increasing his chances of making a major contribution that will repay the government for its investment. But although the 39-year-old has youth on his side, the 65-year-old has experience and the wisdom that comes with it in his favor. The older scientist may avoid the mistakes of younger colleagues. In a less biased, more realistic cost-benefit accounting, youth could be balanced out by wisdom and experience.

Numerous private companies are already discovering that older adults are eager and able to perform a variety of part-time, temporary, or hard-to-fill jobs. Many companies have rehired former employees who were forced to retire 5 or 10 years earlier because of mandatory policies. Many regret letting their loyal, older employees retire because their younger replacements have failed to measure up. Sometimes the companies use the services of temporary help agencies to circumvent company rules about sick pay, pensions, and other fringe benefits.

Such an employee is Bernice Anderson, a 64-year-old retired secretary, who returns to her old job at the Equitable Life Assurance Society in Seattle when her company needs her. "It's a beautiful arrangement; I can use the money and I love the work," she said.

Mrs. Anderson's boss did not want to lose her when she was forced to retire after 16 years with the company, so she signed up with Western Girl, Inc. Equitable Life Assurance pays a fee to the employment agency, which makes sure that it sends Mrs. Anderson instead of another temporary worker when the office calls. Thus Mrs. Anderson can go back to work without losing her pension, and her company is able to retain a valuable employee without violating its retirement policies or generating complicated paper work. Sometimes Mrs. Anderson uses her considerable knowledge of the company to fill in for vacationing secretaries. Sometimes she uses her long-time experience in the life insurance field to help prepare lengthy commercial appraisals.

Other companies discover simply by chance that older workers can perform as well as younger people. They also find that older workers are apt to complain less, show up more regularly, and work willingly for less pay and no fringe benefits at all. Almost without exception, companies that hire older workers are delighted with their efforts. In fact, 40-year-old Jack Heeran, chairman of Circuit Systems Corporation of Villa Park, Illinois, says that he prefers employees who are over 40. "The older worker may go at a slower pace, but over a year's time you get more out of him because he's more steady, conscientious, and always shows up for work," he said. Heeran says he will gladly hire workers in their eighties. But he does have a cutoff point. After a worker passes his 90th birthday, Heeran is reluctant to add him to the payroll. The company, Heeran reports, is doing very well with a respectable number of older adults in its work force.

Few employers are likely to become as committed as Jack Heeran is to hiring older workers. Yet the number who have hired and been pleased with the performance of older adults indicates that companies could be persuaded to stop discriminating against older workers. The job opportunities could be expanded for persons over the customary retirement age if the government launched a "hire the over-65" campaign. At the very least, the federal government, particularly the Administration on Aging, could publicize the experience of companies who hire older adults. The government has enormous persuasive powers when it chooses to use them. It could sponsor television spots, public service announcements, newspaper and magazine articles. It could sponsor talks at conventions or professional gatherings by business executives who know firsthand that older workers are desirable workers.

Congress also can do its part. It can eliminate provisions of laws that encourage the false notion that people over 65 are outdated and passé. It should eliminate the so-called retirement test, the restriction on outside earnings by Social Security recipients. Since interest, dividends, rental income, and private pensions are exempt, the limit on earnings is unfair and discriminatory. Although the restriction may have been useful once, it is no longer. The time has come to re-examine this provision of a law that was originally passed in 1935. The ceiling of $3,000, which went into effect on January 1, 1977, is totally unrealistic in view of the present high prices and inflation. It can extend the Age Discrimination in Employment Act to cover workers over 65. It presently prohibits discrimination in hiring and firing against persons between 40- and 65-years-old who are employed by private industry or who are state government workers. It should be extended to cover federal employees as well. It also forbids discrimination in training programs and promotions to workers in this age category. If the act were broadened to cover persons over 65, older adults would also receive the protection of the Division of Equal Pay and Employment Standards in the Department of Labor.

Private industry should rethink its mandatory retirement policies, with the companies that have rehired workers who were forced to retire in the lead. Forcing capable workers to retire and then rehiring them through temporary help agencies makes little sense. Companies might decide to retain mandatory retirement policies with provisions for employment on a year-to-year basis for those who wish to continue working. Such employees might submit to a yearly evaluation of their work as a precondition for continued employment after 65. Airline pilots, among others, regularly undergo tests of their physical and mental fitness. Anything would be fairer, and therefore preferable, than our present arbitrary and discriminatory retirement policies.

We have become accustomed to mandatory retirement and to bias against older adults on the job. Our thinking needs to be changed along with our policies. Undoubtedly, there will be resistance. The hidebound arguments that have been advanced against equal opportunities for all groups will be used against older adults.

Some will say that older adults, as they once said about women and blacks, are not "fit" for certain jobs. Older adults may not be capable of jobs that require heavy labor or long, tiring hours, in general, but this does not mean that they should not have the chance to apply and be considered for such jobs. The Green Thumb program, which employs older men for exactly this type of work, proves that some people over 65 are not only capable of, but actually thrive on, manual labor. Green Thumb workers, for instance, spend long hours out-of-doors, even in rain and 90-degree heat, planting trees, clearing land, and building recreational facilities.

Others will argue that older adults should not be given equal consideration for jobs because younger people "need" them more. This same argument was advanced against equal employment opportunities for women. Men were said to be more deserving of jobs because they had families to support. But the widespread poverty among older adults proves their need for employment. Like younger workers, they have mortgage payments to meet, food to buy, and medical bills to pay. Their Social Security benefits and pensions have not kept pace with the rising cost of living. If they are capable of working and want employment, they should be able to get it.

Eliminating age discrimination in employment would go a long way toward eliminating age consciousness in our society. Our working environment, where we spend most of our waking hours, helps to shape our attitudes toward people and life in general. If we can learn that older adults are competent and capable in this area, our view of them and old age itself will be more positive. Our respect and esteem for those past middle age will increase. If we can end this form of discrimination, we will be on our way toward an age-irrelevant society.

If we cannot legislate the kind of regard the Abkhasians have for their older people, we can at least strive to create conditions that will encourage respect and honor for older adults. We should seriously contemplate creating, formally and informally, special statuses for older people that would recognize their wisdom, maturity, experience, and special vision. We need older adults to contribute these things to our public life. In Abkhasia, our model of a good society in old age, older adults are able to contribute these things naturally. American and other modern societies are structured in a way that makes this impossible. Therefore, we need to build in these contributions.

A NEW LOOK AND SPIRIT

We need to revive our "elders." Although we have numerous older adults, unlike earlier societies, we have no elders, people whose special value arises from their advanced age. Older adults have a lot to offer. Colleges and universities take note of this when they appoint certain older professors to the status of professor emeritus. These professors may not be actively involved in teaching, but they remain contributing members of the academic community. We also give an informal status of elder statesman to older politicians who may be called on for special public service from time to time. They may be asked to chair presidential commissions, as former Chief Justice Earl Warren was requested to preside over the inquiry into the assassination of President John F. Kennedy, or to handle delicate political negotiations, as Averell Harriman was sought out to head the United States delegation to the peace talks that ended the war in Vietnam.

The contributions of older adults should not be limited to government and academia, and even in these areas they should participate more widely and fully. Older adults have much to offer in other fields. We should take advantage of the depth and range of their vision. We should learn from them the lessons of past blunders and tragedies. Our society is changing so rapidly that we need them now more than ever. Their vast experience can help us to cope with a variety of perplexing problems. They can advise us especially on the human impact of social change. Older architects can help to design livable cities. Doctors and ministers can be valuable resources in helping us to cope with the ethical dimensions of issues such as genetic engineering now emerging from scientific advances. These are some obvious examples, but possibilities exist in every area for every occupational group. Older adults can share their experience with us even if they choose to retire from active participation in their fields.

They can serve on national commissions that are planning for the future. They can be valuable government consultants. They are particularly needed on the local level since smaller communities often lack sufficient resources for solving their social problems. Older adults can work closely with city councils, school boards, mental health centers, and medical and bar associations.

We should seek ways of integrating older adults into our communities. Since public housing for older adults was first build in the mid-1950s, older people have been moving from the community into segregated housing at a steadily accelerating pace. Although low cost housing for older adults is needed, we do not have to isolate the housing from the rest of us. Burgeoning retirement villages are also removing older adults from contact with the young and middle-aged. At the start of the 1960s, an estimated 60 per cent of those over 65 lived in the community and 40 per cent lived in age-segregated housing. If the present exodus of older adults from the community continues, these figures are expected to reverse within a few years. Many older adults no doubt prefer to live with people of their own age, but others do not. They should have the choice of many living arrangements.

We should study the approach adopted by European countries, which encourages older adults to live in the community as long as they are able. Denmark, for example, sets aside an entire floor for older adults in high rise public housing projects. If all generations can live together, a certain number of apartments are also reserved for those over 65 in cooperative apartment houses. The first floor is generally devoted to shops, the second floor to apartments for older adults, and the remaining floors are occupied by individuals and families of all ages. The official state policy is to strive for age-integrated communities.

Great Britain takes a similar approach. In state-owned housing projects a small group of one-story row houses, especially designed to meet the physical needs of older adults, are set aside for those over 65. Other housing projects in Great Britain reserve the ground floor of two-story row houses for older adults and the first floor for families. This encourages easy socializing between the age groups. The older adults often turn into surrogate grandparents for the younger children. The families may call on the older adults for babysitting duties, and the older adults can rely on help from neighbors if they are ill or in need.

Our urban planners should consider the balance of age groups as they design new communities. We have plans for open space and recreational facilities. The generation mix is as important as a residential and commercial mix. This is naturally difficult, although not impossible, to create in established communities. The New Towns springing up around the country offer a valuable and rare opportunity to build an age-integrated community. The builders of New Towns try to plan a community that will include various racial groups and income classes. Equal attention should be given to various age groups.

Some older adults always will have to live in special housing. Nursing homes, for instance, will always be segregated by age. Public housing might be built exclusively for older adults to help them cope with their physical disabilities through specially designed bathrooms and kitchens. But even in these cases, the housing can be part of the larger community. In Norwalk, California, for example, the Lutheran Church has plans for combining a day care center and nursing home. The center for three-, four- and five-year-olds is being built into the Southland Lutheran Home and Geriatrics Center, whose residents include many retired teachers. The home directors hope that many of the teachers will be interested in working with the children and that both will benefit. The older residents may read to the children, tell them stories, and, in general, be friends with them. Many of the boys and girls come from homes where both parents work and have little time to spend with their children. In turn, the children may help rehabilitate the older adults by bringing them into contact with the community again. Many of these older people have been isolated for years.

Public housing projects might be combined with day care centers in a similar manner. Such projects might be built on college campuses, and nursing homes might be built besides churches. The possibilities are limited only by our imagination.

As part of our design for an age-integrated society, we should seek ways to end the unnecessary institutionalization of older adults. Instead of paying to separate families, as we do now, we should pay to keep them together. Although we may not bring back the three-generation household —and it may not be desirable to do so—we can eliminate unnecessary separations. If a family is willing to assume financial responsibility for their older relatives, the government should help. This can be done in a variety of ways. The government might reimburse families for some of the cost of supporting older relatives. It could offer credits on federal income tax for helping out parents or grandparents over 65 if the relatives are living in the family home. This is not a crass way of insuring filial devotion. It simply recognizes that some families would like very much to help their aging relatives, but they are financially unable to do so. Such proposals have been considered by the Senate Special Committee on Aging. Some legislation has even been drafted. The legislation, however, has languished in committee. Commenting on these bills, Val Halamandaris, a staff member of the Senate committee, said, "Certainly if we can give money to institutions to take care of people, we should be able to give money to families to take care of their own."

Throughout this book I have tried to deal with the impact of longevity. The extension of our life-span will have consequences that cannot even be guessed at now. The problems will be large and the challenge great. But a "cure" for aging offers each one of us, and society as a whole, the possibility of a bright new future that is rich and rewarding, filled with human achievement, and deep in experience. It is a future that can surpass anything we have previously imagined. Our social scientists, our political leaders, and we ourselves must be stimulated to address these problems so that such a future will be the old age of all of us.

INDEX